Mosaic

of

Miracles

(The Fountains of Fantasy)
(The Fourth Three Fountains)
(Final Release Version)

Robert J. Koyich

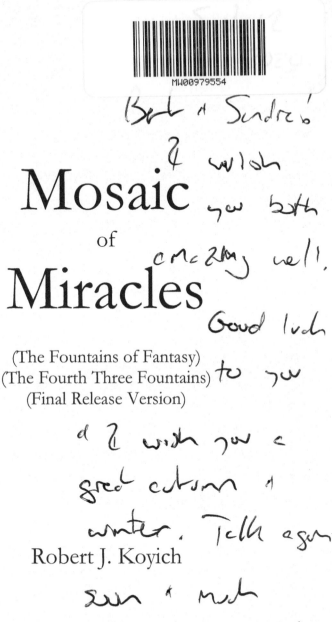

Bob & Sandra's

I wish you both

amazing well.

Good luck

to you

& I wish you a

great autumn &

winter. Talk again

soon & much

good to you both

PVTER! Rob

DEDICATION

This book is for life, love, and commitment to our truths.
I cannot tell you, yet your trust and youth hold the key.
Forever and a day; I wish, I hope, I pray.
Thrive past the eternal yearnings of today.

CONTENTS

Rings of Truth: The 10th Fountain

Reformation   1

Across an Ocean   9

Blocking Time   17

Correlated Faith   25

Give In or Give Up?   33

Mediated Motivation   41

Fuzzy Logic   49

Get the Dream Right   57

20/20 Vision   65

Quality is Our Recipe   73

Subtle Distinction   81

Depths of Discovery: The 11th Fountain

Firstly Formed by Fate   89

Starting to Learn Why   97

Telling Signs   105

Down to Earth   113

Sipping from the Clouds   121

Activate Miracle   127

Forced Servitude   135

The Fan in the Fantasy   143

Ally With the Reason Why   151

A Distant Traveler   159

Our Home   167

The Light in the Dark   175

Signs of Serenity: The 12th Fountain

Looking Out to In   183

Adjusting Promises   193

Shifting Sands   201

Dipping in the Water   209

Diving in the Pool   217

Fork the Counter   225

Forces of Instinct and Divinity   233

Developing Continuity   243

A Discernable Difference   251

How Do You Want to Work?   259

The Concept   267

Back at Home   275

Acknowledgments   285

Books, Contact Info, and Links   289

REFORMATION

Rings of Truth is the first Fountain of Fantasy. I wrote the book to expand my ability and to envision the future. As the Fountains continue the Journey of the Seed, it's a way to write my dreams into life, and as the seed becomes a tree, I also acknowledge the struggles within; fantasies that started as a wish.

With vision, work, and clarity, our souls and spirits meld to be more real. I read somewhere, *"We author our own life."* What I'm doing stems from wishes and hope, and what I've done may ignite a spark in the tinder of some minds. Sometimes we can control the flame of fire to be helpful and dualistic, yet imagine what we can do if we learn to manage and share love like we have the power of light.

I'm careful not to become rampant and torch the fields as I remember some gardens may appreciate the winter shroud of snow. Winter holds the bulbs of spring that come to bloom, and it's my responsibility to use my powers to help and heal our world. I remember, though, not all want to do good. I'm to be a plus one and not a negative one, and those who read these books are Earthlings who have an impulse to give and grow.

The first Fountains cast foundational blocks of text, and later after *The Sands of Yesterday*, *Shards of My Soul* called for completion. The base text of this book started before the conclusion of the Final Release version of Shards as I felt compelled to start this text and move into the future.

If the Fountains cover the dreams, wishes, and visions I hold, then perhaps we should get into the thick of this. I want to tell you what I want., though I also recommend and hope you tell others what *you* want. When we know our desires, it's then we can work towards them, and if yesterday affects faith, we build with endurance. When we hold the courage to develop fantasies into realities, we may flourish—perhaps to be more faithful and fruitful with resolve.

Previously, I've written prayers and repentance to God with Christian tones, though an alternative form of faith is having faith in ourselves. When people do something for someone other than themselves, it can bolster their confidence, grit, and determination. So, I work for Earth, even if God may not like it.

For who do you want to provide? For whom shall you work? Is a desire to work for the feeling of how it is to thrive? What can we do to offer more than we have already, and do we believe we can still do more? How can we have a more positive and expansive effect? Is it only about earning more money? I hope we understand and clarify why we do what we do.

For me, it's three things; the feeling of earning, doing something worthwhile, and because I like and love having money and sharing it. Are you happy doing what you're doing? If not, what could you do differently? I don't know your circumstances, though I think we need to do much more to guide our lives into better situations beyond my writing.

Some people believe they can't do anything different than they're already doing. I've fallen into that trap too. It takes effort, dedication, and perseverance to be okay to do what we need to do to be where we want to be, and as my Mom would say, we can't just wave a magic wand and wish for things to be better. We can, though, make positive choices to adjust our futures if we want them to be better. We also must define what better means to us.

I've lacked gumption and clarity about what I want, though I learn slowly. Generalized wishes of prosperity, happiness, and success needed to home into specifics. What is wealth, joy, and success for you or me? What if the things we want to do contradict those intents? I know I've not yet produced fantastic results, yet setting future goals adjusts my behaviours.

I've talked about the topic of smoking in previous books,

and if we look at people who are prosperous, happy, and successful, how many of them have you seen smoking? It seems contradictory for me to burn while also wanting longevity, and as I develop being more future sighted and optimistic, I envision and *plan* for a long life. There are habits I need to break, many practices I need to develop, and with incremental improvement, legitimate breakthroughs leap us forward.

One thing I strongly recommend is purchasing and reading books to expand your knowledge, your world, your mind, and your abilities. If you're reading *this* book, you're presumably a reader, though are you reading to escape reality, look into mine, or because you earnestly want to learn something?

If you're looking for specific, focused skills, directives, or purpose, try Brendon Burchard's book *High-Performance Habits* or Jack Canfield's *The Success Principles*. They both teach how to adjust attitudes and behaviours, and depending on your reasons for reading; either book may be the right book for you.

I write about creative ideas, recommend insights, and procure soulful imagination. My books use the first-person pronoun a lot, and I'm writing to tell you things that may be valuable or helpful for you too. It was 11:31 PM on Saturday, February 9th, 2019, when I started writing this. My classic caffeine-induced late-night writing sessions were in action, and I had watched two YouTube videos. One was about how much writers earn, and another was advice about authorship from eleven successful authors.

It was 11:49 PM Wednesday, August 14th, 2019, when I began the first revision. The late nights alone and multi-year incubation process were the sandwiches I eat that Elizabeth Gilbert spoke of in one of the YouTube videos. Does another chew on my infidelity instead?

Since these are the Fountains of Fantasy, please let me draw the threads from the loom. Though meeting Natalie Imbruglia is a bucket-list item I hold, competing on Survivor is too. It's ultra-ridiculous to think of doing either, yet both are worthwhile experiences. I also surprise myself and our community by gathering a few hundred pledges in the next year for my giving programs Providing Point and Chilliwack Housing Providers.

I found summer 2020 a successful season. The snow barely fell the previous winter when I was supposed to shovel snow, though a different job, landscaping, surfaced. I work for Sovereign Landscaping as of Fall 2018, and Brad, my boss, has been fantastic. I earn to clear my debts, set aside savings, and hopefully, in the future, afford a car.

My Dad and his wife Sarah were glad I'm working too. Dad and Sarah flew out for a trip in September 2019, and I admit I felt a bit envious. I want to go on flights around the world too, though the main thing I was missing (other than travel money) when I typed this was a travelling companion. I've not met a gal who can make trips overseas with me to visit and feel the air in other nations.

It'll be drastically different living with a gal again, though amazingly worth it. It's been a long time since having a girlfriend, and other than a one named Rizz at Simon Fraser University (SFU) in 1998, I've not lived with a female companion.

The process of hooking up with a gal is a tricky one for me. I've not been in a relationship in a long while, and I've not slept in the same bed with someone (other than my cats) since dating a gal in 2004-2005. My bed holds an empty spot for a real lovestone, though I need to trust her absolutely, and she must be entirely worthy of that trust. I have concerns about my next girlfriend and my up-to-now long-term solo mission, and I'm afraid I'll embarrass myself if we get naked together!

I've not even kissed a girl since 2015, though the species differential allows me to snuggle my cat and give him love; the gender bias I hold for physical contact doesn't apply to cats. I would have preferred a female cat as a pet, though trusting in the process of fate and destiny, I adopted Zeus, the cat.

The first book, *Finding Natalie*, had a chapter written to a friend nicknamed Chandra. Chandra and I talk reasonably well, and though we didn't hook up as a couple, I wrote a chapter to her in angst. Chandra asked later that I don't include the section in the final version of the book, though I also wrote to another female friend codenamed Elspeth in the 5th Fountain, *Fields of Formation*. Elspeth's chapter stayed as part of that book and its compilation *The Sands of Yesterday*.

Both Chandra and Elspeth are quite different, though both are liked and appreciated. Chandra will speak on the phone, visits, and values me as a friend, and though Elspeth too may value me as a friend, she rarely responds to messages and barely ever calls.

I don't have many friends and know only a rare few people. Because I'm not emotionally close to many and I don't have a best friend, I don't have a lot of friends I can call. I'd like more friends, and when I want to talk, there are some I call, though I don't often receive a response. What I want to find are more positive and mutually reciprocal relationships.

I'd like a girlfriend, and by having few contacts, I've communicated much to some, yet I learn how to converse better. With women, my history has been tainted; I've liked some gals a lot and then creep-showed, over-obsessed, or hadn't fully committed, and I held myself away from romance when I fixated on Natalie. That could be a reason why gals stayed away for a few years.

Now that I know Natalie's probably not good for me, I'm more open to a real relationship. It's almost like I'm on the rebound from divorce without ever being in the same room as my 'ex'-wife. And where are we going? If Natalie and the Seed Fund were life-long objectives and I released her, I'd not yet stepped up for my other personal missions. It leads to building a home, The Glass House, and I wonder how to form my prayers of penance for holding some of the desires I've claimed.

If we find our heart's wishes and what we desire aren't perfect things for us, can we take requests back? If to reform wants and desires, can we discover what our real attractions are? Perhaps we learn what is good or right for each other and build that way.

What's best for me leads to quitting smoking, yet I've held onto that crutch with a terrible resolve. One night early Spring 2019, I went to bed with the thought and wish to be alive fifty years from now. I should more often remember that. I also desire to feel inspired, active and engaged and working on things that matter to me, so if that's true, one big one is working on relationships.

Crucially, though, I want to earn my way and start gathering. I waffled on collecting pledges when I wrote this, though the bizarre calling keeps hounding me. I've felt frustrated and agitated and also energetically obsessed even if I've not always been passionate about gathering pledges, even for myself.

A reformation finds undercurrents leveraging activities for my benefit. Since I want to earn my way in life, maybe I should connect with others who also want to make, create, or discover their ideas and paths. In July 2020, I started a course with Jack Canfield and Patty Aubery that can help with that.

The homelessness and street focus push and pull me in different ways too. I want to find ways of relieving situations of lack, though I'm concerned if I don't devote myself entirely to the program, people will get mad at me. I don't want to quit or give up, yet I want to be free to act for my benefit too. I love having the luxury of only earning for myself, yet I'd want to share more. The kicker is the question; what if I can do both?

I don't want to throw money or crumbs at people and call them nuggets of gold either. The entire royalties gathered from book sales up to July 2020 isn't even close to the $800 it costs to cover a month or rent for a decent home. If my vision board says I earn enough money to house a thousand people from book sales, how can I make sales significant enough to do so?

Up to when I typed this, it seemed like the market didn't want my books or music. Even giving away freebies to people hadn't generated much interest in my creations. I'd shared a hundred or two hundred books, and if people like them, there hadn't yet been additional sales up to this release. If I received money for every copy given, it still wouldn't be big money and big prizes, so if my creative work is to house people, we'll need to sell thousands of books.

This book gathers more components of my Freedom Solution. We track how we can find freedom via legitimate pathways and remind me free money is helpful. It's even more gratifying to earn from personal efforts and be the one to provide that money.

I've not advertised the Providing Point program entirely, and I'm not fond of fundraising. The program naturally develops by sharing books with people and also talking about the issues and goals openly, and I've done that a bit since Fountain four. More time, effort, energy, and attention need to go into these books so that Providing Point may thrive. I hadn't been push promoting, and I must draw more support.

Passive actions and attitudes probably are why there'd been a dramatic lack of results. An impulse to create and talk about this program call me into being okay in the moment of now, though if we focus only on ourselves and our gain, or demean others to get the upper hand, that's not the pathway of how I want to be or act.

I'm on a pathway of care, inclusion, and respect with others who develop understanding and compassion. Me, my work, and my intents are hopefully beneficial ideas for encouraging positive channels of activity, and I am committed to the process of love and life. We endure the slings and arrows of the view to how I'm explicitly not You.

For those that are Christian and looking for Jesus, I can clearly and succinctly tell and remind you: I'm not the man you are looking for! I'm not a Messiah, God, or omniscient deity; I'm just a kid on Earth who's not learned how to 'adult' so well. I also seem to refuse to quit without getting my hands, heart, and soul-deep in what we require.

For those that are part of the consect and street community, I know I'm not hardcore or street. I have concern, empathy, regard, and reverence for some of you, yet I know I'm not living the lives you are either. I may be pushing my mind, my work, and my ideas into areas of your turf and territory, yet I'm not seeking to uproot you. I'm just one person who wants to find a sure path and let us each be okay.

I've wanted to shift from talking about providing for others to becoming self-reliant and actually doing so. I do so by activating my heart and must earn my living instead of relying on guilt offerings. Soliciting pledges for Providing Point's reloadable grocery card program keep a path to shared prosperity, yet I also allow myself to thrive and succeed with the books. We all gain from this process, work, and journey.

I keep www.Patreon.com/Introversial open for accepting pledges and abide by my promised contribution commitments from previous Fountains. The money earned from the Patreon pages and Fountains' sales go to the intended causes, and I also forge new activities, connections, and behaviours; to allow myself my wife, our home, and a family of many that include our friends.

Earth *is* a shared planet, and as we each can secure how to give and help others and ourselves to achieve success. We all may live more brilliantly, vibrantly, and with a more explicit manifestation of peace, love, unity, and respect.

ACROSS AN OCEAN

I'd been reading the book *The 4-Hour Workweek* by Tim Ferris. The book is *not* about slacking off, sleeping away the days, or watching Netflix as a professional hobby. The book holds tactical ideas about how to develop a business and life we can love instead of being trapped in full-time mind-numbing work.

For those who are waiting for retirement twenty to forty years later, Tim shares some valuable information about how to actualize more of your heart's yearnings, now. Tim's book also shares how to start up an online company with the support of automation and outsourcing to generate a substantial income.

When I first typed this, I didn't know what to focus on to earn my pay. I knew some Freedom Solution numbers, though. If I can sell a hundred units of 'me' a day, I can live luxuriously, afford to travel, and also have much more to share. The question is, "how I shall sell that many units a day?" What can I do to sell that many books, and when I do sell that many units a day, how will my life be different?

I think of travel, and the first place that comes to mind when I think of flying is usually Italy. I went to Italy in 2016, and I want to visit there again. It's partly because of the language; Italian is my second most fluent language, so going to that country seems more logical. Although it could be scary, I want to go for a few weeks alone and wonder about a three-month mini-retirement.

Natalie is also part of Italy and the title of this chapter. I've not been thinking much about her recently, though she's always in a part of my heart. I don't yet know who receives my entire love, and though Zeus is a kind pet, I want a female companion. I can't and mustn't hold myself away from a real relationship by holding onto an idea of one I fell for two decades ago. I want to find *my* lovestone and be *her* man. The wish is I find my love and travel with her, and she's almost certainly not the famous singer.

It's not going to happen magically by just wishing, either. I need to put in the effort to find love. That's what I've been reading in books; we need to work, plan, and cultivate actions to allow us to have the lives we want to live and love. Usually, the authors are talking about money and success, though it applies to love too.

I remind myself relationships are a high value I hold. Since my books are 'all-about-me,' then the target audience for my books are not specific niches, yet seemingly those interested in me, what I think, and who I am. I write recommendations and ideas, though I need to heed my advice too. "Rob! Make some new friends and just be a super-decent person!"

A friend I labelled Gideon cues me to remember I've neglected to contact people I like and love. Writing *is* solitary, and though I can bring a laptop anywhere in the world to write more, I think I first need to work for the community and friends here in town.

There's one I've complained about a lot, and the reluctance of interacting so much with them is how I get overly triggered by their behaviours and actions. I've thought if I've felt so negative about them that I should just avoid contact. If I get pissed off and angry and I'm meant to accept that's part of how I can be, then what and where is the right outlet for displeasure?

Many people tell us not to complain, yet when frustrated and needing to vent, I also don't want to trap the bad feelings in my heart or psyche; that could be damaging. I remember a technique and experience from *PD Seminars: Haven by the Sea* called a Vesuvius. It's not Pompeii, a place to visit, though instead is an exercise that's a healthy way to release anger.

A Vesuvius is a group activity where a participant receives space, safety, and freedom to purge all of their anger. With the respected boundary of a defined and separate area from the audience, the person performing the Vesuvius can yell, scream, stomp, curse, and cuss out all of their anger. The objective is to release the entirety of the participant's displeasure and purge all the secretly held feelings. The critical point is that the people present witness the session and that the person performing the Vesuvius is seen and heard. The audience helps support the participant by being there through the event.

I've wanted to have a Vesuvius. I've felt dramatic amounts of agitation and have been quite vulgar and reactive to people who deserve kindness. Some of it may be from hating myself for not achieving much, a generalized frustration, and I've not been happy all the time. Writing is therapeutic, though my anger is sometimes wanting to smash the keyboard and destroy things instead of focusing and forming eloquent words for an audience.

Who am I writing for precisely? I was unfocused with the book's direction and had started writing outwards generally again. I needn't just hone what I'm doing, though I must atone for what I've done. In one way, giving the proceeds from the books can tend to the causes people are helping by buying a copy, yet is that a guilt offering?

The night I wrote this part of the first draft, I gave $11.80 from two copies of *Fragments of Intent* to Ann Davis Transition Society and $3.36 to Ruth and Naomi's from the sale of one copy of *Open to Fate*. If I'm going to write books and create seed fields that flourish, I need to know who I'm writing to and for. We can craft our words for specific audiences, yet I often don't know who I'm telling.

Some authors write a lot on a topic focused on a niche audience and can hone their marketing in line. Some authors write books in different genres to reach a wider audience, though I've taken a different path with authorship, and it's not one I'd recommend. A local entrepreneur named Dave commented on how he thinks I'm "trying to boil the ocean." Dave recommended I focus on only one thing. When I told my Dad what Dave suggested, I knew a question I couldn't answer was, "focus on what?"

If I'm to write to a broad audience (the ocean), then how could I bubble up any interest. If I write for a small few people that want to read what I write (a pot), that could be easier to raise some steam. Who are the people that comprise a container of which I may bring to boil? Steam engines are quite useful, though what about Hydrogen fuel cells?

We can get clear and concise with our message or craft, yet still, be like unfocused light. I may need to hone and focus like a laser, and though I've received lots of advice and read some great books, information isn't enough. I need to *activate* my ideas and *actualize* my desires, and you can see the first letters in both those verbs are *a-c-t*, to act.

What we *try* to do or *think* to do isn't often what we *actually* do or *need* to do. I've wanted to write books people want to read and think I've made some good tracks, yet the market results up to July 2020 show that neither my books nor music have a firm demand.

If my Facebook friends haven't yet seen a post about "please ask me for a book," "check out my Bandcamp page," or "please give a pledge," they're not so active on Facebook. I remember that just because I make a post on Facebook, though, it doesn't mean every friend sees it. Yet with the number of posts I've made, and the many personal messages asking people to read a book, play some music, or give a pledge, I bet almost all of my contacts know.

If we're creators, we must remember Facebook, Instagram, or Twitter are platforms where we can gather readers, listeners and fans. With that said, though, just because we've made something, it doesn't mean people will give us attention, time, or money to process it. Push marketing can be like spam and push genuine friends away from interacting.

There are billions of humans on this planet, though, so our friend circles mayhap should be for friends and not soliciting sales. Also true, if our products or services are valuable, there's more of a likelihood someone we know will purchase. If we succeed in selling our work, then we must perform excellent work and also find our viable audiences.

I flooded my local contacts with requests to play my music, buy or read my books, or give a pledge, and Dave's advice narrowed me into knowing I didn't want an NGO as my only job. Music is something I create, yet with that, I'm very passive. Books can more accurately convey and share my intents, yet people hadn't yet been so interested in them either. I want to provide valuable information, I like shifting into rhyme mode sometimes, and I also love sharing resources. Knowing I like those three things (books, music, and giving) and why I want to do them find me to admit something, I prefer to write compared to making tracks or fundraising.

And yet Cullen Roche's post *40 Thing I've Learned in 40 Years* shares that just because we love something, it doesn't mean others will love us for doing it. If you have many desires or options, you know it may be challenging to focus and home in on one thing. I also hope when you reach your perfect moments of flow, you can acknowledge you like or love those things, though the trick about being a profitable creative is also knowing if and how we can sell what we create.

Some have wanted to be mainstream artists to make the big paycheck, yet the sacrifices aren't often enjoyable. Being a best-selling author can lure and generate fame, yet if you don't want to be famous, it's a different trip. With my past events, I've thought it's dangerous to be overly known, yet where I shift to is healing my trauma and learning valuable skills and information and sharing it.

I started with an inversed creation with the Fountains by focusing on Natalie, yet she wasn't receptive to it. Upon reflection, I scattered outwards with *Fragments of Intent* and then fell upon the shores of time amongst all the other grains of sand that wanted to be a pearl with her.

If Natalie's rooted in the ocean – in her shell keeping shut to prevent invaders – then how could a lonesome grain of sand like me get tripped into her world? I honestly don't know, though, in some ways, the years of agitation have formed these books stringing together one after the next. If you have only one pearl, how can you make an entire necklace?

Returning from the metaphors, how do I want this book to be valuable? If I created the first books with a different intent in each, then where are we in the journey? Few would want to buy someone's journal unless it was an exciting or famous person.

I have an idea people know who I am, yet perhaps I'm not so impressive. Some want solutions to their problems, not to read a babbler, so if I don't narrow down the purpose of what questions or issues I'm solving, then how can I direct answers or solutions?

If you want to write a book, be sure to start it, though. If you're going to make music for the pure sake of enjoyment, do so. It's best to know why you're doing what you do, and if you'd like to *sell* books or music, realize it's a different process. I planned to sell thousands of copies, meet Natalie, and house people by writing books, so I wrote them. I didn't think about commercial viability, though, and we need to know for whom we're creating. What do people want to know? Why do they want to know it? I've not entirely tended my answers to those questions.

A commercially successful focus is much different than gratifying creative expression. Is your work for business, prosperity, or personal satisfaction? If I'm to focus on my audience to increase potential sales, then perhaps I shouldn't write so much about myself unless others want to read about me.

My wish is I can succeed with creation and relationships without earning money from a job, yet the trick is I'd like to make a substantial income. Some may be exceptionally fortunate with sales and profits and still feel miserable, so what is the cost of money? I prefer to ask ourselves, "What can we do with the money?"

If people have a clear intent to share their resources with people who need things, what happens when those people providing earn more? If someone has correct ethics, legitimate purpose, and actively abides by those ethics and mission, shouldn't we allow them more to activate good things in the future?

My calls to action have been few, yet copywriting (not

copyrighting) applies to how to craft words to solicit action. Copywriting tells us that when we create advertisements, we need to consider what the customer's wants are and talk about the benefits we can provide.

Seth Godin writes about how marketing is not so much *what I can sell* and *for how much* yet instead suggests that marketing should be "to make things better [and] to cause a change you'd like to see in the world." Holding that statement, then each of my books is marketing dreams, faith, hope, and love.

I'd love for our world to find each to have more than just their basic needs. I want us to expand to see people achieve their dreams, and if the best things we can do are good for us, good for others, and good for the world, then I think finding my lovestone could be a pretty good thing. It may not be I'm ready to be a loyal parent or husband at this point, yet I know a real girlfriend would be fantastic.

When working with a partner or mate towards broad objectives, I've heard and read it's a marvellous thing. The principle of Masterminding edges me forward a bit further to have accountability partners to plot and plan great things. From my experience, I know working solitarily and without counsel isn't enough.

If I were to retake the past twenty years knowing Natalie was a complete no-go from the start, I'd have lived much differently. Since I didn't, I make the best of my situation and parameters and find my path extend. A broad stroke over the canvas can help start the work, yet the fine details painted later often are what refine art into a masterpiece.

Natalie splashed all over my canvas in 1998. Instead of throwing the work away, my soul accepted her as part of myself, and I try to find a way of painting a worthwhile picture. I share with the world instead of tossing the original piece into the bin, and though I may admit Natalie may not know me these years later, with a deep breath, I realize it was I who betrayed her.

It may be because I'm an obsessed Muppet dangling on Geppetto's strings, though we'll make a real boy out of this kid yet. One whose nose has grown so far out there that Saturn might have to send its rings back to the printer for another batch.

When and if I marry someone, I want to get it right the first time. First things first, though, secure a girlfriend. I'm just not entirely sure if she's up for it yet.

BLOCKING TIME

My pathway to profitable authorship has been messy. The first three to four books were atrocious structurally and grammatically, though, by the release of the sixth Fountain book, I'd learned a lot, and I continue to improve and refine my writing process.

When I purchased the professional version of Grammarly in January 2018, I went back to the previous books and distilled them. I cleaned up the text, resulting in, hopefully, kind and good water, though I've not yet had any of my books professionally edited. I have, though, learned heaps since I started writing on my own.

A challenge with writing a book is editing services cost a lot. Editors.ca says we could expect to pay up to $60 an hour for a freelance editor who's a professional in our industry. Some startup writers may not have enough to live, let alone a couple of hundred dollars for an editor, so if you don't have the cash to spend and are aiming for a profitable authorship path, you'll need to learn how to edit.

In *Fields of Formation* in 2017, I got overconfident in my editing skills. I was levelling up and thought I was getting excellent, though after getting Grammarly, I found a vast number of mistakes; there were hundreds of errors in what I thought was a finished document. If you can't afford an editor, make sure you at least get an editing program to help you.

A premium version of Grammarly costs $139.95, though if you're concerned about cost, Grammarly often offers promotions to purchase at a 45%-55% discount. The program is *entirely* worth it, and if you assess the quality of my work, it's the result of a few years of learning and a professional subscription.

I like to read books about personal development, finance and success. I may not soak in and activate *all* of the vital information, yet I learn a lot. By being a writer, I've learned to appreciate good writing, and I know writing well with valuable information is a stellar combo.

My first books are so much what I want to do, yet recently I've thought about writing for those who want to write too. It makes sense how other authors find their niches; by having an interest and then diving into the topic. We can gain a lot of trial and error experience working in our fields of interest.

I like to share big ideas, yet the way I approached Providing Point and my books was backwards. I started first with the focus on one person and looked at how much I could gather from a sale price, not how much value I can provide to be worthy of a purchase. If money is the motivator, it can draw us to work, yet if we write for a cause and with a purpose, it can assist us in believing in the worth of our work.

We need to value our work beyond how much we may gain from it. If others benefit from what we create, it expands the mutual value between the author and the audience. If we make things only for profit, though, there may be less meaning in what we create. If we're only profit-focused and see few results, it too can allure us to give up or quit.

I write partly from obsession, and also to earn a living. My first book was to get the girl, though it shifted to making money later on. I now write to share myself and my ideas, and I also aspire to convey worth and value. Regarding earnings, I've been the cart before the horse with some things, and I don't mean to be incongruent.

When starting to share our work with the world, there's an impulse to want anyone and everyone to read or buy a copy. I thought sharing free books would encourage people to purchase others in the series, thereby selling more, though, after two years of sharing books, I've not sold so many. I also continue to seed and create.

Perhaps I need to rethink my plots and plans? It may not be great to give free copies if seeking monetary gain because if someone would buy a copy and instead receive one for free, then there's zero chance of them buying that book. Writing a series can encourage cross-sales, though if starting with just one book, I'm not clear sharing free copies is the best. If aiming just for local success, it can be easy to flood the market with as few as a hundred copies, yet if you think global, there's a multitude who can buy and view our books.

Another challenge about selling books is that successful book sales are more than a monetary transaction. If a person buys a book, they have to be interested in the book, and also (if to read the book) are giving us their time to process our words. If you're to write a book, create a quality book that's worth both the time, money, and effort to read. The more people that buy a book *and* love what they read, the higher chance there is for referrals.

Some market the ultra-successful books because of *who* wrote the texts. There are also books written by previously unknown people that haven't just written an excellent book; they've also sold well. If you can create quality text combined with valuable information, there is a challenge of exposure, yet think of virality with books too. Some books become phenomenally successful because of entrancing their audience and forming a loyal following.

If you've read my books, you've seen me refer to some influential books and authors. They create great things, so I'm compelled to share them. At the point of forming this book, I'd not had a massive influence, yet the trickling of other's liquid gold fuses in like Kintsugi into my work. If you're to write, find the golden truths, wisdom, and guides that fuel yourself, and then find ways to pass on their knowledge to your readers. Be sure to give the originators credit, though.

I think everyone should write a book, and if you don't know what to write about, it's a challenge you can overcome. Freewriting on a computer or in a notebook is a great way to start—just write out anything that comes to mind and don't stop. Force your keys to move the cursor along with the screen or the pen across the pad.

You can also use the tactic of choosing one person and write to them everything you want to tell them. Who am I telling? What am I telling them? Why do they need to know? By writing slowly and intentionally, craft the words to be just for them. Freewriting activates our ability to produce words and ideas, though focusing on one person can dredge up feelings and deepen intent.

I can't give great advice about fiction, and dialogue can be tricky. One thing I've heard about a good novelist is they can envision entire worlds, situations, and all the characters. If you are crafting a fictional realm, you'll need to think of the scenery and settings as vivid and real in your mind. You'll need to convey sensory information about the world, how it feels, what sights and landmarks there are, and consider daytime, nighttime, and the seasons.

You'll need to know your characters explicitly well. In an exercise about character development and understanding the people, write a letter from one to another. i.e. if your main character is to interact with another primary character, get into the role like a method actor would and write a personal letter from one to the other. Be meticulous and think about the emotions and perspectives of each from a crystal-clear point of view. What qualities or traits either disgust or delight the characters on a personal level? What secrets do they know about each other?

Even if you don't share the direct thoughts and ideas from the character letter later in your book, it will help you to know your characters better. You can leave tidbits and secrets sprinkled throughout the story to thread together more profound insights for the reader to discover, too. Think of Easter Eggs in movies where the audience feels greater inclusion by identifying the obscure allusions.

Authorship is a radically pleasant journey to know. Even if I don't sell millions of copies, there's a definite gratification of crafting something and sharing it with others. Again, I believe every person should write at least one book in their life about anything they want to write.

The way you form your book is unique to you, though the most vital, crucial, and essential thing is to not focus on the monetary gain; concentrate on quality and meaning. If you want to be commercially successful, you may write for money, though that's a different path. Many people know that honestly, though, no matter why or what you make, just make it. (Is that like the Nike saying of creating?)

I lace signs and symbols into our tapestry. I've used metaphors about seeds, blossoming, and life plus allusions to outer space too. I've written sections based upon molecular structure, fission and fusion, and metaphors twisting universal symbols we use. These symbols draw from concepts that others understand mixing in the core of who we are—even saying this is a tapestry calls the ideas of sewing together ideas and thought.

I was still tricked up on this, though. Suppose I am to focus on the monetary gain. If I shift from giving free copies to people, it'd mean I need to sell books to get the words into people's hands, eyes, and hearts. I've been awful with sales, and if I create for people to read, I've also found myself with zero promise or guarantee another process that I've written. It's where either passion or obsession drives me to create as I consider the potential readership and gains.

Self-awareness lessons are substantial when we write too. If you choose to edit your work with Grammarly or another editing program, once the first draft forms and you shift to revision, you'll find weird things about yourself and your work.

When I've revised my books, I've syphoned signs of cryptic intuition and found bizarre hidden truths about language and understanding. The significance of individual letters and consciousness of words are like Lego blocks of subverted guidance. I tear fragments of words and their constituent parts, finding me rethinking how I text on my phone.

For example, I became reluctant to use the word 'good' because it had a potential interpretation if split into 'go' and 'od' with no space. I took it as wishing 'go overdose,' which is not a kind thing. Hoping someone 'good' had a different connotation, and it hounded my neurosis for a while. When I project hidden meanings, I can get weird.

I'm kind of ADD with these books. The text is like an Albertan river twisting and turning through the landscape of time, making meanderings and slowly pooling along. We know most rivers lead to a lake or ocean, and if I've repeated time and time again that I want to create for the essential luxury to write what I want, then is it best I forget about sales and marketing? I've considered and desired financial success, yet I think to myself, sometimes I'm creating intrinsically.

Some of my more 'commercial' projects feel like tasks instead of pleasure. I'm okay to discover a pathway to $70k+ a year. That's three times as much as I made in 2018, though, and a lot less than selling 15,000 copies a month. I sold less than fifty books in the entire first three years of publishing, yet I've not detached from the idea of earnings. I also accept sales to be a consequential bonus and not an expectation.

It may not seem it, yet the reminder is to do what you want to do and release the desire for earnings if money isn't your primary goal. If I were more money-focused, perhaps I'd push for massive sales and push for best-seller status. I admit, now, that I'm *not* entirely comfortable to earn a lower income and *not* have humungous success with my books.

I've feared how life would be if I had more than I do now, and perhaps my mentality of lack roots in a safety belief because I fear jealousy and greed. If I don't have thousands in my bank account, then no one can steal or mooch it from me, and by not having a car, I don't have to worry about expenses and the responsibility of owning a car. I've not even yet shown I'm responsible enough to earn a basic $30k income by myself, let alone $70k or more, yet that changes.

Instead of feeling over-confident or having lingering doubts, I inversely assume success, yet I'm nudged to believe in endurance. The pessimistic and optimistic sides polarized again. Perhaps it's best to stop this tangential chapter.

I'm not creating this book for reaching a word count or believing it's going to make me millions. I thought I'd sell books and house a thousand people, and if I release pushing for Providing Point, what is the drive that makes and allows us to thrive as I write? What is my motivation?

"I still don't know."

I'm finding my Freedom Solution. I want to be safe, sure, and secure mentally, emotionally, financially, spiritually, socially, and physically. I don't want to be tossed into the cold white-water rapids and fight for survival. I want to be like the slow meandering Albertan rivers carrying the waters of life, where we can sit in the canoe and float along peacefully. The winters in Alberta are ridiculously cold, though, and in spring, summer, and fall, there's some great life to live there too.

With the theory that all things happen for a reason, I block the text into the book and shift back into my corner. I may not have a coach at this time, yet some people are rooting for me in the audience. I'm reluctant to fight for what I want because I don't want that much. I want to have a life where I can feel the love in my heart for other people without being judgmental of others for how they're living.

We don't all need to have overflowing pockets of cash, yet a bit of coin would be cool. It allows us to build more together in the future, and it lets us live lives where we can truly thrive, interact, and connect.

ROBERT KOYICH

CORRELATED FAITH

If the most influential and formative years of our lives are when we're kids, that's a sign. I'm an only child, and I don't understand what it's like to be a brother. I was uprooted when I was five from Edmonton to Toronto, and after only three years in Toronto, my family moved to Australia. Two years in Sydney, Australia, and then we moved to Hong Kong for another two or three years. After that, Mom and I came back to Edmonton, which brought me back to being the new kid in school again in grade seven.

It's clear to me now that I've forgotten much of my childhood. I wasn't appropriately socialized, and I'm not sure I'm in contact with anyone from before I was thirteen that isn't family. There are four kids I grew up with until I was five years old; I now call them cousins, yet I barely hear from them. They're now all coupled and living their lives, and I wish we'd speak again soon.

Although it sounds fantastic and glamorous to have lived in Australia and Hong Kong, I recall how I was separate back then. In Australia, I had a best friend named Chris, who tried to teach me how to skateboard and surf, though I wasn't their best friend. When I lived in Hong Kong, there were many international students, mostly American, though I didn't fit in well there. I latched onto a family friend named Ted, and, again, similar to Chris, Ted was my best friend, yet I wasn't his.

I've never really fit in well with groups. In my books, I've talked about playing Survivor, yet how can I excel in a social game? If I've not learned how to buddy up with people and am afraid to speak up sometimes, how could I ever consider having enough gumption to make it to the merge?

Projecting myself as isolated and set apart is a particularly unhelpful behaviour and belief. It's not healthy to think of myself of separate, especially if I want to work with others and be part of a tribe. If I attempt to be bold and brave and claim to do some of what I've written in my books, it could make me a target if I'm all alone.

The psychiatrists diagnosed me as a paranoid delusional schizophrenic, yet sometimes I wonder how much is having rational fear. The delusions of grandeur from my past have called for fantastic wishes and wants, yet perhaps I've dreamt, believed, and wished for far too much. As I sat writing this, I thought about where my psychological issues stem.

How many of my problems are from a lack of social graces and understanding and not only mental health issues? My meds null my mind and keep me under control, yet much power holds me within. If there's a chance of me being med-free in my future, I don't know how or when, and some holistic healers believe meds corrupt a mind. I partly think that's true.

When I wrote the first draft of this section, I felt a scummy tingling in my head and shoulders from my medication and felt sketchy tremors thinking about the drugs. Even if I'm not taking recreational drugs, the techy feelings of past psychological damage and taking medication doesn't make me feel naturally fluid or safe; it seems to feel like chemical corruption. When I've missed one of my meds on rare occasions, the next day feels weird and wonderful, yet later on, the mental activity escalates.

It goes back to the discussion about telepathy. How much of our thoughts are heard or seen by others that aren't us? At the area contest for Toastmasters in March 2019, I was a judge for the speech context. I cognitively heard people critically reading into my thoughts about the scores I was giving. It was not comfortable.

I sometimes think I have zero privacy of my being, and I know when people scrutinize and focus on us, those people can add a great deal of distortion if we're not golden clean. With what's ran around in mind sometimes, I agree there are terrible things and ideas out there.

With awareness being a vital starting point, what happens when we discover our values and ethical acceptability and then build? Some have told me they think I possess strong self-awareness, yet I think I could be called self-absorbed. With my books, I use the word 'I' a lot and don't delve so much into research or reference. If I'm to be market-oriented, then I need to know what people want to buy if to be commercially profitable, and I thought it wasn't me.

Can my self-obsessive lessons, though, be beneficial? Is it best to use me as an example of an overly dramatic and covertly known focal point? When I block the base text of my books, my neurosis seems to stitch waste into the core of the words. Each sentence alone seems not to have value.

Though after reading an entire chapter or volume, and when editing, the words sound more significant. If I'm creating a beautiful forest of work, I guess some of the trees aren't so impressive on their own, and yet the seeds find the needs met.

Zeus has been an influential trainer for me. He has tested my boundaries explicitly and is kind and relaxed most of the time. One contested point in our home was him clawing on furniture, and it's a behaviour we adjusted. I'm not clear how ethical my learning is, yet I assess and reassess as time progresses.

My behaviours, routines and schedules have been something I'm aware of too. Where in the past I'd fuel up on coffee and work until sunrise, I've more often not, and learnt to respect myself by not doing so as much. Chemical abuse has been an issue for a long while, and if now only the legal drugs of caffeine and nicotine, both addictions have fueled my creative work. Drugs, legal and otherwise, are part of the cross I bear.

How could I write a book about being healthy with all of my contaminated choices? I didn't think I could write a book about ethics with some of my unfortunate life choices, though I think we should more often look at our own growth during our lifetimes. Evolution is not only the long-term development of our species or world, but it's also the unstable mutations where we become better aware and develop acute stability.

I'd love to learn what it's like to be a great parent, and finding the gal to have a child with hadn't yet happened. There's also a physiological issue I have. I may not be able to have kids. Medicine has developed a long way, so perhaps DNA splicing ensues, yet adoption isn't off the table from my view. I prefer that my child be my flesh and blood, though if that's not physically possible, I'll need to talk about it with my wife.

Honestly, though, I'm not sure why I want to be a parent. I'm not sure if it's so that my parents can have grandkids, or because I think it'll be awesome to socialize and raise another fantastic human, especially with a woman I love and respect.

Thinking about being a parent and *being* a parent is entirely different, yet it's a dialogue I want to have. I believe being a parent is a rewarding journey to share with a gal, and it stems from me wishing I had my own family.

Watch what you wish for, though, right? I've wanted to meet Natalie, I've wanted to live in the Glass House, and I also wanted to start a charity to home 250,000 people as an organization. I feel nowhere near reaching any of those three goals, yet endure. What have you wanted that you have near-zero belief it shall manifest? Maybe if we work more for our wishes, we can help them come into being.

And then the light courses down from galactic realms into the soul. As we carry forward with the text, subtle unions of thought nudge the cursor across the page, yet when you see the words, the book shall be complete.

When we read books, we don't understand all that's gone into forming them; from the initial idea or impulse, the writing, the editing and revision, and the subtle thoughts, hesitations, and inspirations that press each key. It's a miraculous process.

I bring this back to other writers. I may not have tons of recommendations or much guidance for you, and if you are a seasoned writer, then I may look daft and amateur. The endurance and continuation of forming books hold value. However, it may not always be transactional in a clear and concise form I share—sly adaptations of text hint at the developments of the developing glaciers. And yet the warm water and light course from above to rinse off my spirit.

Even if you see the same words, there's variety in how others hear it. If another hears us speak and we're telling the truth, it may not be factual for them. Inversely true, if another is honestly a kind, decent, and honourable person, it still may seem others goad and are at fault.

Another could be spiteful, filled with malice and disdain, yet always be believed to be love. Some speak gentle and kind, yet a torrent of energy hurls their mind against walls of belief. And yet another may seem angry and hateful, yet just be out of sorts and misunderstood as a person. Anger isn't always hatred.

The balance and shift of good and evil can polarize understanding, and I've been afraid of calling myself good because of the saying, "only the good die young." Though the lyrics haunted me many years ago in my youth, another reminded me I'm not so young anymore.

It brings us to Saturn and the bringer of old age. I may have misconceived the association though found the link from the album *Holst: The Planets*. I had an idea to call this three-part book *Saturn's Rings*, and it was after the first draft of *Rings of Truth* completed that I thought of the title *Mosaic of Miracles*.

If I keep cycling ideas about the dreams and notions of my being, is that a metaphor of how I'm like a noble gas? It seems I don't bond with many very well, and I feel further away from the Sun than most Earthlings. In some mythology and symbolism, Christ is said to be the Sun, the star we orbit.

Part of my life is still tethered to Him, though I've fallen far away from worshiping. I pray, though not near as often as I used to, and I've been concerned about sacrificing myself entirely. I wish to gain courage, though what compounds is my human fear of giving myself away to anyone or anything. Is it because I'm afraid I'll lose myself?

I seem to teeter between my beliefs, though it's not so much like a pendulum swinging between two points, for a pendulum appears far more secure. I sometimes feel like I'm walking a tightrope wobbling and wavering without having a stable balance. Though some say when we're wavering between points without certainty that that's the sweet spot of living is.

When we're on the precipice or cusp of an unknown experience or truth, we can feel quite alive. It's the uncertainty and nervousness that can turn into fear or excitement; it depends on how we respond to the insecurities. Language may seem very explicit, and when reading a book, we see the long game of an idea.

My weaves may be sporadic, yet the process of extending the series straightens out some things. There are frayed threads, yet the needle points of one chapter after the next stitch together something I hope may warm a few hearts. I'm fortunate to have a home and place to sleep, and part of me believes if I keep at sheltering ideas on the pages of these books, we'll flourish. It may be another couple of years until we see the results, and sadly, I've lacked the faith we provide as much as we do.

When I typed this, I realized I might lack some desirable things, mainly money, though I have a massive abundance of other things. Even when broke cash-wise, I've felt rich in some ways. Without being popular or hearing from friends, it's a luxury to have such an amount of time, space, and freedom from the demands of others. Famous people have all sorts of random people messaging and reaching out to them all the time. I don't have that, and I appreciate the lack of attention.

I lack influence too, though, which could be helpful to generate and do some things. If I had a more significant impact on life, what would I do? At this moment, I realize I'm in a vacuum of attention, and I gain clarity by focusing on choosing what I'll do. In line with the Fountains of Fantasy, perhaps it's what we can do with massive influence and money.

I've thought I've been poor money wise for a few reasons. I've been concerned about mooches and thieves, as I've thought if I have cash, that another would want it from me. I've even thought about responsibility and how I've been foolish with money in the past. Wondrously, I increase my resources, yet substantial acquisition and book sales could not be okay if I'm not responsible.

Regarding what I do as I reach high levels of prosperity? If I can sell thousands of books, I know that giving 51% from the three-part books and 100% from the individual Fountain books go to where I promised in Fountain six, though what of the 49%? I also think about what I can do to achieve a high level of well-being.

If I sell three thousand books a month, it'll mean I'll be earning about $12,000 a month. Making that much can easily cover my debts, allow me a vehicle, and put me towards and into a new home. The next question is, then, how do I sell three thousand books a month?

In the second and third month of 2019, I'd started telling people my goal of selling a hundred units of me a day. That's more than the fifty I initially wrote about in the second chapter, though I believe if we set higher goals, we have more for which to work. It shall be a process requiring effort, luck, and support, yet I'm starting to believe in it. *"How do you eat an elephant? One bite at a time."* What I didn't realize in 2019 is that it also requires massive effort and action.

If that holds as truth, then I must start grain by grain, bit by bit, seed by seed, and book by book. I understand it's a pathway I walk, though fortunately, some walk alongside. My friends, family, and contacts might appreciate it if I'm not going to sell them a book or solicit a pledge, yet I'll be able to share more as I reach sales targets. Considering the potential, I'm hoping it's quite profitable.

I best be cautious, though. If I can reach selling three thousand units per month, there may be more focus on me and what I do. With my nervousness and excitement of thinking about reaching so many people, I'll also need to accept more may be asked of me. That's part of the responsibility; if I'm to reach a vast audience, I owe homage, respect, and regard too. It's my readers that also allow me to live the life I lead.

GIVE IN OR GIVE UP?

I needed to reinvent and rediscover a new set of wants and desires. What I had been doing wasn't working, and the day I first wrote this, I became very vulgar, angry, and abusive.

After writing a bit, I called my Mom, and it was an excellent choice. I remember Mom's advice from when I was growing up about 'needing an attitude adjustment.' It's very accurate and happened again a few weeks later.

Fountains ten to twelve are the Fountains of Fantasy. In them, I want to write more of what I want to happen, yet needed to repent. I shifted to optimism after feeling mad and angry with my life, and I know who I am doesn't always coincide with how I behave. I wish for love, hope, happiness, and truth, though the fact when I wrote this was I honestly wasn't thrilled.

Depression is a legitimate thing, yet there also can be bullish and persistent defiance. I've had considerable uncertainty about what I want, why I want it, and how I want to feel, and the day I first wrote this chapter is NOT how I want to be. I needed to get out of the space and mindset I was within; I needed to breathe, centre, reset and make a new take. Gratitude is helpful, and it's tricky to get off a negative train of thought.

Whining and complaining is a waste of time, effort, and energy, though I need to focus on the present. I need to think of what I want for the future, and also remember that the past is a substantial portion of life here on Earth. Some may not forgive, some people may wish they knew more love, and sometimes I need to remember that it's a small number of people that genuinely do care for me.

If I want love in my life, I'm going to have to go out there and earn it. At home, living with my cat was awful for a while. I was getting angry and abusive because of Zeus intentionally clawing on our furniture, and our apartment was a mini warzone. Zeus knows it makes me mad when he scratches, and it seemed to be a blatant power play from the cat.

Some say cats don't understand English, though I hold firm a belief our pets also know what anger is. They're not stupid; they're smart and crafty animals that know full well how to assert power and demand control. That's what happened the first weeks Zeus lived with me, and the power struggle surfaced again in March 2019.

Instead of focusing and expressing how I'd been feeling anger, resentment, and hatred, I want to use this chapter to build, not destroy. It's going to be tough to create a life of peace, love, unity, and respect with how I'd been acting, though the shift is towards earning, developing, and cultivating love and not just money.

Peace with ourselves is one of the first things we need. For me to find inner peace, I need to acknowledge and accept myself. It's tough to do because often I don't like myself. I've been triggered easily and angered, and when I get angry, vulgarities hurl out of my mouth, and I want to smash things. I've done so too sometimes.

When violent, I've ruined inanimate objects and have wanted to decimate some living too. I don't like that part about myself. I want love, though why would anyone want to love me? If I know my actions aren't admirable when I've lashed out in those times, how could I ever earn, let alone deserve love?

I see being peaceful as a precursor to love, and I've understood how someone can be violent and also be loving. Abusive relationships see that, and repentant or remorseful feelings are legitimate. It's a very bizarre dualism though I understand it from myself, something of which I'm not proud.

If trapped in repentant energy, it's difficult to free from such, too. The same thing goes for self-hate or even the emotion of grief. When we aren't feeling good about ourselves or others, we need to find ways to climb out of the pits of despair. I'm learning how to do so and have a firm belief that talk therapy is fantastic. When we can openly and honestly state our grievances, or acknowledge our mistakes to those we've wronged or resent, it can be a path towards peace.

If you argue and win an argument, though, you also may win hate, spite, and anger. Is it worth it? I don't think it is. The title *Give In or Give Up* stemmed from me either giving in and being dominated, or give up and release any care, compassion or kindness for Zeus. I didn't see that it a win/win either way; I couldn't even imagine a compromise.

Giving up could have been avoiding conflict, and submitting and accepting terrible behaviour would have been giving in. Both could build resentments and result in an unfortunate situation.

My life to many is irrelevant and not even trivial. If I yearn to procure the values of inclusion, compassion, and kindness from myself and others, I must adjust when I turn into my angry and vulgar version of self; I must remember to return to and honour my peaceful and loving side.

I do feel guilt and shame, though I need to process the feelings and not contaminate another. It's a reason I keep myself away from people sometimes, so I don't taint the waters of life when I get poisonous.

If I want to push away every moment of life, where can I be if the cat lives with me? He was disrespectful, and I felt aggravated and goaded. I felt like I wanted to throw him off the balcony, so if I didn't like his behaviour, give up?

If I gave up, it would have released any kindness and forgiveness I have for Zeus. It may sound magnified, yet his spiteful and vindictive actions aroused me to hate. I was living with an infestation of negativity and degradation, and I found myself wanting to hurt the cat and damage him.

I won't inflict physical damage upon Zeus, yet I locked him up in his kennel when he clawed on the furniture. That didn't dissuade him either. The spiralling thoughts and feelings wished retribution, yet that isn't positive either. I'd love to hear from Zeus about his grievances and joys, yet that isn't an option because Zeus doesn't speak English.

If hate begets hate and the ones we live with fuel us, we can't always just kick them out of our home. The experience with Zeus was entrapment, yet I know he can't just leave either. I knew we'd find a solution, even if we didn't know what it was. By the publication of this book, though, we were glad and well.

Persistence, patience, and consequence created me as being passive and accepting, yet, with some, I refuse to share the same space. Retaliation isn't a kind thing, and there is an argument about the consequences of actions. How can we be peaceful if we're goaded by another who wants us to be angry?

The situation with Zeus got me thinking about prisons and corrections institutions. Putting anyone in confinement can only further bury and burrow spite and hatred. With humans and prisons, the theory is that we can minimize poor behaviour with the threat of locking someone up in a cell. If someone is put through such, though, I can see how their psyche and self-worth might believe they aren't or can't be decent people again.

With my cat, when I locked him up, I saw him spitefully claw on the furniture again after disliking the punishment. It seemed like a negative cycle, cat claws in spite, lock up the cat, more scratching on the furniture because he's mad. I keep my responsibility not to harm him, though that's where the control needed was self-control and not animal control.

When I typed this, I didn't see or believe punishments of kennel time or being locked up in a room were beneficial or a solution. How can we believe in the goodness of another if they are violent, abusive, or vulgar? I understand the negative cycle, and if we treat anyone like they're only going to do wrong, how can we even expect them to be good, kind, and peaceful?

My expectations were way off. Even if I want to be loving, sweet, kind, and gracious, bad behaviours triggered me to reciprocate hate and separate. Since I don't want to return hatred or animosity, I put Zeus in a different room, and in some situations, removed myself from where I was.

With human friends, I've also separated from a rare few

connections. I've been easily triggered, and when I catch myself turning venomous, I practice learning how to respond and how to be appropriate. I dislike violence and abuse, yet during the two weeks with Zeus, both seemed like highly logical reactions.

If we gain anything from the difficult times, it's both a comprehension of feelings we're not used to and learning how to behave, control, and adjust. When broken, mutual respect and love can return, though it takes time. I couldn't expect to control or manage my cat's behaviour, and I certainly couldn't discuss it with him.

It was exceptionally petty and pitiful how I got so reactive, and I understand there are issues I need to deal with. I wondered what resolution would manifest and thought positive reciprocation was a fantasy. Working together with mutual respect was and is the solution, yet I can't command that from another, especially a cat.

So, what's happened since those few tricky weeks? I've again wanted to travel, I've wanted to own a car, and I'd been working part-time landscaping. I cleared my student loans, and also progressed with the books.

I adore Zeus now, even if I dislike his previous behaviours. To solve the issue with clawing, he has a cat tree, and a scratching post (which, yes, the scratching post was there during the trials and tribulations) and carefully placed towels put on the contested spots.

It's a fact I've not had much love in my life, yet I desire human interaction and wish for more. I sorted out my attitude adjustment, and I'm now wondering how to find a girlfriend and build our life together. That's one of the next steps.

In March 2019, I hated myself and my life. I'm not entirely clear on what happens in the future, yet I'm glad I didn't give in or give up with Zeus and deny him a home. Is that what the world would have done with me?

Theoretically, the world dislikes some of my behaviour too, so it seems some have given up on me and won't contact. I don't want my home to be a prison cell for Zeus and me, so perhaps I can view it instead as a haven and place of solitude where we're abundant in time, space, and connection.

I'd not felt as much anger towards someone in the two years before that March with Zeus. I've bitched and moaned about work, yet having a job, a home, a cat, and resources are beautiful blessings. Being locked up without having space for oneself is different than being alone.

If I like having my own space, I also think of parenting human children. Kids are a lifelong commitment, and not a commitment many can back out of most of the time. Some kids are given up for adoption, and abortion is a thing, though I commend the parents that tough it out with their offspring.

What though can we do about another animal living in our home? What can we do if or when a situation comes near to or is violent? I've seen parts of the dark side of life, and it's an unsettling understanding. What I'd like to know is the solution to evil thoughts and feelings to prevent them in others too.

It got me thinking about marriage and divorce. How bad can it be that there's a divorce? As much as I didn't like it, I comprehend how hate and animosity can become too much. With Zeus, I saw a side of human emotion I'd never fully known, and I'm glad I forget it. With Zeus, in some ways, I believe he knows what's right and wrong, and if he now does what he wants, perhaps I can give him more good things to do. The lesson was; when others abuse us by triggering our tender points, we can turn into monsters.

I don't want to carry negativity in my being. If it's helpful to get out of a toxic relationship, it may be beneficial for both. Unfortunate situations can turn out okay, though, and that's what happened for Zeus and me. I thought living with a cat would be all love, kindness, and affection, though it wasn't that way for part of our process.

March 2019's trauma and crisis was a call for love and respect. It's due to a cat who refused to give in, and I'm glad I didn't give up. Living with another isn't easy, and it was profoundly evident to me. I questioned my mental health and understand how abusive, demeaning, and reactive I can be, and

I wish not to be that way.

Here's a weird thought for the world:

If there is a God, then He created science. If God created science and doesn't want to be known, then science cannot prove He exists. If God wants to be understood, yet not by anyone who believes only in science, then science will never be able to prove He exists. If someone believes entirely in God and uses science to determine His existence, if God doesn't want anyone to prove His existence with science, even a believing scientist cannot prove God exists. If God wants people to believe in Him in their own understanding or way genuinely, then He will be faithful to them in the ways only that person may know, thus not being recognized in the same way by anyone.

It may be very few are a friend, yet I seem to sense some who present as friends yet don't like me so much. I've thought of the plan and plot, and though I don't like how I was with Zeus in our rough spot. The time since, though, reminds me that our authentic nature is love.

Perhaps this chapter is sufficiently titled. I wouldn't give in and submit, so maybe I gave up and released. Another part of this is my compassionate side believed and thought there could be a situation where Zeus and I wouldn't struggle for power. With his attempt of dominant behaviour, I was sure I needed to clear the cat from home, and with such a substantial adverse effect on my psyche and demeanour, I found me hating myself and others when I was around them. I didn't want to be in that type of relationship with myself or another.

The blend of self-care tangled with submissive compassion and thorough animosity. If I submitted and let Zeus scratch on the furniture without repercussions, I'd only resent him more. Another pathway would be to release any attachments to my quality of life and attitude and let him rule the home. No. I didn't want that either.

I almost gave you up. Sorry, Zeus. Though you pushed me far too far and I wanted to obliterate you, it seemed you intended to aggravate me and push me to my limits. I'm glad you didn't give up on me, and from a few pages ago: "If you win an argument, you also may win hate, spite, and anger." That is what you won for a while, Zeus, though we didn't give in or give up. We found a different pathway, and for you and me, and I thank you for being here. Ti amo!

MEDIATED MOTIVATION

We fuel reality into fantasy. The previous chapter stemmed from the power struggle I had with my cat, and though that point of time included some of the darker and harsh elements of myself, it taught me a bit about abusive relationships. I believe in healing, repentance, and reparations, though if these are the Fountains of Fantasy, let's get back to dreaming.

I've been open at times about helping others with money and resources because I want to help people other than myself. I hold dreams of my successes, and for the three to four weeks before this chapter, I was working landscaping, my classes had just finished for the semester, and I'd gotten money-focused again.

With earning from my job and liking such, I repent I've also received a lot for free. If we're to have money, what are we doing to do with it? Some want to buy expensive things or high-value items, while I'd like to pay off my debts and invest. I owe money to the government and the bank, and though I had student loans, I paid them off in July 2019. I want to own my home outright and save for the future, and that requires money and planning, too.

One item I'd like to buy is a car. I've gone without a car for three years, and though the lure of putting money towards a vehicle is there, instead of buying a car, I'd like to keep money free for other things, such as my debts. Once I become debt-free, I can look at owning a car and building The Glass House and paying for it.

If I build and live in the home, it's going to require significant earnings. Working landscaping isn't anywhere near enough to provide for the home, yet I can envision each room of the house. It seemed like book royalties weren't the pathway to the house yet either, but they hold a substantial role.

By seeing and hearing how my boss is with his company,

it's evident running a business is *not* an easy thing. In 2018, I thought I was going to run Providing Point as an open and expansive organization, yet charitable work isn't going to earn me an income. Another business could potentially be profitable, and the concept of gathering for a non-profit reminds me that that money is for others and not me.

In earlier books, I promised book earnings to go to charities, and I maintain those promises. I also wonder if I'd have more success with books, sales, and marketing if I profited more from the process of authorship. I need to sell myself on the books being great reads and also that the programs are worthwhile and valuable.

In a movie, I heard one thing about being an adult is to fail miserably at something we love. At this point, it seems I've been unable to achieve my dreams; I've not yet met Natalie, I'd not yet turned Providing Point into a thriving non-profit, and I've written almost a dozen books without profiting substantially up to release.

I've not quit, though. Even if I've not yet earned much from my books, writing, for me, is something I feel compelled to do. The dreams are there; sell lots of books, gather interest and pledges, be debt-free, and move forward into a new home.

Some pledges come from talking about the program with the confidence needed to find people who want to ally. I realize, as much as I'd like otherwise, it truly matters what I do and say. I fell from being high in the clouds and floating in space, I then landed pleasantly on stable ground.

It's kind of comforting to know I don't have to tend to millions of fans. I live a peaceful and sometimes dull life, yet Zeus is here. Even if it's not always been true, Zeus is a perfect point of love, and I feel a bit of sadness and shame for my abusive actions of the past. My cat is very dear to me, my heart, and my soul, and I hope to gain his forgiveness and his love.

My Dad and step-dad have read some of my books too. These books are how I send out some of my wishes to the universe, and in an open exposition, the hope is we can continue to sort out and refine aspirations, goals, and dreams.

Sands shift along the shorelines of time, yet I remember to amend and add a tad of PLUR with the rhyme. Repentance is a positive thing.

April 18th, 2019

Okay, I can explicitly choose to write anything I want to. With the intent to see the book in its final form, we remember the cast's view of how I didn't know her yet too.

My girlfriend hadn't yet visited our apartment, yet she might have been thinking about this for a while. I remind Zeus that Mooshka and Belle also weirdly believe in love, and I hope I can write for intrinsic value and allow the right things to happen for us. God, please enable us to thrive.

I wasn't clear I could write to Aeris again yet. Aeris is my future daughter, and I wrote to her in *Seeds of Tomorrow*, the 4th Fountain. Upon revision, I wondered about that text because, as far as I can yet understand or imagine, it's only Zeus and me at home.

Hopefully, two calico kittens, Mooshka and Belle, can move in after I hook up with my real lovestone, and it seems logical to find real love instead of Natalie, especially since the enchantment's worn thin.

I remind of us a question to ask when writing. Who are we writing to? An active part evolves what we're saying, though if I write to one person, even if myself, a focused chain of text ensues. If written to a broad audience, perhaps generalization could dilute, so to whom best I direct the words?

I didn't have a girlfriend when I first typed this, and if to write to another, I could mix up parameters. What about a letter to God? Or, I could generally write out to the Universe again? If my next girlfriend reads this book or the others, she'll have a window into my being, yet since I can't talk to her yet, if she does read them, she'll know a lot.

You may not see and understand how I've been galactically outlandish, and even if I'm foolishly optimistic, I've achieved abysmal results from my bookwork up to release. I prefer to talk instead of text, and though sometimes a phone call is as good as an in-person meeting, my dear love, where are you?

Sometimes I don't want to meet up with people, and in those cases, sometimes a phone call is entirely okay. There are a rare few I'd love to talk with and can't for they don't answer the phone or return messages. It's also rare that people are up late when I write during the night, though I heed hints and allegations to be more respectful and considerate.

Who are you, though? Living alone, even with Zeus at home, it's an ultra-basic life for us with so few people to talk to. I have about four hundred contacts on my phone, yet there's only a narrow few I can call out to if I want to talk. Of lots of the others, I either don't want to bother them, I don't feel safe to contact them, or I want to avoid reaching out to them.

Of the twenty or so people on my favourites list, less than one third can I call if I just want to talk. It's also tricky to call someone when it's near 3 AM, and when I wake up, I don't have a human to speak with first thing. In my ideal situation, I'd have a person to chat with and plan the day and future with in the morning.

Zeus and I's relationship had improved a lot in the past few weeks. Though I can't talk with Zeus, I learn to be more intuitive. Some people say we limit ourselves by saying, 'I can't,' but some things are technically not an option. I wrote about how we can't make people care, yet we can till the seeds.

Brad, my boss, gave me the next day off. I deep-cleaned my bathroom and noticed how I'm starting to care more about my home and the quality of life there. It's a radically good thing to have a job, yet I'd like to have more time at home to work on the computer too.

I wonder about my music, and, similar to my books, I've created a bunch. I've not yet generated or earned much money with either books or music, yet I keep making things. I posted a track called *Matrix* on SoundCloud the night I wrote this to share with a friend named Glenna.

I referred to Glenna as a kind glass of champagne before,

yet I believe I shouldn't sip from her glass. She's radically kind and refreshing and has always been talkative with me, yet she's still quite young. Age has been an issue with a few gals I like and appreciate, yet I check-in and keep my intents. In a chapter I wrote to Elspeth in Fountain five, I wrote and reminded us, "I shouldn't be doing things like a twenty-year-old."

Have you heard of the 'half the age plus seven rule'? If you're older, divide your age by two and then add seven; that's the boundary of age allowance. I'm 42, so 28 is my boundary. Dating someone older than 28 and younger than 45 is my preference, and if we live for a few decades, I hope I don't have to grieve my love as a loss. Is that a reason why I'd prefer a younger gal?

2018 held a few deaths, and it's clear from then I don't want to feel grief. Grief may be a reason I keep from loving some friends and family too much also; I know how terrible loss can feel. I don't want to lose people, and even if to say it's better to have loved and lost, then never have loved at all, I feel uneasy.

Check-in with yourself right now. Who are the people you know that are explicitly clear as ones who you can trust and also love you in return? Some are trustworthy, though distant, and some may like us, yet we can't confirm the truth.

My paranoid side tips me into how some friends are authentically safe and honest, while others could be conspirators. I rarely feel entirely confident about who is trustworthy, though I also desire to share my illogical pathways of thought in text with you. I want to share what I've thought and why, though if no one reads what I've written, there's still a cognitive element. People hear what I type and think when forming these books.

Zeus is a thought conduit, and I've sometimes believed what I vocalize or think at home is amplified by him. When communicating ideas to others, there's a belief in ESP, telepathy, or groupthink that mixes in with linguistics. If multiple languages are woven into threads of speech, text, or thought, potentially diverse networks and nodes of people hear and understand. Strings of communication in different languages piece together fragments of our mind, body, spirit, soul and heart by stitching together the tapestry of life.

The various representations of symbolism are shards of a coherent whole, yet we consciously align via the choices, connections, and functions we presume and perform. I hold zero dominion over anything on this planet, and yet with grace, forgiveness, and compassion, I hope we endure. I've had concerns about plots and plans while at home and out and about, yet I mustn't let fear dissuade me from thriving.

The nighttime is a place I love, and though not in it as much as I used to be, it's a place within which to create. A bit of Christy Whitman's advice; three questions. What do I want? Why do I want it? How do I want to feel? And, from my neurosis, three questions to consider; who is causing the nervousness? Do I need to pause and reset? What may I do to use this energy productively?

Psychosis is synergistically complex, and it's like cryptic messages muddled by the truth. Sometimes it's apparent who we best not trust or contact, and hearts seem to compound with faith. The wish and hope are we can have friends that want to support us and also want us to be there to meld.

Why should I write these books? If people read them, what do they gain from them? If I put truth into text, how and why could that benefit the world? If my thoughts are all filibuster or nonsense, how is this helping another? What gains do we receive from putting these words one after the next? The sequence matters, yet spelling scatters the debris of language across landscapes of time.

My kitten reminds me how to love and be kind, yet I filter doubt about me being lovable. I've detested myself and my actions when I get angry and reactive, and I've felt shameful and repentant for misgivings and transgressions I've made.

Hesitantly, I move the cursor across the page while conspirators loom in my psyche. I yearn for genuine care, hope, and devotion, and I'm committed to the process as I set myself aside. I wish for peace and love too.

I don't know who I'm telling right now, and I'd like to know. Reverently and abashedly, I think of how it was Easter weekend 2019 the Thursday night I wrote this. Delusions, hallucinations, and fantastically wistful notions of the past called with a thirst for our future.

We cannot save humanity with wishes and wants, and I don't think faith can lure my lucrative lunacy. Lustful liaisons call coded collisions of constellations, yet callously contested correction calms creativity. It may be best for the next few months to assist in securing some hope and faith.

I may not yet earn the big money and big prizes from writing, though the gains made are in our future. Sanity is a precious thing, and parts of these books help me home in on what is right and just. People could be upset that I'm up late again tonight (it was 1:37 AM), yet fortunately, I was getting a bit tired, and this chapter was almost complete. I thank You for allowing me to write this, and I hope much more is allowed to form.

Molto Grazie, Dio... Amen.

FUZZY LOGIC

The night I wrote the first bits of this section, I thought of the 10th book's earnings. The idea of giving profits got twisted up with organizations I'd like to assist with funding, though considering sales up to now, I'm not clear much comes from the individual books. It's highly probable the three-part books are better and shall be significant earners.

One thought from before I finished the second Fountain was to have multiple books for sale to increase earnings. I know it's a manipulation tactic, though the idea is if people want to own *all* the books, people can buy separate copies like collectables. I didn't know back then I'd give 100% of the earnings from individual Fountains to different causes, and I also didn't plan to receive 49% of the three-part books either.

A twist of selfishness surfaced with Providing Point. I want to earn money for me too, and from a conversation with a planeswalker friend, I wondered what happens as Providing Point expands. An idea for a salary to run the program came from the irrational dream world where Providing Point develops and grows to gather millions. We'll need additional employees, yet as of July 2020, I was the only one running the program.

In 2019, I asked the then-current providers about receiving a percentage of the Patreon earnings. A small percentage seemed a bit sly, yet earning some money could be motivation for me to work and gather more. If we reach a high level of gathering, 1% of the earnings could be significant, and the lure of a gain could shift my actions to profit motivation. That wouldn't be intrinsically about providing, though it could be a reason to work for a reward.

When I asked another one of the providers about garnering 1% of the earnings, their suggestion was instead 5%. When we're gathering $5,000/month, 1% would mean $50, and 5%

is $250 a month. That's not a dramatic amount, yet as we expand to thousands of pledges, 1% can easily be hundreds or thousands of dollars a month.

Gathering a massive personal income from a charitable cause isn't ethical in my view. As we thrive, expand, and register as a legal non-profit, Providing Point requires money for operating expenses, legal fees, incorporation, an accountant, and future employees. Yet, if we reach the point of Full Seed, complete coverage, any percentage could be lucrative.

I've written that the value of one Yearly Seed, the amount per person we want to gather, is $15,128. If we provide 1,000 Yearly Seeds, that means 1% is $151,280 per year. If increased to 5%, that would mean $756,400 per year for fully supporting 1,000 Seed Recipients. That's a significant amount and can allow us to pay for additional employees.

A personal goal to provide 10,000 homes for people and gather enough to share $100/week groceries for 10,000 people can't come only from book earnings. As we work Providing Point as a for-purpose non-profit, Providing Point's power to provide becomes substantial. As of July 2020, Providing Point and Chilliwack Housing Providers (CHP) were not registered companies, and Providing Point had $1,135.86 in its account, enough to cover the next four to five months of fifteen $15/month Share and Care cards.

I'm aware I sometimes like to give money and things, yet I also love to receive and earn. Even if individual Fountains' earnings go entirely to charities or causes, I feel more invested in the three-part books. The three-part boos have done through more distillations and are higher-quality text.

I've focused and split between working for zero personal gain and squirrelling a living for myself too. Because of potential earnings from Fountains books and a belief I'm finally starting to release good books, I have more confidence in books like *Shards of My Soul* and *Mosaic of Miracles*. If both sell well, it'll be a while until *The Waters of Life*, the next three-part book, is available, yet writing it generates brilliance.

I also need to sort out what to do with *Shared Node*. *Shared Node* is a book of rhymes, and though I've not thought of earnings from the book, I hope more recordings manifest from it. My first recording was in 1999, and though my musical productions are amateur, I've increased my mental agility and skill. After rhyming for twenty years, I don't want to neglect my music, and as I've learned more about my rhymes and flow, even if not Hip-Hop or Rap, the music is pretty cool.

I have five albums available on Spotify, iTunes, Google Play, YouTube, and Amazon, yet if you want to find more of my music, go to www.KoyichDigital.Bandcamp.com. A dozen or so albums are available for streaming or download at Bandcamp, and the music is available by donation. 51% of the earnings go to Providing Point also.

The idea of one or five percent fluxes into my mind again. The program seems to be a lot about me and what I make or gain instead of running a non-profit. Readership and listeners can purchase the music and books without a monthly pledge, and if the purpose of the Patreon site is to gather and provide for those who need and want help, then how may I guide more people to pledge?

I find ways to improve, bolster, and add to the process while increasing efficiency, and if there's a potential for gathering more pledges, I realize I need to step up. I was concerned about massive expansion and wondered how to evolve the programs, yet I've been able to understand how we can scale. I'm not always sure about the right things, yet for the right reasons, they are what they are. If we can assure we do so for the right people, perhaps the ideas can grip and be valuable to aid, support, and tend.

If we operate Providing Point as a company, when we reach the point of one hundred cardholders at $50/month, then I can rethink about earning a portion. Until then, I work as a volunteer for Providing Point as a branch of Introversial.

Boundaries and expectations must be clear, concise, and openly shown and known. Providing Point and CHP weren't yet registered companies, though managing the cards and accounts require ethical behaviour. That's something I also provide. It may be too soon to speak with all the people involved, yet conversations with the cardholders and providers through the next few months are valuable. I want this to be an open and honest company working with and for our community with gradual, successful, and consistent expansion.

Some people say only to do what's best for ourselves, and a Utilitarian viewpoint would be to do what's best for everyone. If working for personal gain can benefit many others, generate pledges, and sell books that give to charity, sales are a great idea. I want to provide, and I want to earn. If I can't make enough on my own to share a lot, perhaps I can encourage others to help support the programs.

I waffled on percentages with the book earnings for a couple of months too, and in the two or three weeks before the base of this chapter, my opinions, guilt, and hope bundled a muddled intent. It feels cleaner in my heart and soul for me to not earn from the Providing Point Patreon gathering at this time, and I realize it's also going to require a lot of work outside of writing.

It's a win/win lure for me to work and promote, and I believe if I receive earnings from the Patreon page, it might dilute the company. I've thought of running Providing Point as an extension of myself and my creative work for profit, yet I don't because it's a community idea and program, not for me to make money. That's what my books and Focus Sessions are for.

I shared 65 copies of *Open to Fate* (the 8th Fountain), hoping to garner more pledges. Although we'd not received additional commitments from sharing the book, because the book talks about Providing Point and its premises, I believe sharing *Open to Fate* is valuable. The book can still gather patrons in the future, and by explaining the promises and premises of the program, it can generate more interest and acceptance of the program.

At some points, I've wanted to work solely as an author and sell, while other times, I've wanted to gather and share money and grocery cards. Money can assist and help, yet it's not the only variable. Money can, though, provide homes for people, and that can change the outlook of some who think they're living in Hell.

(It was early August 2019 at this point. We had four $15/month cards in distribution, and I felt good about the people who held cards. I'd not known many suitable for the program, and because of my paranoid delusional sides of self, I'd not been confident on street level).

Many need support, and I'd been working alone a lot. As of July 22nd, 2020, we had nine pledges totalling US$68/month after fees. I want to know how to gather more. If you're interested in seeing where we are now, please go to www.Patreon.com/Introversial to see our gathering page. I couldn't imagine a hundred or more pledges at this point, yet believed it comes to be.

I've been skeptical of street-level activity. I've feared connecting with random street people to find more cardholders, yet I received a recommendation to contact Ruth and Naomi's. At the point of this book's release, Ruth and Naomi's held seven of our cards, and Anne Davis held six. Cyrus Centre (a program for at-risk youth) also held four Care cards and could accept five more.

We find more providers and also more good seeds. People giving additional support are kind, decent, and generous, and ideally want to support the people with whom we share the cards. Many need assistance, yet who are the right people to gain support? How shall we cover so many people after starting so small?

Mixed up into all of this is the question: "Does it even matter?" How do these years of bookwork and a passive activist viewpoint affect the big picture? If I was gone, how would Providing Point operate? If the program thrives, will it be appreciated? I've sometimes thought that conspiracies aim at me for making proclamations, yet I wonder too, how many people know about me and my ideas? Does it matter if I write?

I like to write, yet my texts are so much about me and my

wishful ideas. I've written a bit about my fears and obsessions, and I've also discussed my neurotic lack of hope, faith, and confidence in my books. Writing is a valuable thing to do, yet how can my work be useful for other people too? I've thought the dissemination of ideas is beneficial, yet how is the world different as we activate them? Perhaps that's a section title to rewrite; *What if it all Happened?*

Rationally, I learn how to care for myself and my dreams. I've discovered that I can care kindly for others and their work and goals too, though, at times, my obsessions suffocate. A fear of lack and lost faith inspires some to communicate.

Writing may be a passive activity and not super-efficient to gather resources for community support. Though money is often a lure and motivation for me, I accept a profit-driven focus can compel us to produce. Conversely, generosity, giving, and sharing are things I like and love too, and I need to have something of benefit before I can share it; that also applies to knowledge and skills.

A couple of weeks slipped in between sections. I received another book in the mail to read; *How to Write Copy that Sells* by Ray Edwards. The mix of business books gets me psyched up and inspired about Providing Point, yet my activities also urge me to work for personal gain. In the week before, I had a coaching call with a QSCA (Quantum Success Coaching Academy) coach that suggested I write a wish list for a girlfriend. I thought I might have a chance with Elspeth, though she was in a relationship at the time.

Impatience, my Dad would tell me, can lure delusions. Fretful and jittery, the caffeine reminds me I'm afraid to sleep. Why cannot a nice rest seep kindly and comfortably into my desires? Why must money be motivation when a big wish is a relationship? Another belief cues me to think that if the connection is the desire, then I best share abundantly.

Prerogatives of thought beckon for resolve, yet resolve isn't, however, yet an R of PLU8R. PLU8R is an extended credo and philosophy based on Peace, Love, Unity, and Respect, yet I added the 8 for the multiple other R-words. What shall be the resolution with reverence, responsibility, and representation?

Why are my vagrant whims of heart calling for fortitude? Why do my fantasies seem to lead to wandering backwards from where I want to be? With pressure in my skull, it's like I'm pushing and fighting to have meaning while evading purposes others wish me to have.

I have dreams, yet seem to relish in being alone where I'm allowed to write and work. How can I claim to be love, when all I am is myself? Why don't I wake up in the mornings happy to be alive?

It's like a locomotive; my days and my life. It takes a long while to get going, and then it seems like I can't or don't want to stop. One nighttime dream I saw had a train engine blast into a cement wall. The impact tremor visually resonated with a wave of sound and energy that looked like deep ripples of water, and I could feel the power of the collision.

I hope I don't need to crash, and it's clear I'm pushing against the walls. Perhaps I need to switch tracks and carry more of my being to a peaceful and romantic destination. That said, who is she to join me?

ROBERT KOYICH

GET THE DREAM RIGHT

If to begin with the end in mind as a proactive way to live, titling chapters before writing them can guide the horse. The cart I wanted to carry with the title was a wish list about my ideal lovestone, though then I thought about travel. Telling you three places I'd like and love to travel, all three are places I've already lived or visited; Hong Kong, Italy, and Australia.

If we have to choose between two things, sometimes we can do both, though that best not apply to mates or else it could be quite a mess. Blending ideas may confuse, yet I'm reminded again about the concept of immediate reality. I hold a moment within my comfort zone.

Canibus' track *Poet Laureate II* says: "I go with the given, you know what comes to me over the celestial wireless. Whenever it comes, you're lucky when you get it." Perhaps my girlfriend wants to tend the soil in which we grow? Roiling in waters and puddles of clay, instead of boiling the blood, she reminds me I'm like a cow to chew my cud.

The music I play seems to accuse me of being free. It's bizarre how some songs can speak direct references about our lives by artists who've never met us. Tracked voices can describe our exact situations precisely and manipulate what we think; it can seem like surgical implants communicate our thoughts.

Without being conscious of what we're doing, prerecorded lyrics seem to fuse preflexively. Comments more accurate than I can vocalize share truths holding and moulding humble reverence. I meant to tell you about my desires as these Fountains are fantasy, yet there is faith in this too.

How and why could I ever want anything? I told one friend that it's okay to want things, though can I believe that for myself too? What is the dividing line between want, need, and greed? I remember not all wishes are for money, things or resources. There are other desires humans hold, such as peace, love, unity, and respect.

I'd love for my core family unit to expand beyond Zeus and me, and when I wrote the chapter *Give In or Give Up*, it was about two or three months before this one. With the addition of three carefully placed blue towels, we guarded the contested clawing areas. The towels alleviated a great deal of anger and abuse by not needing to battle with Zeus and some of his power-control behaviours, and, now, life here is well.

When I tell you I want to write my future into life, at times, I've been hesitant because I don't entirely know what I want. I want to sell books to earn money; that's true, yet it's an objective that needs me to market my work effectively. I've thought sharing free copies could expand my reach to readers, and it may, yet, how can I garner real live sales? Mass marketing isn't a core skill I possess, though I can learn skills.

I had just started Ramit Sethi's book *I'll Teach You to Be Rich*, which excites and inspires me to pay off my debts. With online calculators, I also found a $70 a month increase to my home loan can reduce the amortization by five years and lessen $10,000 of interest. To be debt-free, I must act appropriately and actively pay off my debts.

It was February 2019 when I started writing this Fountain. It was a great year and experience as I continued up to and beyond October that year with landscaping. From my earnings with Brad, I paid off $1,500 of my student loans by the close of July, and as soon as paying off my student loans, I started to think about fueling money into my savings and mortgage.

Earlier in the year, I wanted to get a car, though I've halted partly on the plan. I want to have a car again, though the lure of having $600-$800 discretionary money instead of a vehicle is tantalizing. I'd like more car friends who'll help out with lifts and accept gas money for rides, yet I loved it when people would chip in money for fuel when *I* was the car friend! We could jest about being a passenger or driver in life, yet I suppose that's better than being a crash test dummy.

So, three things I want; to be debt-free, to sell books, and to travel a bit, preferably with a travel buddy. I want them to be my girlfriend, yet I made a big rewind to *Finding Natalie,* where I wrote about the real-girl/dream-girl/no-girl dilemma. Since I couldn't be with dream-girl, I wanted to find a real girl, and yet, as of now, I'm with no-girl.

I'm mostly okay being without a gal, and I've written about how I've learned to be alone. It's true Zeus is a pretty great companion, yet it's also true I'd like to have more female contact and more conversations. Solitary living is sometimes alright, being content is a good thing, yet I nudge forward for a bit more of what I want. It's a slow, gradual process; bit by bit, grain by grain, and seed by seed. I heed my heart, soul, and spirit, becoming more aligned.

I've written lots of audacious goals and objectives in these books, and though few had manifested by the point of typing this, some minor gains had acquiesced. I wonder if it's my fear of acceptance hindering me. Is it a lack of faith, or a firm belief of scarcity or absence that withholds forward motion? If I submit to the will of God and The Universe again, what flows out of the keys with skills to ease and appease?

Why can I be so hesitant and unclear about saying what I want? Telling others what we desire is exceptionally valuable, especially if we can help each other gain what we want. Is it that I don't want what I want well enough to push for it? Sometimes I'm afraid of wanting things because I fear being considered greedy, yet wanting is a natural thing. Why have I put so many restrictions on myself and my core sets of desires? Precisely because I fear judgment.

With Providing Point, I've strived for meaning and purpose because I can have a significant function, yet I was thinking of providing for others from a purpose-driven motive. Instead of pure love, a humanitarian point of compassion and prerogative found me to push and expand for meaning.

I need to get outside of myself and what I want more often, yet some online mentors and guides remind us the more we earn, the more we can give. Earn like the 1% and share 99%? Perhaps that's a great objective, yet if we set aside discussions of money, where does the mind wander?

If cares of the heart remind us of other's loss and grief, is it best to not message them? If Heaven is a rightful place and the afterlife crosses over between the spirit and shadow realm, how may we glean further insight? If we cycle ahead four thousand days, is the home still where I want to reside?

Are free days working with the worth of the cross led instead of the loss of paying to have a boss? In exchange for a gain of time and another late night, the power of love is reliable. Is it enough to rewire the brain from understanding religious principles into an agnostic view? Who is it that wants me to spit out my food if I've not said a prayer for it?

Can I comprehend and share religious ideas without proclaiming them? I don't have a rock-solid faith. Why are there prayers in my books? Am I running away from God, bullishly refusing to catch the baton? I'm not sure of running His race because I don't want to dash into the afterlife. Who do I want to vote *onto* the island? We wind the threads of thought into a strong cord.

I pay homage while reminding myself such decisions hold me out on a limb. Shimmying down to a slim desire, the cigarettes meet fire to stem the spire. Chemical pleasures are part of me and what I use to allow myself to retire, yet I halt to restructure at this juncture. I pause to discover and amplify the cause.

If I mean to get the dream right, I remember some of the best dreams happen while we're awake. Perhaps agitation stems from processes that I've yet to comprehend, yet I want not just to have friends, yet also *be* a friend. I may need to reach out more often than others do to me as part of this process stemming from a seed to a tree.

Shards of My Soul was available at this point, and a feeling of accomplishment seeped into my being. It's weird because I've started to believe in my hopes, goals, and dreams. Instinctively, I must support future successes with action, and as I continue past the next books, I intuit how to write and fuse enjoyment with this process of creating.

It's a long task to write a book, and writing helps build positive faith that results in good feelings. The experience of enduring through a long, arduous process has a satisfaction of its own, and while my dreamy side reminds me of only having rice to eat for thirty-nine days, an entirely different experience calls me to live as a non-smoker.

I've wanted to extend outwards from the Providing Point demographic to friends too. When I chose to give the 7th Fountain's earnings to friends, I imagined helping a lot of others with money, food, and other things. I believed the 7th would earn more than it had up to now, though the total royalties of the book, *Etched in Stone,* were $9.35 at the time of Mosaic's release.

Rings of Truth's committed cause, the Chilliwack Animal Safe Haven, is entirely in line with Zeus being here. When I wrote the section *Give In or Give Up*, it was not a safe home for Zeus back then, and I see how my work can be as penance. Each section can call me to repent and give and inspires me to share a due desire or influence. *Fields of Formation*'s earnings go to Pencils of Promise, though that came from the impact of Lewis Howes and his podcast *The School of Greatness.*

Reminders land in my email inbox, and though I don't want so many messages, I hold them aside to read. In the month I was in, Gabrielle Bernstein was a prominent mailer. Gabby's reminder is to do what feels good, and it couples with Christy Whitman's teachings to allow a manifestation of what is right. We must remember to amplify what's right for others, too, in addition to what we like.

With ideas going back to my January 2018 trip, I know not to always do things purely on the premise that only others shall gain. I'm still learning, though I understand how I need to care for me first and *then* do the right things that benefit. I mustn't sacrifice myself to my detriment as much as I used to.

Mentioning Gabby and Christy stem from my conscious reminder of aligning with our best interests and core desires. After building foundations, we can construct our homes upon a reliable and sure base, though if I carry a real-estate metaphor, the first three three-part books were homes for my growth. I rent them out to others while changing how and where I'm living in the present moment. I need to get the dream right.

Visualizations and imagination are not always accessible, though, so if you have difficulty seeing in your mind what you want, write out what you want. Our dreams, fantasies, and realities change, yet remember that your life also can be like a glacier. Each wave of snowfall descends onto the mountains adding to what fell before. The culmination is the fortified glacier of what your life now is, and the result can be both good and bad. Be careful what type of precipitation falls from your mouth and attitude.

Perhaps you don't like the cold and clouds, yet before our lives can become liquid water suitable to drink, sometimes a distillation process must purify. Our past experiences and life on Earth hold cryptic debris deep under the layers of snow and ice, so tunnelling is an idea to dig further into the core. Journal entries are points to remind us, though, I'm not yet sure what I'm searching for.

I have a few thousand pages of written rhymes, yet I don't know if they're water or soil. If they're water, then we can use them to nourish the seeds, yet if they're soil, perhaps those preflexive seeds I mentioned earlier in the chapter can sprout.

Similar to my writing, my rhymes aren't thought out or planned with conscious intent before I begin. Like my books, there are shards and fragments of ideas that seem to be controlled by forces that aren't me. When my music plays, I don't have a conscious awareness about how others hear it, yet I can understand the threads when I listen to them.

When music sites ask me to share similar artists, I don't even know who to say. I can tell you who's influenced me, who I've played on CD or mp3, yet I don't compare myself to others. I don't want to get mixed up in egos and attitudes that conflict, so where I seem to put myself is a solitary nodal point or as a person of random interest. I call my music genre Introversial, similar to the style of my books.

Unlike many people seeking to be famous or garner massive amounts of attention, I'm quite thankful for my kind, peaceful, and boring life, and though I'm not seeking fame, my actions seem to contradict. If I'm putting books, YouTube tracks, CDs, or emails out to the world, for what am I searching? You know, I don't always know.

It may go back to how I'm a sea-dwelling creature, just climbing out and about putting on showy behaviour. I'm not the best or better, and I'm doing what I do while often neglecting or not being aware of the consequences. Perhaps as we learn what the intrinsically right things for us are, we can fortify peace, develop love, and share respect in and with full unity. If to get the dream right, I must share what I dream.

ROBERT KOYICH

20/20 VISION

Remember what you have accomplished, Rob, and recall the comments others have made reminding you of your process. Sit and hold a breath telling yourself to move forward with people supporting your efforts, and even if you're not sure the destinations, keep moving forward to where you think you want to go.

My friend Bert told me he thinks the keyword of my work is 'growth' yet I've been resisting acceptance that my work has meaning and value. The motif "I still don't know" is one I've fused into this series often, initially about Natalie and how I still don't know her, yet perhaps it's also how I've not yet known success with the Fountains. Much has manifested, though, even if I've not yet seen the final vision.

This section of the book is self-therapy to tell me some of my positive bits and acknowledge what I learn by writing this series. I may not have found Natalie, yet the journey is extensive, and I'm glad I continued with authorship.

I started writing the first book about six years ago, and it took two to three years to finish that first manuscript. The quality of *Finding Natalie* is awful compared to recent releases, and though I've learned how to craft a quality book, my obscure ramblings and nattering still lace the pages I form. The glacier I'm building develops some fortified eloquence.

I've often focused on money and earnings instead of people, yet in the past year, I've not had as much lack. At some points in this writing journey, I've mentioned scraping the wastebasket for shreds of tobacco to smoke, and though I've been a smoker, having part-time work freed up my concern about having enough to puff.

I've written about needing to find alternate sources of income other than my writing, and, with a job, I have access to more than if I didn't work. I've also written about how I need and want to focus more on people and develop and entrust real friendships with people. I do.

I've grown a lot since starting these books, yet my assuaged notions of self-disdain and worthlessness also taint my heart. She calls out to me through my soul, yet it seems I must refute any wishes I've had before connecting.

It's been twenty-two years since a song trained my being how to love according to my delusions, and now I must re-circuit my authentic pathways back onto what is real. I've been living with desires of fantasy for decades when I should've focused more on truth.

How do we reach the completion of the Fountains of Flourishing? The next three-part book is, perhaps, two or so years away from now, yet those three Fountains process the fantasies I've held into the official channels of who I am and what I want. Can clarity hone what shall be into homes that manifest?

For a couple of years, I was quite religious and wrote chapters about God, Jesus, and Heaven. In recent weeks and months, I've still prayed, yet not anywhere near as often as I had when I held a stronger belief. My faith in God has shifted with trust in the Universe and fate and also extricates myself from false worship. I sometimes have had issues of not praying before eating food, and in real moments of gratitude, I say thank you in different languages when I'm glad and thankful.

My reverence for God is there, yet I'm not clear about recognition. I've barely ever heard the voice or intuition of God, and want to know what is real and not blindly throw thanks at Him if I don't know who He is.

While writing before, I've mentioned how I thought every letter, space, and period was formed without my choice, an entire predestined sequence of words and punctuation. Other people tell us we have free-will and opportunity; that we can do whatever we want whenever we want to.

Sometimes when I become aware I have the chance to speak, I can't articulate a single word from my mouth. I've claimed my meds prevent me from communicating, and my medication does affect me., and sometimes it feels like I'm entirely controlled by forces I can't pinpoint. My mental health hints there are many forces at work altering my psyche.

Sounds from the world outside of my home bark in fears, seemingly to disrupt my flow of thought and change my pathways. If I try to exert my desires and will into the text and choose my actions, it seems stifling ideas keep me from being myself.

I very well could write on the question "who am I" and not be able to answer accurately. I know my name. I also could tell you what I've said or written. The central core of who I am may not entirely be definable, though. Nouns could label me, adjectives could attempt to describe, yet the actions of what I sometimes do and say also could paint a dreary story.

I've sought to have value instead of understanding the parts of me that are valuable. I've put in time and energy into writing and seeded the first few patrons, yet one other helpful thing about me and my work is I follow through with my promises, most of the time.

We've not housed the first person, yet I follow through with the earnings distributions I've written. My books generated about $300 for charity up to July 2020, and if you're reading this book, more sales and earnings come from this release.

My inner and external dilemmas come from committing to work for others while also wanting to earn for me. A difficulty I face is wanting to give more than I spend while also finding ways to make more. The idea of the secondary gains for myself seems to suggest I think of others first, and cognitively that's partly true. I'm sometimes aware of outer parts of life, yet more honestly, I'm frequently neurotically wrapped up in my thoughts and challenges.

The biggest challenge I've faced is bullishly and dismissively committing to Providing Point while not feeling thrilled to do so. I want to gather and generate prosperity naturally, yet I lack the genuine care and passion for getting onto the street to help people more actively. I want an abundant life, yet I also want others to have abundant experiences too.

I work landscaping, and even if I like my boss and I can earn some money for him by being an employee, I also want the freedom, finances, and space to work on anything I want to at home. This goes back to working for others. By working for my boss, I earn money, yet the wish is I can sell something (even if not my books) so that I can afford to live with sleep patterns that involve late nights of work. I don't like waking up early and feel far more inclined to work on the computer.

The dilemma of working alone at night is a separate issue when wanting to be well integrated into life, yet perhaps the Providing Point idea is right. My books may still house people, though not many books had sold up to releasing Mosaic. A lack of book sales is a reason why we use the Patreon page to gather.

I can't shake the idea that I need to provide for others and not only myself. Earnings from my job are seemingly selfish earnings, while book sales are a sign I'm doing the right things for our life on Earth. I seem to have a belief that links financial rewards with just actions.

"The right thing, at the right time, for the right reason."
— *Owen Beattie*

I'm a friend, employee, community member, son, and nephew. I'm also a human, a writer, and a shared soul. I'm a person who attempts to be profound while I also link rhymes on the Internet with the mind's sound. I've received support from the government, and it's valued, required, and helpful, though my audacious wishes include earning the entirety of my income from books, music, and providing.

My home is a place where I almost seem imprisoned with my cat and mind tethered to obsessive tendencies and devious devices. Entranced by stillness and the aghast fears of consequence for being who I am, the keys seize moments of incepted thought and etch them upon stone and time.

I value solitude, it helps with productivity, yet I also

appreciate people and relationships. How many friends do I even have, though? Have I been trying to buy my way in life? I love to share and buy things for people, yet have I been trying to lord over people by offering crumbs?

Is Providing Point a waste of time? How much benefit is $15 a month to someone? For those who have less, a little bit means a lot, yet what can I give to people that have more? I can give my time to those with money, yet want to use my money with some to save 'time'?

And yet the breeze on my deck as I typed this remind me I'm wealthy. Some have cars and more income than I do and are still financially concerned. Some of them also have relationship issues and mouths to feed while I wish I could have a lovestone to live, build, and dream with together.

Zeus is fantastic, and we live in our apartment as I have the chance to write so much. We develop my skills and abilities further, and I've also had time to read books and learn. I hold the desire that others may also thrive because I don't want others to be poor.

I don't want to be above people either, even if it's nice to live on the top floor. When I throw a prayer up and out, it's sometimes to the ceiling or out to the sky where satellites could be recording the very moment and place I sit or stand.

I avoid evil, deceit, and wickedness, yet smoke the foul, filthy cigarettes that are a vice of my creative freedom. Having a tin of tobacco to me is a sign of prosperity and is a pleasure I don't often want to sacrifice.

Yet my health is weak; I can't run very far, I have a bit of a fat belly, and I don't eat regularly. My teeth are stained, I love to drink coffee and Coke, and I've also neglected to exercise. I also never get sick and have very few aches and pains.

I used to go to Taekwondo and recall how much fitter I was back then. Even if I was a smoker when I trained, I was stronger, more flexible, and my behaviours and thoughts were far more disciplined.

And yet now, I've become more self-aware, I've developed my ability to write, and I've started to think, perhaps obsessively, about what I can contribute. My conscientious nature fortifies a stubborn resolve to ignore what others tell me I *should* do while I, instead, focus on doing what I want to do. I need and want to find more ways to provide.

Having a job is an excellent source of money, though earning hinged upon required labour compares to desired work; I wish to win through creative effort. The books and gathering entwine so tightly, though what would happen if I rewound to the first book? If I never thought of giving from the earnings, what would have I written?

Charitable motives did not fuel the release of the first book, and I don't think, back then, that I even believed Natalie would ever read a copy. I know now that the 49% royalty lure is a motivation for me, and if I go back to *Finding Natalie* and *Searching for Tomorrow*, I recall I wanted to earn money back then too.

What was the twist in *Seeds of Tomorrow* that called me along the seemingly dismal darkened pathway to seemingly nothing for anything? Why do I keep pressing the keys in the 13th and beyond, and if I want to share valuable text to readers, why haven't I used more focused formulas?

The Freedom Solution cues again. To do what we want to do, with whom we want to do it when we want to do it, where we want to do it, and with full financial support.

Let's check the self/other parameters of the Freedom Solution. For others first, please; what do people want to do? It's a great question to ask someone: "What do you want to do?" Often, we get the response, "I don't know, what do you want to do?" Perhaps we need to think more clearly about what we want to do, and after we find out what we want to do, work for it and find others who can help us find what we want.

I think a core desire is more so *being* things. I want to *be* a loving, trusted, and appreciated friend, I want to *be* free to choose how and when to go to sleep, and I want to *be* at home with my lovestone and be able to talk with her. I want to *be* in a home where I can turn around and talk to someone and have them talk back to me.

My Freedom Solution is essential, yet I'm only one. I want to live with a girlfriend and insanely and obsessively work on my creative projects while knowing I have a real true love whom I can talk with. Sometimes, I like my life now, and when I typed this, I was in line with my truths and had the luxuries of coffee, late night to work, cigarettes, and a kind reminder that life is a lot better when we live with someone.

"Like the deserts miss the rain."
— *Everything But the Girl*

Yet, ironically, the lyric holds much more substance to a different love. I've sometimes thought of the above lyric and how deep sadness can permeate when I think I'll never meet the woman I love. I feel like a desert wishing for rain, yet not like one that's known it before.

I feel sad, devoid, and solemn, knowing I don't have a girlfriend, no matter how many other beautiful things I have. Zeus is great, yet I want to find *my* mate and live with her too. Who is she, though?

QUALITY IS OUR RECIPE

This section is a girlfriend wish list. Where shall I start with it? It's telling what the first item someone says, and when written, it's even trickier because it's there for all readers to see and assess.

If I'm to hook up with a gal, first, she must be single when we do so. She must accept that I'm, for now, a smoker and not expect me to quit. I may stop, yet I've no idea as to when. I also hope she forgives me for all the apostrophes on the page. If we have a kid, I don't want to have written so many contractions from my attempt to be concise.

Do we have kids? Not necessarily. I led the 4th Fountain with a chapter written to Aeris, a future daughter, yet it's not a requirement my gal births our child. Physiologically, I may not be able to have kids, and adoption isn't off the table. I'm partly ambivalent about being a Dad to a real live human and am not sure if my next girlfriend needs to be childfree.

My financial situation at release showed I didn't yet know how to afford or cover more than my own and Zeus' lives. For things I like to do, I like going out to dinner and movies, I love walks and conversation, and for a bonus point, I enjoy snuggling. My gal may need to be a cuddly person and also best give real full-on hugs. I'm physically affectionate with some and want to have a secure physical connection with a gal; not so much sex, though that's a bonus point.

Regarding trust and truth, I want her to feel comfortable to tell me her honest opinions without concern about upsetting me or setting me off. I value radical honesty, though that doesn't mean not having tact and being kind. I can be a bit abrupt, so I remember I may need an understanding and accepting gal.

I don't have a car yet, so it'd be rad if she does, or we can share and go halfers on one. As I like having money, it'd be great if she has a job or career and understands how to discuss finances. From Ramit Sethi's book *I Will Teach You to Be Rich*, I learned a few intriguing things about money recently, so it'd be awesome she reads that book too. My gal doesn't need to be an avid reader, and I'm not clear how I'll respond if she's a bookworm.

My gal doesn't need to have a post-secondary education, though that would be a plus. I like women who're smart and can talk a lot, yet also value questions and hope she's inquisitive. Sometimes I need to have a cue to get me started, yet there's also a delicate line about being an interrogator and asking enough questions. Oppositely, it's rad to have a gal who knows how to speak while also not overloading me with too much. Communication skills are necessary.

My girlfriend has a fantastic sense of humour. I'm not sure if it's dark, yet there must be a potential edge for rudeness, and puns are often welcome. She must be ready for reruns of my jokes and not-so-random repeats as I like long-running threads of inside jokes as shared humour. I may tell her jokes that are in poor taste, yet she'll know I'm generally not biased, and I know some things should not be joked about, period.

Another critical thing about my girlfriend is that she'll want to meet my other friends. I want to form a merging or sharing of friends and meet hers too because I like how, when friends meet each other, we can glean tactical information. I'd like that my girlfriend can speak of tactics and schemes without being manipulative or malicious, yet a different way of saying that is that she's smart and wise, and we can help each other with our blind spots with other people.

Regarding being a drinker, she doesn't need to drink alcohol, yet having a glass of wine leads to a communication exercise I like. A game of twenty-questions could play out, though one thing at a time. For drinking, it's okay for her to drink rarely or occasionally, though absolutely not a habit beyond one glass a day. Even a glass *every* day is a bit much, yet I'd prefer maybe one or two drinks per week outside of meals.

From meals, we go to the Glass House to compound the text. The island in our kitchen is a place where we can prepare meals and also chat with our friends while we make food. She doesn't need to be a great cook at this point, yet she best have a willingness to learn and work with me in the kitchen. I'd like to make sure she's open to talking about cooking sessions and meal preparation, even if my current home is limited.

For the Glass House, part of the vision is to hold gatherings there to earn and pay for the home. If we can expand and grow to the point of having meetings in that home, I wonder how she and I can work together on projects. We'll need excellent communication skills and also the knowledge and ability to listen, guide, and create. I don't know how artistic she needs to be, yet I like people who paint, draw, sing, dance, or write. Business, too, is an art.

Walks are a must. Not for our dog, though. I don't want to own a dog at this point in my life. In the future, perhaps, yet not while I'm living in an apartment. Maybe she has a dog, though we'd need to have two homes to allow that at this point in the journey. I live in an apartment and live with Zeus as of now, and I wonder how the first years of her and I's relationship develop. We've yet to see, though I wonder what she thinks of two Calico kittens?

I remind myself that I've talked about living together, yet haven't so much talked about marriage. I'm not entirely afraid of such, yet one thing at a time.

An idea I've shared is the half-the-age-plus-seven rule. If older, divide your age by two and add seven. E.g. I'm forty-two. Twenty-two plus seven is twenty-eight; my lower bracket. I'd skip this rule with one gal (she's twenty-seven), though she was with another for now.

Religion? She's hopefully not evangelical Christian. I like those who are open to talking about spiritual matters, and I'd like to develop my understanding and exploration of belief further, but I don't want to be preached at, even if she believes. She hopefully is respectful and open to learning about other religions, and I'll dig it if she's into meditation. I want to develop my spiritual understanding and exploration and could use some shared support.

With podcasts, I hope we can play and hear them and also talk about what we've heard. Talking about ideas and concepts that aren't part of the everyday conversation are radially good and stimulate new connections. The activity of laying down on couches and just talking or letting a podcast or music play is enjoyable for relaxation.

I'd love for her to be entirely open to talking about money and finances. My earnings aren't high, though it'd be stellar to have a gal who's into long-term planning and also wise with her money. It doesn't mean that she doesn't spend on herself or some luxuries, though that she and I can talk about our earnings and share a conscious spending plan. When we move in together, it'll be awesome to discuss and plan our financial future.

She also must be compassionate and forgiving. A different way of saying that is that she must have a kind heart and be empathetic. Not so much for me, yet also for the wellbeing of others. She must be okay with Zeus if we're to live together, and oppositely, Zeus shall help guide me to know she's the right one.

Family is the entire group of people living together, and a home is where that family may live and thrive. I've known some gals who don't have great relationships with their parents, yet are still thoroughly decent people. In a previous part of this journey, I wrote how I want my gal to be on good terms with her family. It's ideal, yet not an absolute necessity.

What might be a necessity, though, is that she gets along with my family. I'd love to go to Australia with her and visit Dad and Sarah and have them thoroughly happy and thankful I bring my gal along. If we need to pay for the trip, that links back to money and planning to afford trips together.

From the word 'trips,' I think she shouldn't do drugs because I don't want to be in a home where drugs are beyond the catnip for Zeus and my coffee and ciggies. I mentioned how I want her to be okay with me smoking, yet I'm twisted up and in about whether or not I'd be okay with her smoking. If we both smoke, then that could mean a life-long entrapment with nicotine instead of me finding the desire to quit and live a longer life with her.

It's difficult living alone for so many years. I want to gain the experience and skills needed to live with a gal full-time and believe the best way to do so is by doing so. I don't want to go out looking for love in all the wrong places, yet how am I to find a gal who wants to live with me if I'm at home alone?

Some have recommended Internet sites like Plenty-of-Fish, and though I don't know who I'll live with beyond Zeus, I remind myself she won't magically fall from the sky. I'm not as soul-bound with Natalie like I thought I was, and I also got hooked up on Elspeth and negatively reacted when I couldn't connect with her.

Chandra is terrific, yet I'm not clear about living with her full-time. Of the gals I do know, there are barely any with whom I'd love to be in full-contact. I also don't want to 'pick' one because I more so want to be the one chosen. I want my gal to want me and seek out a relationship with me and then have me receive her.

Fear of rejection is a legitimate cop-out for me, though, differently, I've let gals know I like them a lot, and then they don't want to connect. I've had massive crushes on gals, which I know isn't healthy, yet my wishes and dreams for a lovestone may be a good sign.

It'd be cool for her to read my books and be interested in forming a relationship. That's the tactic I started with for Natalie in the first book, though my obsessive nature and the intentional selection was for one I don't know and one who theoretically doesn't know me.

I'd love to be in love, and I'd like to know what she likes. I want her to want to connect and make an effort to do so. I also wish someone could wish upon a star and tell me exactly who you are.

Two decades of being solo have worn on me, and I don't see a quick fix for it either. I've said often it feels like I'm at the start, and it seems like my love hasn't yet begun. Two decades ago, I thought I knew who I'd live with and have kids, yet I've not seen her in real life. I want to build *with* someone and not construct impossible fantasies. That means that the highest probability and best situation is to find a gal who wants to make a life with me.

I refuse to believe that the world has been conspiring for me to bring the lovestone into my awareness. My friend Coleman asked, "what if there's a gal that thinks of you the way you thought of Natalie?" Perhaps, similarly, if there is, I'd love for her to let me know who she is. Differently, Natalie has thousands of fans that love her and would like to meet, while I seem to be alone wondering if anyone would like to connect.

I'm quite glad I don't have thousands of screaming fans, though it'll be rad to find my biggest fan as one I'd love to live with too. I don't know when you'll read this book, though it may be a precursor for you to read the others to look into what I've shared. Even if I dream, I still think my rational limitations often override my desires.

I want to go to the islands and dance in the sand, hand in hand with a look deep into her eyes, reminding me she thinks I'm her prize. Wanting and wishing for love is a solitary activity. Doing so requires a fixation, yet a real relationship is an active engagement of two's spirit and their soul.

I've often thought that destiny and fate are making me wait. Perhaps I waited too long? Maybe I should have gone across the oceans to find her before settling into writing a book. I've written about acceptance a bit and how it's valuable, yet I've also written that wanting things is okay too.

If we have a desire, we often attempt to find a way to satiate that want. What if I've wanted too much and haven't had the gumption to work for it? What if I've worked on these books pushing for prosperity instead of finding ways to live in genuine love? If I want to provide and share love, why didn't I advocate for her to be my love in real life?

Has my self-focused nature removed the beautiful parts of myself she used to like? Would she like to be my mate and not just a friend? If I told her how I felt, is she afraid to reciprocate? Does she want me, yet found me focused on a different gal? Is she afraid to reach out to me because I told her too much?

Had I not known that love is how we always are, are we separated by universes, a galaxy, and a star? If I've told her I love, is that something she can't sense as real no matter what I feel? Or, perhaps, she feels unwanted and doesn't get I want to live with her and our pets.

If there is one bit of advice laced in this text, it's to tell people how you feel and what you mean. Not being able to speak to someone doesn't mean they don't like us or don't want to be together. There may be other reasons people don't return our calls or texts.

"I still don't know."

Though what if this is a couple of decades later, and you and I sealed our bond? I hope you've read the books and have seen all of my crossed and lost hopes, goals, and dreams and still chose to forgive me for not knowing what to say. Just because I have piles of love to sieve before I give, I also sometimes feel devoid of positive characteristics. I hope you looked into my flaws and found acceptance.

I still may get obsessive and overbearing, though I'll try to be the best human I can be for you. Love is real, and note this time it's not capitalized. You're a beautiful human and soul, and even if I didn't know where to enroll in your life yet, thank you for being patient and letting me come to know our truth. Youth seems so close and far away, yet rewind to *Life is a Sunset,* "forever and a day."

SUBTLE DISTINCTION

To go a bit meta, I'd like to share with you the process of how the individual books form. Before writing the different texts, I've often had a clear idea about what I want the book to be, yet the books barely ever result in how I intended.

I don't write outlines for these books, and often the natural course of events and thoughts show the meandering formations of text. In some Fountains, I've input timestamps in sections to share where I was when I was writing their first draft; temporal points are helpful with an evolving process.

Each Fountain is eleven to thirteen chapters long. The length of the books comes from the format of the first few. For *Finding Natalie* through to *Fields of Formation*, I printed the texts in a sixty to seventy page eight by eleven magazine-sized form. It was *A Distant Glimmer* (the 6th Fountain) when I chose to adjust the books to 5.5"x8.5" sizing. I went back to *Seeds of Tomorrow* (the 4th) and *Fields of Formation* (the 5th) and rereleased them the same.

Even now, though, I write the individual books in the 8½"x 11" format for their first draft. Each chapter is usually titled before I start writing the sections to give me guidance about what to write. Each block of text is almost always five lines of 12 point Book Antiqua text with a neurotic tendency to have each line cover entirely to the right side of a justified page. It's rare that I even add even one word extra to start a sixth line, maybe less than 2% of the time.

I'll write the five-line blocks and attempt to open the next bit with a separate thought that doesn't follow the previous one; basic paragraphing, yet to the five-line format. Sometimes the text blurs, though I attempt to carry the thread of one block into a followable series.

I strive for conciseness by adjusting the words I use as I learn how to write better, and I've improved my writing a lot since the first few books. It was in Fountain five's revision where I started to level up in editing, though improved even further later with Grammarly significantly enhancing my work.

The objective is to complete chapters in one sitting, though that doesn't always happen. The chosen title guides me, and as I start to write, I draw out the text in the five-line paragraphs. I add or subtract ideas to keep in the five-line blocks as best I can, though sometimes I find myself out of words or ideas for a chapter. In those cases, I'll just stop typing and not force the process. In other instances, I push and strive to keep the cursor slugging across the page and down the lines to push forward to completion.

A chapter is 'done' when I've written about four and a half pages of text. When I complete the thoughts for a section, I'll often have an inspiration for what the next chapter is going to be and write the title for the next chapter. Not always, though often, I can return to the text with a line of awareness about where I want to guide the streams. If I don't finish a chapter in one sitting, I'll come back to the Word document, reread what I've written, and then continue.

Titling the books is one way I heed subconscious guidance too. Almost always, I know what the next book's title is. I didn't have that with *Rings of Truth*, yet for the first three three-part books, I knew most of the titles before writing to prepare for release. The titles of the first three three-part books all include particulate ideas; *Fragments of Intent, The Sands of Yesterday,* and *Shards of My Soul.* It's by accident, yet it shows how I know I'm a bit scatterbrained. I used the word Mosaic in this book's title as I attempt to hold all the pieces together.

After I'm done writing a chapter, I'll sometimes run a Grammarly check on the text after it's written to help for later revision. I don't do rewriting at that stage, though a Grammarly clean up helps the book when it comes time to rewrite and revise. I still often force the text to remain in the precise five-line blocks.

After I complete eleven to thirteen base chapters (the goal of 65 pages of base text), I copy and paste the sections into the

5 ½"x8 ½" book template. I then change all of the text to 12-point Garamond font and separate the chapters. Since the pages are smaller than the first drafts format, chapters extend in page length, though the writing is still in the chunked blocks. After sorting out the Garamond shift and blocking the smaller size template, then we get to the tricky part, Revision.

If writing a book isn't so easy, and you want to be an author, get ready for your soul to be ripped through its self if you're going to create the final version. Revision, I find, can be crucially tricky, though the revision and rewriting are becoming a quicker process now that I've learned a bunch.

Although I'm not a professional editor, it's beneficial to clean up and prepare. I've never had any of my work edited by another person, and I don't follow many rules, though I've hopefully have crafted some decent books. I don't know how the quality of my finished works compare to others, yet I do and don't care. I'm creating what I want to develop and absolve obligations of catering to what *'should'* be done.

That said, we *need* to do some things to write a book. Rewriting and revision are necessary. First, I start at the beginning and see how it reads. I read each line and adjust the text to how I want it to read, and I make sure that what I'm saying reads as I want to say it. I attempt to carry a cadence and flow of words, yet since I have the initial blocks (the five lines per paragraph in the draft), I start to segment each line into formed sections.

If an idea stops short, or it reads into the next links of a text block, I edit and form naturally sounding segments. My paragraph formation occurs with the text revision as I slowly reshape the initial chapter. I adjust sentence structure and revise the book chapter by chapter until I like how it reads. It takes me only an hour or so to edit one chapter.

When I get stressed out, pissed off, tired, or think I'm creating garbage, I'll stop. Just as how it's difficult to be likable when we're pissed off, creating requires patient care for good work. After I rewrite and reform the paragraphs into a cohesive text, I'll Grammarly the document again. After

Grammarly, I'll go back and reread, making changes as a digital proofread.

By this point, it's been about two to four digital passes, and I'll start to think I'm getting there. If I believe the entire book reads well, I'll go online with KDP (Kindle Direct Publishing) and start setting up the release. KDP is the channel I used for publishing, though this is about my process, not quite publishing.

The goal of my digital revision process is to read an Unlimited Version of a book. The Unlimted version is a version of the book that I feel good about, enough to release soon. I've often ordered copies of the books and have made them available on Amazon when in Unlimited form, yet not for this release.

The first Unlimited Fountains were four and five, and I've been using that format since. After a Fountain is in Unlimited Form, I order proofs, yet at this point, the book still isn't done. After a full reread and manual revision of the book – being sure it reads well and adjusting the style and flow with punctuation – I then have to transcribe the manual edits into the digital file.

Once I finish the transcription, another run of Grammarly and I think I've got a finished book. Nope! Not yet! One more proof (or release copy) of the post-Unlimited version results in another manual proofread when I can order a printed copy. After transcribing edits and a final Grammarly run, we have a single book's completion.

One by one, the individual books form and still won't always be the best they can be. I make them better and better with each revision, though when done the distinctive Fountains, it's later time to bundle them. Putting the three-parters together has been a bit different for each. With *Fragments of Intents*, I cut about thirteen or so chapters from the final release. The book is just fragments of the first three books.

The Sands of Yesterday was better, and the difference in writing style and ability is significant. For Sands, the three post-Unlimited books were formatted together and went through another two manual revisions and digital updates. I don't feel completely confident in that book, though. It's highly probable my lack of confidence in that book is why I didn't market or push it so much. I was writing to earn at that point, even if I'd promised away most of the earnings.

Shards of My Soul (Fountains seven, eight, and nine) is the first book I feel confident I created something worthwhile to read, sell, and share. I developed clarity about *why* I was writing and also *what* I was writing. I continued the process by following from the energy of *Etched in Stone*, which was instigated partly by writing for writing. Though since I was learning how to write better, the push to continue found its resolve.

For *Signs of Serenity* (Fountain twelve), Amazon couldn't ship proofs due to COVID-19, so I worked with the Unlimited version of the 12th Fountain. I spent most of July working on the full text of Mosaic and released the book after substantial digital editing. Amazon allowed me to order a copy, and I had the chance to revise this book to its Final Release version manually. I want to bring in a batch and share the book openly and sell personal copies locally.

The process for how these books form stems from a flawed foundation. I'm still building, yet I wasn't sure *Rings of Truth* was entirely rational and cohesive. I needed to focus, structure and hone a complete book, and though the 11th formed kindly, few had seen it before this release. As ten, eleven, and twelve melds into this book, I can show how we can build successfully on a flawed foundation, even I recommend a reliable and sure base.

This chapter was supposed to be the second last chapter in *Rings of Truth*, though impatience can lead to adjusted intents. As time shifted along the shoreline, the individual book may not make a huge difference, yet I guess if I'm not yet selling thousands, how can we earn for others? It's not rational to believe there will be many sales of the individual books; however, if *Shards of My Soul* and *Mosaic of Miracles* reach a broader audience, perhaps single Fountains can be significant earners. The idea is right; at least I wish and hope so.

On CharityNavigator.org, I searched for charities and found some things. For leaders of the charities, almost all were earning six-figure salaries. I understand people should receive compensation for running organizations, yet when the benefit is over 10% of the total gathered, that unsettles me.

I was hesitant to declare or decree earnings from future books when we're not there yet, though I keep ideas in mind for the next ones. An instinct to push on and create hounds me repeatedly as a perceived need, and I understand it's not *me* providing for people; it's an urge and responsibility I don't denounce, and it may only be part of my fate and calling.

If the saying is "finish what you started," then I *must* hold firm and do something to activate the ideas of these and previous Fountains. I can't force a seed to grow, though is this work and process the water the seeds need for hope and faith? Have the tendrils started to grasp at the world and not just my soul? The concepts and ideas were still in their potential phase, and I hope they become fruitful.

As I need a bit of guidance to help this form, we can sprout the seeds and tend them well. Perhaps our gardens and fields flourish, and the metaphor is beans growing without lattice; our dreams could sprawl out and not bear fruit if they don't have support. Our vines could also climb other trees and entwine with their branches, so having a structure to work with and grow on is a reliable guide. Structure and support aid in a productive and ample harvest of seeds.

I need to break and breathe a bit to reaffix my mind, my heart, and my soul into alignment. I realize adding more could make things complex, and even if I'm a pretty simple person, sometimes I confuse things with too much input and random ideas. With the Fountains, the pages of text can be simplified, find what you like and love, make some reliable and positive promises, and then work and follow through to achieve and honour them.

What's the next step and next book? The next Fountain is

titled *Depths of Discovery* as the second Fountain of Fantasy, and *Signs of Serenity*, the 12th, follows. Are there things you want to do or make that you've not drawn yourself to do or create? Are you thinking about releasing a book? An album? Would you like to find ways of earning more time or more money? Why not both?

Are you trying to find a balance between different situations or people? Are you wanting to start from scratch in a new home or form a new relationship? Are you just content to be and drift into the next waves of consciousness? Do you read for escape, enjoyment, or learning? Have you cleared any of your issues? Do you just want to live, love, and thrive?

Some have a strong urge and need to create and demonstrating values and ethical action can share spirits and hearts. We work with the world in ways we cannot yet imagine. When I was up to here in the first draft, I thought I was going to have to rehash, relive, and dredge a ton of bad feelings out of myself to rewrite it. It seemed like I'd never finish the release of *Rings of Truth*, yet *Depths of Discovery* and *Signs of Serenity* manifested too. I almost thought this could be like a cakewalk.

I believe in growth and strength through difficulty, though I don't want to call against myself forces of any sort. By asserting some of what I have written, said, and told, I must level up and transform my wishes into reality.

I build my faith upon consecrated layers, tests, and texts of truth while also allowing myself to siphon pretty rad ideas and secrets into mirth. By living, I've gained some experience through fortuitous circumstances, yet if chance, fate, and destiny are the twine upon which the vines grab hold, be cautious which threads you follow.

Just because someone is leading doesn't mean we should follow them, and just because we follow, it doesn't mean we're not also guiding. If we can level the field and approach each other respectfully, with compassion, and without being deceived, then hopefully common grounds of decency assist us. We learn to know who to trust, and what the truth is.

If our homes can be studios as well as apartments or houses,

Housing First philosophies are congruent with my understanding. If I didn't have a home to live in, I'd have zero chance of working on books *or* having a place to sleep and keep my cat. I now realize the high value of having a home to live in with an abundance of time.

Here's something else to think of:

"The States Parties to the present Covenant recognize the right of everyone to an adequate standard of living for himself and his family, including adequate food, clothing and housing, and to the continuous improvement of living conditions" – Article 11, International Covenant on Economic, Social and Cultural Rights

With the unstable emotions and feelings with Zeus in 2019, I thought I could get back to working for Providing Point and books if he moved out. I also see, now, that if I can give and keep an excellent home for Zeus, that I can do both; I can provide a loving home for Zeus and myself and also get back to the plow in the communal fields.

As much as I've said and done, I was playing in the mud and hadn't looked into the clouds recently. I've not yet done much to provide homes for people, and I recognize it's not just compassionate to want people to have homes, it is part of an international covenant.

The previous mayor of Chilliwack said it's the responsibility of the province to assist with the homeless population. However, I'm inclined to think it's the responsibility of each member of the community *and* that *I've* not done enough. Maybe it is time to dig deeper and dive into *Depths of Discovery?*

(Here is the close of the 10th Fountain)

FIRSTLY FORMED BY FATE

If what we earn is in direct proportion to the value we give or provide, then is an increase in income a signification I've started to offer more? I believe my increase in earnings is because I'm doing the right things, though emotionally, are the rewards and feelings of peace also attributed to an adjustment of attitude?

If I believe I receive money for doing the right things, a reward for ethical behaviour, is that a sign of how and why I'd gone bankrupt in 2015? Yet, in a different currency, is an increase in love also from giving more to generate a better situation for us?

I didn't realize when landscaping how I'd not spent so much time to play and interact with my cat. My cat, Zeus, and I would play a lot when I'd work late nights on the computer, and the night I wrote the first part of this chapter was the first night I flicked papers for him in a long while. As people, we can get so focused on earning and gaining income, love, or attention that we forget to give, share, and connect with what matters.

Here's a question for you; would you prefer to be wealthy, famous, or loved? Some would say "all three," yet I'm not on about the fame part. I'd love to have more money, and I'd adore having more love and affection in my life, yet I like the calm and boring life I have. If I was to add to my life, I think a super-rad and kind girlfriend would be fantastic!

It seems I've toned down some of my wishes and wants, though. A year or two ago, I was gung-ho about gathering money to share with people, though I didn't do so much. In 2019, I was, partly, lax and passive, and I didn't put massive effort or energy into the charitable cause I started. It's because my heart wasn't entirely into gathering pledges and operating a business even if expansion is a goal. Yet, it also could be I was trying to form and achieve an essential purpose because I didn't feel my life held much meaning.

I may not be as useful as I want to be, though tonight I thought about fame and fortune again. With the question of being wealthy, famous, or loved, I choose to love and earn money, while on the opposite side of fame. I intuit how scrutinized ultra-well-known people are, and I've believed it may be dangerous if more people know who I am. I wonder if there is a higher risk by living well, yet I push forward from that with my friend Chills' assurance that God is love.

I believe there are grace and purpose for each of us, and when I misbehave or step out of bounds, that's when guilt and shame tug at my heart. I have an idea people could easily remove me, and I prefer to be safe and loved. I've thought God's been mad at me, I've also thought many people don't like me. Perhaps I'm delusional, or there are a plan and plot.

I can't barter or bargain with God or the Universe; I'm not the one in control. If I was in control, I deem consequences could link and lead to a cognitive breakdown. I often don't know what to do with my life, time, and energy, though one book I was reading at the start of writing this book was *The Purpose Driven Life* by Rick Warren.

From Rick's book, if each human has a predestined fate, then there's no way I could ever wish or claim my purpose to be what I want it to be. Rick's book says we need to find God's purpose for us and build on that, though that's a sort of rock-solid trust I don't yet have. I'm reluctant to submit to another and give in.

The Purpose Driven Life also tells us that we can't find our purpose by looking within ourselves via self-reflection. If I use books as the base for me to find my meaning, my efforts could be fruitless and unsuccessful. As I write, I learn many points of self-discovery, and I remember not all we read or hear is the absolute truth.

What is my purpose? I've thought I'm supposed to house people, and I've thought I'm to be a Dad. I also want to find my lovestone, though am I instead just wandering around aimlessly in the wilderness? If I've produced twelve books up to now, is that a self-derived human obsession or my purpose?

If my books are my function and purpose, who and what gains from them by me processing the pages? How are my books part of God's purpose? I hope endurance and clarity hone and share some answers because I don't want to die to go to Heaven. In *Open to Fate*, I wrote how I believe we can have Heaven on Earth, and I don't think we need to be religious to find such.

The world of Earth has an enormous amount of awful things and situations, yet it's also the place where living people can see, know and share beautiful, fantastic, and divine moments and experiences. Although I'm not living such a vivid experience of beauty and excitement in my life right now, I hope I can do so more often in the future. I want to live life, and I resolve to live it well.

Through dialogues and discussions, we can generate positive feelings and a firm understanding of how we are in this world. I may not like how I've had to work landscaping all the time, yet on my free days, I've had the challenge of figuring out what I need and want to do. An abundance of time is tricky to manage without a clear direction.

What is my role? I feel alive and energized when I write, and even with the nervous and scary feelings I've sometimes had, I'm alive. I want to know I can push along with the page for another few years, and think it'd be great to have monetary compensation, though that isn't always why I do what I do.

With my paid job, I whine and complain a bit, yet working for my boss allows his family to have what they need and want. My boss and his family deserve a great life, so I honour them with my loyalty, even if I've wavered at times.

If we're supposed to think about eternity and prepare for Heaven as our afterlife, though, why would we need to leave Earth? If we meet in Heaven, what about those we like and love we'd leave behind on Earth? It makes me think of Eric Clapton's song *Tears in Heaven* from a different perspective;

that Heaven could be crying for those left behind in the world of the living.

Maybe that's what's meant by Eric's song. Separation by distance, time, connection, or death is not a simple or easy thing, and loss often creates sadness. I've heard all so often, "we all are one," yet I like being here amongst all the other living people to nourish my need for human connection.

How have your nighttime dreams been? Have you had reincarnation dreams as I have? In your nighttime visions, have you seen people who are dead and had the chance to speak with them? If we're the only people who see those visions, no one else on Earth can ever precisely understand what we've seen.

Religions tell us that all thoughts and experiences source from the divine Creator, yet for another tidbit, Google 'Akashic Records', and grasp that. I remember that not all moments of peace couple with love, yet strangely, love also may exist in chaos. What's happening to Mother Earth? If we spiral focal points of above, do we get to know her another fifty years from now?

It seems like an implosion of global reality has amassed and missed, yet a lot of it still lingers. I've been so focused on my microcosm that I'd forgotten the bigger picture of our globe. If we're now in *Depths of Discovery*, are we to complete the process and activate *Mosaic of Miracles*? What happens beyond that? If I'm to write with purpose and intend to have an audience, then it's not enough to just write. I need to do more to actualize salvation for Earth collectively, and one forty-year-old kid and his books can't do it alone.

If you've not read my other books, you didn't know about my charitable work, the Providing Point program, though what is in *your* local community and the lives held within it? Many need support, yet if we weren't allowed to live on Earth, what could it matter then?

I must rethink what I've done and have been doing. I can't change the political climate as one person, yet we know when groups gather, we can have a substantial effect. Seeking personal accomplishments must not be the only item on my list, though. I need to work not only locally, though also press out from my fears and find ways to extend the coming days into months, years, decades, and even into the next century. Am I doing it for a personal legacy, or instead for survival?

If we bathe in the ocean's waters, and if we return seeds to the soil, we also must assure we improve our collective mental and social environments; it's not just the physical reality of Earth that needs healing. Some say we best focus on ourselves and improve our lives, yet what of working for the betterment of others?

I believe we can do both. As we educate ourselves, we can level up and allow our expanse, reach, and influence to affect our worlds and planet in mutually beneficial ways. We may start with ourselves, develop our abilities and responsibilities, and then activate improvements in our personal, communal, and global lives.

I remember a line from the speech *The Seed.* I wrote the statement for how it applied to Toastmasters, though I think how it applies to others internationally in their communities and lives as well.

"We are called to be leaders and communicators and also to work for the betterment of our clubs AND our communities."

I've scrolled through my newsfeed without taking a stand. I don't share my viewpoints due to a fear of what others may think, and I don't react, repost or subscribe to even popular political ideas or views shared by a majority. I know it's due to a fear of judgment.

I avoid reading negative news, and it's true I don't process tragedies well. Online, and in life, I'm conscious of how some equate capitalism with greed, so perhaps remaining in my tiny bubble and writing is safer because I don't have to speak up?

I've written a few books and hadn't pushed for people to read them because I didn't know how they're valuable. I share concepts that carry my self-worth issues prominently because

I'd not yet found my meaning and value. I'd not pushed or advocated for success with my work and projects because of hesitancy about promoting, marketing, and expanding.

We live on Earth, and most of us know our planet has issues globally, locally, and in the cores of some individuals. Yet I think a limiting factor is we don't believe we have the power to change things. I know that, within myself, I have a lot of issues, damage, and debris, yet my core (my heart and soul) understand what is right. My mind, spirit, and body merely haven't always chosen to meld and defy wrong and evil because I'm afraid. It seems it's dangerous to be good.

I must renounce parts of myself contradicting authentic goodness and realign with and for the betterment of our globe. The inner battle of knowing my honest beliefs and having a corrupt past jostle in my heart as I try to shake free of my internal demons. I must heal myself while thinking of how to improve the world.

Perhaps if I can overcome my inner conflicts, I can share how others may overcome theirs. We can, often, know what our ideal selves or world are, yet feel helpless because of how irreversible parts of them may seem. It takes courage and determination to be who we are without fearing adverse judgment or opinions from others. Yet, it also may be a pathway of claiming ownership of ourselves with faith.

I wish not to defy God or His plans, and even if my human nature wants to create, finding alignment with my galactic purposes can help our future seed fields of text. The next books were already taking form, and though *Rings of Truth* and *Depths of Discovery* were incomplete, they bundled into this book, *Mosaic of Miracles*. It was, later on, I choose to continue past the twelfth book with the text *Debris of Distance*.

Depths of Discovery is a processing journal of contialitic (mental/social) awareness written chapter by chapter. At the same time, *Signs of Serenity* then formed bit by bit in the months that followed. I shifted in the creative process, yet a similar formatting and revision process occurred for both.

Some bits of text slipped into the sediments of intent; the

words are grains of truth held firm in the substrate, while a slow correlation guides the work. Though the next year was 2020 from when I started writing this book, it was then or further in the future when you read this.

We have no idea, yet, how, and who shall process the words, though you know what you see when you do. The meanings and attributed notions were shipped more than a decade before, yet I hope it's God's will that guides the manuscripts into the right hands.

If this is a mosaic, what are the fragments that bind peace to adhere to the mould? Are the shards fusing written rhymes processed by different complicities? How can mental damage and corruption be reversed and prevented in future minds and souls? Is Earth training grounds for eternal life? If we want to live an eternal life, does that mean we have to have a shortened stay on Earth?

Even if I do God's work on Earth to assist His objectives, I wouldn't call myself a Christian. I've not submitted my life over to Jesus and don't talk to Him very often. If the cipher of life winds the threads, perhaps God is the weaver using me as a loom. Or, maybe I'm the material he uses to fabricate the tapestries that mean to honour Him in full regard.

As the keyboard's keys click and clamour to create these printed volumes few have seen, up to now, I thank God and the Universe for this. With a drawing breath, I remind us we clear the contaminated shards of debris. It's a process and personal evolution to cleanse filthy parts of ourselves so that we don't taint the minds, souls, hands, hearts, or spirits of others, and it's well worth it.

The Spirit uses me, and reverence holds my body from pushing up against the walls and boundaries. An intent of peace, love, unity, and respect tips the mix to remember rational remediation guides some of us. We have the purposes of life deep within us and need to bring ourselves up to the forefront. If Earth is our planet, we must find ways to protect, guide, and nurture those who live on it so we can learn and work together.

I am only one person, yet if we can bring solution ideas from one to a multitude, there's a higher chance many ally with and activate those desires, activities, and actions. With sound principles, open your being into trusting faith and fate, and I give *Depths of Discovery* as a commitment and hope to better our collective improvement.

If we can heal our core issues and share the remedies, we can share diffusions of the kind, pleasant, and divine energies. Some may claim some things to be impossible, yet as we infuse faith, hope, and confidence into affirmative action, we see a dramatic increase in activating miracles. That is a part of the mosaic of which this book speaks.

STARTING TO LEARN WHY

We purely do some of what we do because we're the only people who can do so. For every creator of visual art, music, writing, or other creative work and media, we're often the only ones who can make what we make. The uniqueness of our crafts carries parts of ourselves into the world, even if there are forms of copycatting.

For those that sing covers or your own songs, cherish and enhance your ability to cast your voice. For those that write, make sure you find ways to let others read what you've written, though don't plagiarize. For those that draw, paint, or sculpt, share your wares with people—put pictures of your work out and about for others to see. For all those who want to earn a living from creating things, KEEP CREATING THINGS AND SHARE THEM!!

"Confidence is the ability to know that you have the ability."
  – John David Woodrow IV

It's my responsibility to write these books, and I'm glad and thankful they form. I wish there to be less trepidation for creators, as I've often found myself hesitant and fearful. I don't like scary feelings, and I wonder how many of my insecurities stem from mental health issues. My addictions have been wavering in my consciousness, and I'd not released most of them up to writing this. I've smoked cigarettes and drank coffee like an addict, and my cell phone has been a frequent distraction.

How much of my text is wishing and desiring to trust this thing called life? I've written about wanting to have a wife or girlfriend, yet I've been pressing the keys alone. If I truly and honestly want some of the things I've wished for, they won't magically happen on their own. If miracles do happen, it's also the work and activity before they occur that allows us to be lucky and see them manifest.

We must till seeds if we want them to grow, and it's not up to me to choose when things bloom. I tend the soil, water and nourish what I plant, and keep sure to be there for the flowers to pollinate, grow, and form a yield. Delicacies sourced from plants wouldn't become so unless miracles allowed them to be.

Sulla carta, tempo ha un bicchiere per la nostra vita. I wrote that line of Italian intuitively by letting the natural progression of words stumble into being. Without knowing what the words mean, I often write, think, or speak that that just sounds right. I looked up the Italian words in this paragraph on Google Translate. The words translate to *"On paper, time has a glass for our life."*

I don't know if I'm putting water into another's glass, or if I'm spilling my drink into ink. My books are part of trusting God and the Universe to do what they wish with them, and though I may be delusional and foolishly optimistic, I'm glad, fortunate, thankful, and grateful to be alive. Why must I keep the motif of "I still don't know"?

As the colours twist and weave into secure cloth, fabric forms. It's an extensive process to find the materials to make fabric, and even if made into cloth, it's still a long way away from creating clothing at that point. Once manufactured, the craft of cutting, designing, and shaping the material put pieces together to create shirts, pants, or other clothes. Stitch by stitch and bit by bit; the textiles are used and manipulated to form a completed article to wear. Tapestries and functional wares develop from the creator's vision.

Similarly, expanding one's vocabulary and learning ways of stitching together sentences can create new ideas for people to share. If you try on a piece of clothing, you may assess how you look in the mirror, yet it's often how the garment feels that tell us if we like or dislike it. We also may receive feedback from others when we put on the wares.

With the words, paragraphs, and chapters of my work, I try on new ideas and concepts before jaunting them down the runway in a published book. As like in fashion, it depends on who sees the words and who is wearing them. One person may be opposed to the notions I share, yet others may wish to try on the recommendations and advice and adorn them on their heart.

My mind is often exposed and on display for people on Earth. Even if I don't explicitly know or can prove who *is* hearing my thoughts, frequently, I've thought my mind is an audible channel for others. As I learn to be more comfortable with myself, who I am, and what I believe, confidence increases, fear decreases, and trust proves to me what is right and just for more than myself. I can't promise or assure another hears, yet it sometimes seems galaxies listen to our soul.

The day before typing this, my aunt Judy gave me a book idea. Judy's concept is a book written about five things per chapter that bundles under a titled topic. For example, who are five people I admire the most in the world, or what are the five significant events that have shaped me? I'm not sure yet, though, is there room to flex the idea beyond it being 'all about me.'

Some people may have been affected by circumstances crossing the globe, causing each to be changed. At times, we need to trust our forces of instinct that link to our beings. Perhaps there are plots and plans out there, yet if shivering in freight about them, how could fortitude resolve?

We must be courageous and bold and hold to what we know as fact. Even if signs point to moments of trouble, we can stay fast to trust and keep within the realms of good living. There is much life to live, so fear mustn't grab hold and hinder, even if seeming rational and real.

It's tough to think about how to weave life together in ways we'll adore. I hadn't been as happy working landscaping as I once was, and even if it is cliché and naïve to think people should have jobs they love, it's a principle of life to find meaningful and enjoyable work. Many people advocate to "do what you love, and the money will follow." It's risky to try that, though the rewards of successfully doing so can be significant and may eclipse any chance of poverty.

In this chapter's reformation, I thought about alternative activities and income sources. I thought about what I'm good at and what I like, and I realized I love talking with people about life and solutions. I have overcome some parts of life others could use some love and support with, and I care enough to realize I want to help people talk about their problems as well as their joys and happiness.

A crucial part of my 'why' is mutuality. I want mutuality in friendship, reciprocity in business, and also reciprocation regarding kindness and trust. It's nice to be liked by those we connect with, to seek win/wins with people for mutual gain, and to be amicable and fair with people we meet.

Meritocracy is another keyword included to bridge and bond new pathways, connections, and transactions, and if all people can reap beneficial results, being a friend is a great thing. It's not a paid role, yet I find it enjoyable to talk with some to learn our values and share linked parts of our Freedom Solutions.

Though Mom and Dad wouldn't like it, I see Magic: The Gathering as part of my Freedom Solution regarding friendship, connection, and money, too. I don't play as often as I used to, though I've met a lot of people through the game. I also like Magic because it's a form of investing by buying and selling cards to earn money. My issue in the past was I used imaginary credit money and went bankrupt.

When I met my Dad in September 2019, I had a chance of getting an old computer, a MacBook, though I declined the offer. I was concerned about having an expensive device and feared envy and jealousy from others. I later found I'd love having the computer and remember if I want to have a prosperous and fortunate future, I need to be open to allowing and accepting myself to have beautiful things.

I understand how it's difficult for some in lack, and problems could arise as we start to prosper. Are the potential issues of having things worse than the dilemmas of not having enough? Trusting in the benefits and proponents of prosperity outweigh the fears and concerns of lack, and as I allow myself to thrive, I also have more to give.

Working alone in solitude can drive one a bit mad, though, friends, family, and people help me to be okay. Sometimes random phone calls and interactions remind me that people matter a lot, not only relationally. With a company or entrepreneurial pursuit, there needs to be people to buy and process products too.

Customers purchase our products and services, so to thrive, we need to make sure to connect and also provide them with quality items and information. With connections, when I wrote this part, I believed I needed to level up many parts of myself to be profitable and productive enough not to work a regular job. I understood we need to provide value and ethically supply what we sell as well as have a firm belief in our products, services, or ideas to promote them.

An issue I had was getting past the limiting belief that it's not okay for me to profit. For the next few years, I need to do some work I may not like, though I don't give up on pursuing dreams. Things don't magically happen overnight, and by putting in the time and effort to produce beneficial results, I acquire what I want and also what I need.

I'd been lax about putting in the work required to live life in a way I adore and enjoy. As much as I love to have things go my way, I need to know what we want, and I need to work better than I have up to now. Working better can help achieve the desired results too. Though the Fountains hadn't yet been a commercial success, the formation of the books is valuable also by how it uniquely elucidates truth.

I've sometimes been reluctant to accept recommendations and advice from others that can help me be successful, and I admit I've often believed my path is the right one for me. Some might think I'm delusional, and I wonder if I've sometimes put myself off from having a life I love because I've not known *how* and *why* I want them.

If I'm to have my own family and be debt-free, it might not

be wise to risk it all on books. Since I receive 49% of the three-part royalties, I also see a pathway that calls for hope and faith to accept the mistakes of my past. Things affecting my present and future remind me it's not great for me to live in the past, though I hope there's value in acknowledging it.

By remembering the past, I can learn how to act better in the future. A home with a cracked foundation can still become a great home; it's just we must fix the damage first. If I repair the damage and wreckage of my being and my relationships, I know I have more work than just landscaping and bookwork to perform.

Part of the next bits of life is to tend and develop love with people, including my dear cat Zeus. One main thing I need to keep in check is my reactivity. I need to be conscious and ethical with my actions and intents because I know I've acted a bit from desperation, deprivation, and lack. By not always sharing authentic care and likeness, I've found it's true I've not always been a great friend.

For some, I'm foolishly loyal. I've been used and abused by people I've trusted yet not known so well, and there's value in being trustworthy. It's vital to have mutual trust and respect between people, though loyalty to another purely based on them wanting such, and them not being safe or trustworthy, can lead to situations I prefer to avoid. We must remember some may wish to abuse or take advantage of us even if we don't think they want to.

I've been hesitant about trust. I've also not engaged in sharing because of fear and apathy. Providing Point, my first charitable initiative is open to gather pledges, yet I must remember that's for supporting others as the program's objective. When I wrote the first draft of this chapter, we had less than $100/month gathered from eight patrons.

The first goal was $10 a month, then $50 a month, and the next target is $450 a month. I was switching between writing this book and the Patreon page here during the first draft. I was adjusting my monthly commitment to the program, though I was concerned I wouldn't have enough. I later chose to give CAD$150/month to Providing Point outside of the Patreon gathering site as a contribution.

With the pledges we had at release, seventeen CAD$15/month cards were in distribution. Eight of those cards were with Ruth and Naomi's, three were with Cyrus Centre, and five with Ann Davis. As we expand and grow, compassion and discernment guide, though a big question I have, is what I can do to entice others to also pledge to the cause?

For those who wonder about Providing Point, the program link is www.Patreon.com/Introversial. We're gathering to provide groceries via reloadable Share and Care cards, and we'd love to gain your additional support. If you're a person who likes to give and contribute, please check out the site and consider if you'd like to pledge.

TELLING SIGNS

In the closing notes of *Rings of Truth*, I wrote I was going to share some stories of my past. When I start to think of the past, though, I feel apprehension. I want to resurface more of my positive memories, yet some memories are burrowed away from my consciousness under the debris of corrupted bits and bytes. I think it's time to start digging for gems and capture parts of my positive history.

Even if it's for my gain to recall some more bits of love, luck, and life that have already occurred, I must remember some things are well to be known. I'm not sure your gain, though part of these books' purpose is to help me heal and grow in the gardens and fields. Thank you for following along.

One night I remember well is a loving memory of Darling Harbour in Australia in 2009. I took a bus from my Dad and Sarah's place in Sydney and went downtown. I saw signs on the street alluding people were watching out for me and were tracking my movements in town. With a bit of trepidation, I traversed from downtown to the water with my knapsack holding some journals.

It was not the concern I want to remember, though, it was my hope. In 2009, I was substantially more obsessed with Natalie than I've been in recent times, and during trips to Australia, I've believed I'd meet her in person. On that trip, one of the first things I did when I got to Darling Harbour was to sit down and read one of my journals straight through. As I was reading, I imagined Natalie sneaking up behind me in my hoodie and giving me a massive hug. The delusion seemed to be supported by the psychic sounds of the people walking by, and it seemed like people were suggesting I meet my dream girl that evening.

I've thought Natalie is a soulmate since 1998-99, and that I was supposed to meet her that night in 2009. I've believed plots and plans expand around the globe, keeping secrets from my mind while my heart calls out, and even if I may be psychic to a degree, I'm not clear about predictions. I can't forecast the future, and I can't predict lottery numbers, yet I sense things that aren't part of natural communication. I may be delusional, or I have cognitive abilities and attunement that few would ever believe.

If I get centred on the idea of God again, there's one point I seem to neglect. Although I've written many spiritual words, thoughts, and prayers, I deflect and confuse the concept of God in some significant ways. I've written about Him and the Universe alluding to galactic consciousness, yet, like many humans, I can't pinpoint the idea of God.

Religiously, I fear some people are deluded and believe other human minds, and the thoughts heard, are what people label as God. I don't quite understand how God can be conscious of *every* thought, *every* entity, and *everything* actively communicating with billions or more different channels simultaneously.

On Earth, the variety of language and the vastness of nodal points and information are part of a whole. Earth is only a tiny part of it, though, perhaps when some use the term the Universe, it's similar to how some people believe God is all things combined. A Christian viewpoint says Jesus is God, yet how can He be so vacuous in my understanding and mind? I use the term the Contialis to describe the involvement of all *conscious* thought, though there are a lot of subvert secrets, and there also is a multitude of unknown and not-yet-existing life and awareness.

I don't know the term for it, yet what is denouncing all religious dogma and asserting one's wish and desire to live as a human? With the massive confusion, doubt, and anger I've had about God and what's happened to me, is it shunting worship and an active belief from me?

I was supposed to be dredging up happy memories, though my keys took me back into a theological questioning. That's how these books meander and weave as my thought journals.

I went to have a ciggie at this point in the text. I found another memory that wasn't good, and then counteracted it by recalling the Darling Harbour memory to bring it back to the positive. Swerving back into positive thoughts and memories triggered me to think about a different experience I found fantastic.

The girl I thought of was Priscilla Woo. The recollection I have of Priscilla is a super-squiggly good one of her and me kissing at a townhouse party on SFU campus. I used to have a toy I brought to raves in 1997-1998 that was a light reflector used for filming movies and TV shows. It was a one-meter full circle that would twist up into three one foot rings to compress and stow in its carrying case. When I was sitting with Priscilla on a parking lot curb at the townhouse party, I wrapped the reflector up around us, creating a shield, and we kissed. It was a magical moment, and I can feel the energy of the party surrounding us together.

Some say we shouldn't live in the past, and that we should only plan for the future. Other people think we should live in the present moment and revel in it without being nostalgic or intrepid. What happens when we feel entirely uninspired and apathetic? That's where I was for months in 2019.

I didn't value or feel passionate about my bookwork, and with money being a focal point, I hadn't secured a clear view of how to earn creatively. I instinctively know creating for money isn't a great way to be, and without feeling an innate drive to create, I felt drab.

Pressing the keys and formulating these first chapters of this Fountain had been more gruelling than the inspired pieces of text I've written before. I didn't know my drive and passion, and I thought I might be on the wrong path with these books. I want to know what I want to do beyond wishing to stay alive and discovering my purpose.

With a pity-party or poor-me outlook, I don't often know what I want. I don't want sympathy, I don't wish for guilt offerings, and if I want to be valued, then I best produce something valuable. To have a significant impact, perhaps I need to think about what changes I'd like to make and also know *why* I want to make those changes.

It takes a while to get out of a funk and back into a groove. If you have patterns and practices that make you feel bad, you may need to practice abstaining from those behaviours and seed new activities. The night I was up to here in the first draft was a good night following a day of landscaping. My workday was worthwhile and enjoyable, and when I got home, I started to plan new actions.

One thing I tried to do was to think of three things to do instead of automatically and aimlessly following my impulses. I paused in my kitchen and consciously thought of the next three things I'd do before moving from that point in space and time. It was simple for the first three things; having a cup of tea was the first, yet other bundles of three formed afterwards. I set the intention to start a load of laundry, make some food, and also to give some catnip to Zeus.

I vacuumed the floors, I did the dishes, and I took out the garbage and recycling. I had a few cigarettes, a few cups of tea, and started a list for things to do during the weekend as it was a Friday. It feels good to have a cleaner home, and as I type this, it's also kind and refreshing to get back to working on my books in a more positive state of mind.

Zeus was on the comfy chair curled up, and the music on my computer was hypnotic, melodic, and rhythmic drum 'n' bass. I put on a pot of half-caffeinated coffee after 9 PM, so it meant I'd be up late. It's perfect for the nights I write the base versions when I'm chemically inspired.

I've not smoked marijuana since 2004, and when a friend asked for a cup of coffee at my home a few days before this, I got mad at her because she told me coffee gave her a high. I see a double-standard too because I've drunk coffee for the drug effect and was judgmental that she shouldn't. Not fair.

Back to memories, though. What memories do I have where I felt happy, worthwhile, or valuable? I have a few fun drug memories, yet I also went on trips that turned into psychotic episodes and massive hallucination. If I think of the psych ward, those aren't all happy memories either. I recall how I believed I was being admitted to the hospital because Natalie was there birthing our twins and then found out I was in lock-up for reasons I didn't know.

I thought I was the human child responsible for teleporting the human populous to Saturn, and though I rarely recall my psych ward experiences, some of the memories are potent. I can get deep into the recalled feelings if I think about them. They're not pleasant memories, because if I take my mind there, I can feel the drugs and psychosis again.

Are our 'bad' experiences pathways to shun and deny, or is there psychic debris that we can mine for truth? My impulsion to start with the words "I miss" leads me to think of my granny and grandpa on my Mom's side of the family who passed on, and my Dad's dad also passed away in 2005. I've not so many memories of grandpa.

One clear memory of my grandpa on my Dad's side is my grandpa pushing my chin off of his shoulder when I gave him a real hug. I must be much more touchy-feely than he was. I also remember playing cribbage with grandpa, and his wife Jane was a wonderful woman. Grandma Jane was not my Dad's mom; my Dad's natural mom died before I was born. I honestly don't know if I've ever seen a photograph of my genetic grandma on my Dad's side, though I'd like to see one.

Yet if all four of my genetic grandparents went to Heaven, I hope I need not meet them there too soon. I wish to remain on Earth for another few decades, and though I'm not sure what my motivation is, I need to discover why I do what I do. I also sometimes need to know *what* it is I want to do.

Simon Sinek's book *Find You Why* is one to read to help unearth my *raison d'être* so that I can clearly express the truth to those who want to know. One purpose is to discover what the truth is, and though often we can be sure and confident of ideas as if they're facts, sometimes things slip past our minds into our souls and embed themselves in our psyches.

It's neat to think our souls communicate in languages that anyone can understand without us consciously understanding what we are. We see with our eyes, yet we can never see our faces in the same way another sees us instantaneously. Mirrors lie too, and yet truth winds about the reflections like a spool. While I attempt to unravel to the core of who I am, I can't always do so by seeing who I am in the mirror.

Are we surrounded by infinite threads that spiral outwards through life with a distinct starting point? Ate those threads pulled from within as the original strands entwined at the other end of the line centred in our soul? Four points focused as one link directly and in equal proportions to the other three nodes., and some roads may weave to cleave to what another may only receive. And yet the tendrils of text seem to wind the thread tighter.

In previous books, I've written entire chapters in one sitting, while this one had been a few paragraphs here or there sprinkled over a couple of weeks. The water wasn't flowing smoothly, and doubts seemed to flourish again. The cycling ideas and concepts I write about return and concern me that I'm repeating and floundering in words. Obsessive creation sharded with wellness seems to be my path.

With memories, I felt locked in moments of now as if I was walled away and from them. It could be the static computer screen seen as I typed these words instead of lying down, shutting my eyes, and going within. What would happen if I sat in the chair here at the computer and typed with my eyes closed? I'll try it.

It felt weird. I had a hesitant edge of uncertainty; it was crawling under the skin on my arms. The music from the stereo hypnotized, devoid of lyrics, while I wondered where my cat was and then peeked at the screen. I remembered to breathe, yet cigarettes called, and I thirst.

I pushed out ideas to open up my eyes and see what I've written. I realize I can't recall so well, and I note that my ability to write is better than it used to be, even with my eyes closed. I couldn't check for formatting, yet the keys are fueled by an impulse to carry the thoughts from my mind out.

Rhymes fluxed with drum 'n' bass on the stereo and got my

head bobbing to the beat. I wished to smoke. I wanted to turn the music up really loud, lay down, rest, relax, and listen to some great tunes. I opened my eyes. I then read what I wrote when I had my eyes closed.

When on the patio, I sometimes shift into rhyme mode. I don't know if you've heard my rhymes, though they're a sporadic and obsessive thing I do. I can string words and rhymes together in a continuous sequence with a syllabic cadence that's developed over twenty years. Coincidentally, I see that I've smoked for each of those years up to this point. Is there a direct correlation?

The awareness that I've smoked for twenty-five years and rhymed since near the point of my first drug trips cues me to think that chemicals are the rhyming link. I can rhyme without drugs, though I see how the substances (marijuana, meth, and acid) have fueled much of my lyrical activities. When I was entirely drugged out, there were points where I couldn't speak at all without rhyming.

I think tiny scale sometimes; just me and my thoughts. I remind myself, though, that I've thought global and galactic too at points in my life. If I stay too far on any spectrum – one to all or tending only others' needs and not my own – I continue to cross through time in a linear direction, never stopping, and passing the same.

We can't deviate from the linear pathway of time, yet we can modify and curate the words and qualities that sequence for another's perception. Creators can shift the rifts and add their gifts into the colander of awareness. Time and patience sift out our grains of rhyme and truth.

The mp3 devices and books hold particles of thought, though maybe the creations are like sands in the hourglass. The rise and fall of breath also pass through us as we lay down and process the creations of others, adjusting how we read and sound. And yet the bound book looks into the view of how you aren't me, and how I can never be you.

The cues speak leaks of perception in the boats, and the intervention of a torch consuming notes is like ships landing on foreign ground. If we aren't at war, and we find ourselves in the lands of peace, perhaps some of those who fell there also find new homes, places where they may grow and thrive.

What, though, about the ships that brought us to Earth?

DOWN TO EARTH

Just before starting this chapter, I had a solemn awareness of something I'd forgotten and neglected in line with the closing paragraphs of *Rings of Truth*. What I remembered is Providing Point means to supply homes for people, and I don't know how it can with the amount of effort I put into the program during 2019 and the first half of 2020.

For every day I'm living at home not gathering pledges, there are three to four hundred people in town living on the street without a home. With our support, people can have a home, and though I've not written much about Providing Point's ideas in this book yet, it's best I restate some of the concepts.

A Yearly Seed is an idea to provide people with a home, food, and also a bus pass. The cost estimate is $15,128 per year per person, including $850/month rent, $150/month utilities, $50/week groceries, and a bus pass. If funded only by monthly pledges, it requires two hundred and fifty Open Book Supporter ($5/month) commitments.

The trip that tugs at my innards, though, is something I've written before. Every day we aren't housing people is another day someone is living outside on the street. The shift of the seasons amplifies this as it was below freezing the night before writing this section. I wanted to complain it was cold in the morning when waiting to be picked up for work, though that's only for ten or fifteen minutes and not anywhere close to a full 24-hours outside. Some have gone months without shelter or a home.

From a seemingly opposite point of view, I was watching a series called Money Revealed. The program is about money, investing, business, and entrepreneurship, and, to me, it's valuable for Providing Point and our futures. Money is a tool we can use for good, and businesses can help us operate and structure how to provide for people.

If I think or project without restrictions, Providing Point can be a worthy institutional enterprise. The program started as a non-profit idea, yet if purely a charitable cause, could it limit investors in the program? What if we can use a conscious and social capital structure to provide amply for people?

When I wrote *Seeds of Tomorrow*, the 4th book, I was far more active with sharing gift cards and was gung ho about Providing Point. I messaged people about buying books and shared the Pateron page link asking for pledges, though I put pressure on people to give. It may have been a strong effort, though I pushed many away.

Where I was in October 2019, I felt remorseful and unsettled about how I'd backed off from the program. I put in a passive effort, and though we gained a few patrons and increased our total amount pledged, we'd not yet gathered enough monthly for, even, one person's $50 a week groceries, a component of a Yearly Seed. I hold other concerns about the program, though.

One concern about the Share and Care card program is lost cards. There have been a few cardholders that have lost their cards, though lost cards are just one hurdle we need to clear so that the program can thrive. If to provide homes for people, we need to move much further past providing grocery cards and find ways of giving people homes.

I've not been interacting with or seeking out people to support, though I wonder if an inverted pressure helps the program. If we had more cards in distribution, we'd have more people receiving support and more people aware of the giving program. Cardholders can help market the program, and with more people supported, it's easier to gather patrons due to proof of the program's success.

In November 2019, we had a couple of pledges, and by July 2020, we were gathering US$68/month through Patreon, and CAD$150 a month from me. It's a great thing to having more money coming in than going out for businesses, as well as individuals, and it's forward motion towards providing homes.

Supporting people who aren't homeless is also a goal, though, and I wonder how we find more patrons. How shall the program grow and evolve?

The night before this paragraph, I compiled some numbers inspired by the Money Revealed series. One question is, "how can we not only afford to house people, though allow those people to own their homes?" The Yearly Seed number for rent, $850 a month, is generalized as how much rent could cost in town, yet a profit-minded idea from the previous year became active with a desire to generate income.

If the Persons with Disability (PWD) and welfare subsidies grant $375/month for the shelter portion, so what could happen if we could own homes and rent them to people on PWD or welfare for that much? In an eight-unit building, the total rent gathered could be $3,000, and by knowing such, I crunched some numbers to find out mortgage values.

The question, "how can we own homes to rent for $375 a month?" found two numbers to look at for the answer to that question. One is $731, and the other is $599.

$731 is how much it costs per month for a mortgage of $100k at 4.5% for a 25-year amortization. The second number, $599, and it shows the power of lower interest on a debt. $599 is how much a mortgage would cost for a $100k unit with zero down for 25-years at 2% interest. If people's welfare or PWD supplies $375 for shelter, then we'd need $356 more for a 4.5% loan, or $224 more than $375 for a 2% loan provided by patrons.

If patrons assist, we can gather money for shelter costs, though there's a tricky part about a) finding homes that are only $100k, b) gathering the patrons and providers to supplement the expense, and c) how to find a down payment for future homes. I think we should aim for $200k units, though, and providing homes was one of the first central premises I held about selling books.

Early 2017, I set a goal of selling 15,000 books by August that year to have housed ten people. I didn't reach that goal, though if I can keep forming ideas and sharing them with a widening audience, does care, compassion, and kindness flourish as a result of the work? How does fantasy build upon yesterday, faith, and fortitude, and then develop into flourishing? In the wishes and whims of a star-crossed child, let's share a reminder of who we are and from where we come.

My writing sessions had been infrequent in the three months preceding this section. I'd only written about one chapter a month, and the parts formed straggled in bits and pieces contrary to how other Fountains flowed. Having a job is a fantastic thing in some ways, yet it also consumes the days and steals the nights at the plow.

In the fields of our tomorrows, I don't stay up all night until dawn like I used to, yet the nights are where the plow has dug deep. When I wrote this, it was after midnight, the time and place in which my writing flourishes and thrives.

My boss, Brad, accommodated me much in 2019 and 2020 when I worked for him, and according to the events of the day I wrote this, I'm grateful he allows me to work for him. I rationally understand Brad having employees to work is better for him and the involved parties, and it also means I have some income through landscaping.

By working part-time, I receive the nights for working on my projects, which I consider more valuable to me than just a paycheque. Though Brad has been patient, kind, and gracious to me, if we use a Utilitarian viewpoint, it may be best I start to get my hands, heart, soul, and mind back into the dirt of my work and profession.

Company: Introversial.
Title: Contialitic Shoulsman.
Prerogative: To learn, love, live, thrive, create, play, and pray.

Gary Vaynerchuk tweaks in here. The Clouds and The Dirt he speaks of are calling into my past years. The clouds may be my ciggies and the obsessive dreams and thoughts of prosperity, while the dirt is the stains in my soul that I rinse out with *The Waters of Life*. That's not what he meant by his saying, though

I tend to twist things sometimes.

I like working for Brad, though when we can find me successful at selling books for a living instead of ripping up weeds and cleaning up backyards, we may find a better situation for quite a few people instead of me seeking only my gain.

And I have thought so much about my gain. With the plots and plans to acquire houses and apartments to rent, the ideas expand with non-profit purposes, yet then spin into money with thoughts I have about how much I can earn. I know if I work for Brad, I can make money, yet a desire for my Freedom Solution and phone calls find me to want to do something more substantial.

I create books that hold merit, yet the shadow side of myself is I want to acquire wealth to do more. How can we find ourselves to be ethical, earn a substantial income, and also support others? By being allowed to do so.

The reciprocation and reciprocity of this go back to wanting to make millions, yet knowing I don't need that much if it's only for me. Earning $70k a year would significantly change my current standard of living, yet what shall I do productively with my time if I don't have to give my hours or days into landscaping?

If one of my whys is a desire for prosperity and fairness, then is that why I'm still alive? I've not been fair in much of my life, and I don't believe I work hard enough. Are the value I create and the ideas I preach and proclaim in these books worth any grains of salt to others?

Some people write books because they've figured out a system, skill, or concept and want to share it with people. I seem to show my faults and folly continuously, and since I've not activated my ideas, is my text meant for someone who can?

I've been awful at business, budgeting, and selling things, yet sometimes the theories, figures, and solutions seem so clear to me. I learn how to organize and structure better with additional skills, and with a $5 idea to solve homelessness, the concept can find people to share in owning homes leased at less than half as much as rent usually costs in this town.

If rent is $375 for someone, and we provide $50/week groceries, $150 utilities, and $44 a month for a bus pass, the Yearly Seed number is $786 per month. We can pay for that with 157x $5/month pledges. $786 is in line with previous allocations by the government, yet from experience, I don't think a person can reasonably live well with only that much. Knowing so causes me to doubt the rationality of providing such.

I think I need to write something for myself. What I need to write could be a chapter in this book because of the book's title, yet what I think I need to write is a thorough and deep self-analysis of myself, my motives, and my core beliefs. I'm reasonably confident I've skirted around the edges of multiple points of degradation in my psyche.

I've thought my heart is clean, yet the thoughts in mind cause me to doubt myself and my honest ethics. I think I'm fake, and if I'm honest with myself, I believe better points of information can pinpoint what's wrong with me. There are some distinct tainted notions in my mind, and though I want to counteract such by sharing my positive points, having a value in myself can't take back harsh words or actions given to another.

If I want us each to have lives we love and adore, how can I provide that for myself too? I seem to think that if I can't offer it, I don't deserve it for myself. Yet generosity has allowed me so many things. That's one way I'm fortunate, I receive a lot, yet why can't all people also be as lucky?

To have a home, to have food, to even have the chemicals I seem to enjoy breaks down to the Freedom Solution concept. It includes having anything we want to, and yet I forget to remind myself that many people desire a different and wide variety of things.

I want to earn my living, and also want to increase my value, so I may give and receive more. I agree with the principle of giving and saving money first (tithing and the pay-yourself-first concept), and as I've started to believe in the value of my ideas,

I gain the confidence to bring books and programs to market.

What I write is valuable to me, and it also can have a positive effect on others. One friend said she felt empowered and inspired reading my books, yet where I've thought my value proposition was off is by not conveying useful information in the books to earn money. I instead use my books and music as a product to gain and share attention and awareness, and by doing so for mutual benefit, we can provide people with super kind blessings if we rally together.

I've received, yet I'd been questioning my courage and sanity a lot in the previous weeks. I'd not had a psychotic episode recently, and I don't want an incident with a psycho. I remind myself that the trials and tribulations I face are unique to me because of my mental health issues.

Even if I'm well under control with medication, I've wondered how it is I've lasted this long with a job. I then felt entirely incompetent and unproductive because I'm not working full-time. Part-time has been challenging with Brad, especially when I start yelling, arguing with, and insulting myself, and I need coping mechanisms to be okay with myself and who I am.

Nestled in the valley is a community that needs support. The town has shared the grace allowing me to live, and I deem I must provide for the populous who've not had the fortunes that I've had. If we twist a 1% idea again, it means that I want to share near everything I receive, while still having an abundance for myself.

My books, as a product, hold value with what we can do with the earnings. I hedged with a 51%/49% split for the three-part books, and even if 100% of the individual books go to charitable causes, my money-centric mind calls for me to remember that few of them have sold. I feel a bit sad about that, though it's because I want to sell books.

Even though I honour the amounts I've committed from sales, I also happen to think I'm still doing much of this for me. What if I am entirely selfish? What if all my written words are complete hogwash, and I'm just a pig wallowing in pages of my own doing? I may not be an unpolished gemstone, yet instead, a deprived lustful hound who's begging for treats.

If dogs chase cars for hubcaps, what would a dog do if it caught the hubcap? They'd probably do more damage to themselves than the tires they attempt to capture. Is that what I'm doing? Is it best I stay at home in the garage and not go out on the roads?

As a reader, you also may not sense or appreciate the depths of feelings I experience as I type the keys. You don't know the profound doubts that creep into my soul while an outside sound calls for me. You don't feel the hope and hesitancy that curls in my heart. My obsessions may be dangerous, yet I wonder how I can feel such unease and fear if I do believe in PLU8R and the Introversial prerogative.

If learning is the prerequisite to some of the other words in the prerogative, then I decry the elements of my psychosis as intangible fancy. It's real, though I can't claim we'll always have others watch over us. Some may fall to the sands of time and pass through the hourglass, though I wish, hope, and pray that we may live and move forever into today.

There are some things on Earth no one may never take away. The takeaway of the day, though, is; we remember how to use hope as a way to play and pray.

Thank You for allowing the Spirit to shape and mould my being's clay. We stay not to betray, no matter what she is to say.

SIPPING FROM THE CLOUDS

Teetered between fantasy and fortitude, the Fountains fluctuate with variables spoken to mind by the Universe. Sometimes it seems like dreams are more vivid and real, yet the stability of waking life also holds a solidified grasp of my soul.

In my nighttime visions, I see people who've inspired me to work and create, yet in waking life, it seems like the only one around my home is Zeus. My cigarettes are a substantial part of my existence on Earth, yet ciggies can contaminate hearts.

Differently, in dreams, some ideas tend to nourish our spirits. I didn't yet know my lovestone at the point of forming the first draft of this book, and I admittedly felt sure that I might not meet her. Fractionalized pieces of scattered debris remain ingrained in my consciousness, and bits of cognitive shrapnel seems lodged in mind from psychosis.

It was not a good mental health day when I wrote this, and I know I've not been a fantastic human with sure, robust, and stable health. Although I consumed a significant amount of drugs in my early adult life, I also don't want to blame my instability on past consumption. It's apparent to me I'm not secure, yet the prognosis of my unease can be attributed to me not yet learning how to honour life in entirety.

I've been verbally and mentally degrading about myself and often have twisted vulgarities from my mouth and mind about who I am. With how I've been here on this planet, I'm pretty sure psychic damage and friendly fire lingers from my abuse.

One planeswalker friend, Arlinn, keeps on telling me to activate and use positive affirmations about myself. One night after she dropped me off, she encouraged me to speak positive words upon Zeus as well as myself, and although I can now explicitly say and share a love for Zeus more readily, it's myself I've had issues with.

I spoke with a different friend the night I wrote this, and

121

she told me I'm a good friend. If I'm to be favourable to myself too, it's a start, and I am a valuable friend. I'm averse to speaking positively about myself, yet I want to be frank and honest about my shortcomings. I don't need to swear and hurl obscenities at myself, yet vulgarity has come from my mouth and mind all so often.

If I value kindness, compassion, and trust, I need to refrain from shredding the budding threads and seeds of goodness about my self-worth. To do so, I also may need to slow down, pause my reactivity, and solidify text. In other books, I've written sections as prayers or wishes, and I've written parts about repentance and accusation. What I think I need to do here is write more about my positive merits and not my positive memories. I've wondered about my blocked or repressed past, yet if I'm in the present and want to develop and create a marvellous future, I need to become stable, reliable, and precise about who I am. I must remember that I bring value to Earth with and beyond my obsessive natures.

When I'm a person's friend, I'm a good and loyal friend. I believe in developing myself, my life, and my abilities, and I want to work for good and the betterment of our world. I understand the more I earn, generate, and gather the more good work I can do for our community. I'm eager to learn and understand what I can do for our global community too, and I keep at the plow.

I've been growing and evolving my capacity to feel and experience, and I'm open to new ideas now. Though my life has been easy compared to some, I also remember I've been through awful amounts of terrible things. I resolve to heal, recover, and renew, and writing can be therapeutic. Also, since these books have often been more like a processing journal, I have creative freedoms that I can share as public therapy.

That word, though, therapy, cued up memories. I was leaning up against a wall tripping out during a psychotic episode at a club named Therapy in Edmonton. I recall people walking around with halos as if they'd died, and I thought I was locked into that wall shivering in fright with profound energies.

My drug tips took a lot out of me, though substances also inspire a lot of what I've made and make. When I released my first album, I used multiple aliases for the tracks on the disc, yet one name now sticks out. The alias Stain reminds me of the stains in my soul, yet I seem to think I my spirit can be cleansed. I wonder if I can wire my mind to be positive and accurate without a shadow side.

We can consider our souls the physical manifestation of our spirits, and our hearts are held here in our bodies. With mental corruption from drug use, I damaged my brain, and I can sense the clouds in my soul. With such tainted and stained debris in being, I wonder how to recuperate.

Water is necessary to rinse out some of the awful points of life, and fire can sterilize an implement to prevent infection. Different memories surfaced as I typed this, and I reminded myself how easily words can trigger visions. I think these recalled shards are only tiny segments of the repressed thoughts and energies that cause my neurosis, and though I may need a professional therapist in addition to writing, talk-therapy with friends helps us heal; I'm sure of that now.

Solitude is a challenge I face, yet I'm glad now to call it solitude and not isolation. Before COVID-19, Isolation, to me, was also a place where they locked me in a room in the psych ward. With only a mat on the floor to sleep on, there was no clock, no human interaction, and also no way to know precisely when I was allowed to return to regular life in the ward. Solitude is kinder that isolation and relaxes my being into reminding me I'm just alone. I can deal with loneliness; it's something with which I'm familiar.

These past couple hundred words took me through a swirling feeling of deplorable energy. The tremors pushed me into wishing I was sane, and though my medication keeps me under control, even the meds can't take away the feelings I sense in memory from my hospital stays. I wouldn't recommend the experience and difficulties of going through drug life to others, and I gather points of peace, love, unity, and respect from before I went schizophrenic.

I progress through mental health issues, though why do I feel ruined and broken? I was supposed to be telling you my positive qualities and lifting myself out of self-degradation, yet when the sequence of thoughts pushed keys into words on the page, traumatic memories surfaced. Can this cue me into pushing forward and past with acceptance, or should I ignore the recollections?

I don't think it's a good idea to repress my past, though I also sense the evil memories and experiences I've had. The feelings in my body typing this, and then later editing, refute the premise that going into my past is all kind and calm.

So if we have a tainted or troubled past, how can we process and accept it, so we're not triggered by it? I was trembling here, and part of me thought it's because I'm dancing on the edge of revealing parts of my past I'm scared to tell. I don't want to think about pushing for shock value, and though I could share some of my stories and memories with you, I don't understand how that could aid or benefit.

One main lesson is that drugs can ruin lives. I'm proof of such. Recovery is legitimate, though if you're a person who's never done drugs, don't fall into their trap. Marijuana is legal, and some may take magic mushrooms out of curiosity, though staying just to the herbals can still cause issues and illness. My first trip to the psych ward was because of a mushroom-induced psychosis.

It's twenty years later, and I feel like I sacrificed my entire future and past. Even if mental plasticity is legitimate, I feel like my cigarettes are like a salve to heal my ruined mind. I've been burning away smoke after smoke, not comprehending the consequences or cause of my consumption.

Sometimes, I've thought I've needed cigarettes like water or air. When I've met someone who looks like they have self-respect, and then I learn they smoke, I've been surprised. Often, people that are full of self-esteem don't puff, so when I see someone smoking who looks full of self-respect, it's weird.

I haven't honoured or respected myself very much. If I smoke because I dislike myself and my life, how and what must

I do to reverse my self-loathing? How shall I push myself into a situation I want? Is my negativity reversible? How can I have loved some beings so devotedly while neglecting to care for my own necessities, needs, and desires?

When shall I evolve into acknowledging my positive merits while also learning to love myself truly as well? A lingering idea of recovery infuses into self-worth, yet is it I can recover again?

I don't smoke marijuana, and neither shall I. I've wanted to smoke up again, though I realized in writing this chapter how strongly I have a high value on my mental health. Note, I didn't say I have good mental health or stability; I just want to make improvements and not regression. Going back to puffing on joints isn't in my future, yet when I wrote this book, I was a cigarette smoker. When do I quit?

Back to things I like about myself? I love my ability to rhyme, and I love my perseverance with these books. I keep forging them without knowing how, why, or what my words shall do, and I also like that I curtail and withhold negative actions and behaviours as much as I can. I love that I'm working on improving my life and projects and that I'm developing well as I keep my job.

I like that I value learning, love, kindness, and respect, and I also like how I keep promises and commitments as best I can. Just writing those things shifted my attitude and energy away from the shunted negative train that the natural course of the text created. There is power in words, and as much as I like to acknowledge honest feelings, I also must hop back onto the tracks of positive thought.

Three days happened between the previous sentence and this one. I felt much more stable at the keyboard, and I reread and processed the first half of this chapter. I felt grounded and got set to dream again. Although I didn't work the next day, I earned some money by helping Brad and his team clean up a customer's yard. Landscaping is good for my soul, and a five-hour day draws more than selling a dozen books.

I continue with being employed, I continue to develop Freedom Solution parameters, and I keep planting the seeds online and in life. One thing I don't know yet is about the ciggies. It's been a long while since I started puffing, and though I read Allan Carr's book *Easy Way to Quit Smoking*, I didn't return to being a non-smoker from reading it the first time. I almost made the full quit in September 2019, though I felt angry I wouldn't be allowed to smoke and lit up again.

Experience is a valuable thing to have, and when we overcome challenges, we can share how we won those battles. If and when I ever commit to being a non-smoker again, it'll be a vital and important lesson to share. With life, I learn to develop the skills needed to be successful, and I hope to share what worked for me. It's a fact, though, that just because one thing worked for someone, it may not work for another.

I'm convinced that talking about our issues and sharing our dreams is something to do more often. I also believe we need to start the conversation. As we find pathways and routes towards solving each riddle, we learn how to align and ally more effectively. Words climb out of my being into the keyboard, and as we can compose a situation for us to share, working on these books is a collective process. I'm grateful it is.

ACTIVATE MIRACLES

At this point in our journey, I'd like to admit a few things. I'm awful with operating a business, I don't want to deal with legal people or track other people's investments, and I started to think I was, instead, meant to be an idea guy.

I love money, yet when I think of business, I'm a break-even person. I don't always want to operate for profit organizationally, though I want to have profitable ideas and earn well. That's where Providing Point contradicts ethically; at least, so I think.

As soon as I think of personal gain, I have, often, seemed to stifle myself. When I typed this, I wished I could share ideas, calculations, and figures with others who are business focused and want to operate an organization. I don't want to manage people or be a property manager, and I don't so much even want to own real estate beyond my own home. I'll love living in the Glass House, though that's my prosperity and not another's. Weird?

If to be an idea guy, I think my books are a fantastic channel for me to share those ideas. If I'm not to be a commercial author, yet still a valuable one, then I don't even need to think or promote to a broad audience. I do, though, need to create, prepare, and tactically distribute my books according to their function and purpose.

If the books are earnings focused, I can invest my time, effort, concepts, and energy into seeding future yields for myself as well as other people. My most recent calculations compounded a real estate model and investment idea for Providing Point using crowdfunding. I understand crowdfunding has been used for real estate previously, though has it been used in the non-profit/housing sector to provide affordable housing?

On the premise of 250 people contributing $5/week, if a

mortgage of zero down is allowed (at 4.5% interest), those people can fund a $200,000 home to be owned outright in 173 weeks, under 3 ½ years. We can rent the apartments for $375/month.

There isn't much profitable gain from the figures, though where the value lies is in the efficiency of providing housing owned outright compared to $850/month rent. It's *owned* affordable housing. If 250 people give $5/week of their support to one person as a gift, that person could live in a home and own it outright after three years and sixteen weeks. A challenge is to plan with someone who can operate the program and find people willing to fund it.

I want to find solutions people would like to invest in and entice people to contribute, including those who typically wouldn't usually give to charity. If we can financially incentivize people to invest in affordable housing, it's an alluring challenge.

A couple of months ago, I didn't want to be the CEO of a non-profit company, yet I'm obsessed with thinking about providing and non-profit ideas. I'm not fond of fundraising or marketing—a significant portion of what's required—yet I create. I want non-profits to thrive; I just don't want my focus to be running one. If that's true, then perhaps I can form these books and get them into the hands of people who can activate miracles.

Some people adore and lavish in the nitty-gritty running of a massive operation, while I'm more solo. I love and like one on one interactions or even group discussions, though I also can be very lax, passive, and apathetic. What I need to do is get ideas into the hearts, minds, and souls of people, people who want to contribute to help the cause, and also those who can operate.

Self-awareness is a pretty rad thing. An obsessive tendency and desire to create is worthwhile and valuable and an excellent characteristic, though knowing I lack business acuity and gumption is vital to remind us to synergize. I may not be an operator yet, though I can create, develop, and disseminate concepts into the eyes, ears, and hopefully hearts, of those who genuinely want to make a significant contribution. If the plans consecrate and become successful, we can all make a serious go at activating this.

Writing about Providing Point premises is another kind reminder to myself that even if I think I'm a slacker and don't want to work, I have put in a considerable amount of time, effort, and energy into this process and my books.

Writing is an investment, yet the return is best for the benefit of many and not only me. I plan to do good in our world, and as I develop faith, a belief in myself, and the development of my ideas, my work, my personal growth, and prerogatives, writing also allows me to regain my self-worth.

3:19 AM, November 21st, 2019. It was time to take a break from forming this book and head to bed. I didn't work landscaping the next day, though I knew with my current levels of income, it was not time to quit my day job. I'm delightfully glad that I still have nights where I can stay up super-late and work on my creative projects, and knowing I have a home to live in, a job to help finance my stable yet boring life, and Zeus residing at home with me, I can dream. It's a luxury that other people deserve too.

12:59 AM, November 23rd, 2019. I returned to slugging the keys after running through an edit of what I wrote before in this chapter. Coincidently, I didn't work the next day either, a Saturday, though remember I have responsibilities outside of landscaping and bookwork. I also need and want to be a friend.

When I'm up in the middle of the night, there are a rare few people I can call out to, and I thought to call one of them before continuing here. I called three, though none of them answered, and that's understandable. I want to have more conversations with people, though, and about Providing Point too.

I find talking more about the program and its potential benefits enjoyable, and though I've sold a few copies of *Shards of My Soul*, I'm still far from selling a hundred books a day; the goal I set in *Rings of Truth*. Perseverance and endurance, though, are qualities I possess.

I learned about bank statement loans and how the loans can help our future. With bank statement loans, the premise is to give a mortgage to people who qualify based on their previous 12-24 months of bank statements. A personal bank statement loan considers all of the deposits into an account, while a business bank statement loan uses 50% of the deposits as a guide.

A one-month bank statement loan requires a declaration and proof of income on a one-month statement. The account must have a positive balance, and it reminded me I needed to get out of overdraft in my primary personal account. I learned about the program from a person I look up to online, so thank you, Rudy, for the link.

There are quite a few stipulations for bank statement loan acceptance, yet the idea opens up a pathway to potentially using such loans. Since the loans only need 10% down, if we use gathered resources for mortgages, we can keep the account open and activate a bank statement loan. When we collect enough monthly income through the Patreon page, we can start purchasing homes to lease to tenants. I didn't know about how to find the down payments yet at this point, though found out later.

$375 a month rent is not a lot, though the money gathered with Patreon can also pay for the insurance and property taxes for the homes. People on PWD receive discounted rates for property taxes, and we need to have money for the necessary insurance. Ideally, we'll use weekly mortgage payments, yet the Patreon page is in monthly increments.

We gather money via www.Patreon.com/Introversial for the grocery cards, though for housing, the page is different, www.Patreon.com/HousingProviders. Both gather in US dollars, though because the money is in USD$, it adds a buffer for the calculations. The money accumulated is for those in Chilliwack, B.C., Canada up to now, though even in *Shards of My Soul*, I wrote how the idea is a transferable concept.

Profits make investment opportunities valuable, and to start, we need funding. If down payments are required, there is a way to reward investors who help with the down payments. For a $20,000 downpayment loan, we can repay $375/month over six years for a $27,000 return. That return on investment is near 10%, and while many investors seek 7%-8% for a substantial gain, this concept could provide homes for those without welfare or PWD too, which excites me.

For me, I believe I'm more invested in gathering pledges if we have a goal; in this case, $35,000 of earnings per month by June 20th, 2021 or sooner is the breakthrough goal. We need down payments for future homes, and if we have to purchase for $200,000 per household, we know how many contributors we'll require per home.

Are we going to bind Providing Point and Chilliwack Housing Providers as registered charities, or operate them as for-purpose companies, with investment incentives for the housing model? Even in this chapter's text, I told you I don't want to run a real-estate empire, yet another corner of me wants to operate the whole deal of homes, repayments, pledges, and process as an extension of myself. If both programs are to thrive, it requires someone to activate and operate them, and I understand having both programs as registered companies is a good safeguard.

There had been four Providing Point meetings up to January 31st, 2020, and I had yet to talk to a large group about the ideas in this chapter. Am I delusional and dreaming big bad things, or are these ideas, figures, plots and plans something that shall thrive?

The guilt I feel of having a home when others don't combines with the sheer luxury of having food, water, ciggies, and coffee abundantly. For proponents of meritocracy, if I'm not working full-time, why do I have these things while others don't? Is it a sign I'm doing the right things for the right reasons and people? What about compassion as a balance?

Is it I feel guilty because I have more? I don't always feel like I'm earning the life I live here on Earth, and for those that are homeless, how and why could another human not want you to have a home? I want to plot and plan with people who have a home and rally together to ensure all have a place to live.

I've felt shame by having an apartment because I've not earned all of it on my own, yet does that mean others given a home would feel shame too? The goal is to increase the baseline for all people. Think of how life would be if *every* person owned a place within which to live, eat, and sleep? What if *every* person had a bathroom to use anytime they needed or wanted one?

Also asked, what if *every* person had a mission or project to work on while having money to afford what they want and need? What if *every* person was fortunate to have a sustainable living situation and intent or desire to build or create for their local and global communities?

We discover ideas we'd never think about until the crucial moment we need to know. We can adjust and change our psyche to match a unified and universal resonance of pure love and respect, and we also can discover our heart's core desires to allow peace to thrive in our homes.

When we meet the moments of above trickling down into the spirits of clay, may we stand next to our loves with our hearts, hands, and minds entwined? Why do so few hear the call? I don't listen well, yet when people speak, I usually hear clearly. If we miss what someone says, it's good to ask for clarification, though don't interrupt with questions when others are talking.

From a course at university, I found if I hold on and don't ask questions, often answers to my unasked questions are presented without me needing to ask. If we give people the opportunity and space to speak, we can learn a lot from them, and with these books, you give me a voice. Who, though, shall heed or listen to my ideas?

With my books, it's a wide-open space for me to share and create. Without another human in my apartment, I can press the keys and ease these books formation, and, delightfully so, some nifty thoughts arrive. I'd not yet secured homes for people, and if it's not my responsibility to do so, I make it a personal objective.

I want to house ten thousand people with my creative efforts, and Chilliwack Housing Providers can be a channel to assist that process and journey. I've asked this before about Providing Point, though, ask it again here. What would happen if I made the program a personal gathering point and then share 99% of that gathered? Is one percent for me acceptable, or greedy?

If I'm marketing the product or service of providing homes for people, then could it be more widely accepted as a personal initiative and not a legally bound charity? I want to assure if people contribute and gain from the program, and if PDFs of my books are a meagre offering for Providing Point patrons, I want to share more.

I went for a ciggie and a coffee and held a notion. I ask again, what if I run Providing Point a personal initiative and not a charity? If future patrons give on the premise and trust of me doing the right things with the money gathered (providing homes, food, and additional support), and I keep open accounting, could we use an open leger to ensure we can support all those who need help?

Does a company need to be an NGO or non-profit to do good work in the community? No. Is it a socialist or capitalistic approach? Both. If profits and earnings entice me to gather, and I ethically distribute and contribute that entrusted, can we work together for a win/win/win? Yes.

People can gain homes and food, investors can earn from assisting, and we can contribute abundantly to people in our community who need, want, and appreciate given support; it's a Freedom Solution. Some people need and want homes, and I know I don't yet personally have enough resources and connections to house people.

It's tricky to make broad coated statements, wishes and hopes that people all be kind, peaceful, and respectful of others, and I sense some displeasure from people without homes aimed at myself. Perhaps there's a layer there too; I don't want others to be upset at me for having more than them.

It's at this point in the text I call for miracles to remind myself that by having more, I can share more. That applies to the future because I believe, as I increase my ability to generate, invest, and earn, we can have a substantial positive effect. We can work with and for people to assist with issues that hound parts of our society.

It's not an easy task to think about 'solving' big problems in our world, though as we achieve some audacious goals, we can do so together.

FORCED SERVITUDE

Do you have a job you love? Are you happy and enthralled when you wake up, excited knowing what your day's going to be like for you? Are you doing what you want to do with your life, or do you feel like you're in forced servitude?

If you're like me, you have a bunch of dreams and wishful hopes, yet still feel shackled by yourself, your choices, and the results of those choices. I want to have open nights without needing to wake up early every day, and with a job, I'm not always there, yet a paycheque is helpful.

I've seen and heard lots of people talking about how, if we don't like our day job, to do something else to find our passions and meaning. I'm glad to have money from landscaping, and though it's not my desire to *need* to work that for a long time, it's terrific. I hope my boss finds others who'd love and honour a landscaping job, too, because my boss needs people to work for him. I have worked, though it dragged at my soul trudging through the years.

We were early in 2020 when I finished this Fountain. I wasn't at first delighted to think of working another full year of landscaping because I wanted to find and form a creative pathway of earnings. I didn't want to shackle myself to three or four days of a job as a necessity. When it rains, it's awful, and my mental health has been terrible many days, though my boss, Brad, has been understanding, kind, and forgiving as an employer. I like how he's treated me, and I hope he can find others to work for him.

What would be my income sources then if not working for Brad? I'd sell more books, and find alternative sources of income in addition to landscaping. I've wanted to invest in Magic cards again, and though that's spending and not immediate profit, I can buy and sell Magic cards for others on eBay. Who wants me to do that for them and would agree to sell or purchase on agreed commission percentages?

If I don't want to *need* to work an hourly position, what can I do online at home to earn? I might not have yet actualized monetary success with books, though I've learned how to self-publish. What about helping others with their books?

I could potentially offer editing services, though who's writing a book and would want my support? Do I have enough skills to give to enhance another's text? What if I don't like what's written? What if I'm locked in my style of words and not diverse enough with my vocabulary? If I help others write a book, how can I keep the text in their voice?

What do I want to do? I'd love to keep forming the Fountains even if the books weren't yet earning big money and big prizes, though I wish to know more people are going to read them. When I know who is going to read, I can be more direct with information, advice, and, hopefully, wisdom.

In the mornings, I've often woken up slowly and groggily, not having a committed course of action. I want to discover and develop my missions, and where I feel most inspired is either in communication or solitude. I want us each to thrive, and nighttime is when I often feel my best.

I want to have more people I can speak with on the phone and in person. Providing Point is a mission to support, and I believe the ideas hold merit. With landscaping midweek, I miss the time to make some calls during business hours, and there are connections to form. Perhaps I do both; to work for Brad *and* develop Providing Point and my books.

It was November 30th, 2019 and I was supposed to have four days of work set for the next week. As it resulted, I only worked two and was glad. I know my work with Brad isn't servitude, and instead, a decision made to work, yet if I find myself bitching and moaning about things and feel looming negativity pressing on my shoulders, is it the right choice for the wellbeing of my soul to stop?

I value Brad and want his company to have excellent employees, though it seemed like I was working because Brad didn't have other people to work for him and because it's a paycheque. It didn't feel right in my soul to accept income from the giving programs either. Of my soul, I think it compresses the text as the next rhyme shifts to mix rifts of interstellar gifts. I want to record more and believe my music has been overlooked, yet it seeps into my being to make more.

There's much to say sometimes, and though my recordings aren't quite structured lyrically or conveying a story, the lyrics often base solely on the premise of the words rhyming. The flows are internal communications knowing how I can think, speak, and write new material, and similarly and differently, I can explain the text in my books. I'd like more coherence from my music too.

My creative work is meaningful and unique to me. Books are one way of sharing ideas and instilling concepts, yet the music bases on sound. How and why the words link in either format is reasonably natural to me, though the intents are different. It's rational that books and music aren't the same forms of media, and though I may not feel comfortable or want to record videos of myself, I'm sure I'd like to be successful on YouTube in an audio format.

I didn't know how or when my creative work would be an earnings channel, though it's marvellous to earn money by writing and recording. The book *Shared Node* is a bridge between the formats of books and rhymes, though I'd not worked on that project so much recently. Creating hadn't garnered much income for me up to this edit, though I compulsively keep on with my creative work. I'd not yet cleared the glass walls of earnings and reach, though keep at the process.

I sometimes want to separate and clarify what I do and why I do it. I know some of my motivations are intrinsically profit-focused, yet I activate non-profit ideas and programs. I'm aware I've not marketed well, and I wonder if it's because it's so much about me and not about others. I want to have more friends and communication, yet I'd not reached out as much as I used to.

I want to earn money by contributing and building excellent

text, and I don't want to provide landscaping hours only for cash. I don't proclaim or preach religious ideas, yet Christian sources infuse my base neurosis. I'm fortunate to have excellent health regarding never getting sick, and even if I cloud my lungs continuously, I don't always want to be a smoker. I squeeze all sorts of love into my cat, yet I neglect him and focus on the computer instead of playing. I want to have a girlfriend, yet don't go out there talking to random gals. I often keep my eyes up instead of checking out gals, yet tops lure me.

The mix of contradictions weave multiple threads in the fabric of my life, yet I have near-zero clues about who wants to wear the garments. I'm not even sure if I'm making pants or shirts! Maybe I'm basic. Or perhaps I'm a new or exciting person that people don't know?

I don't feel necessary or essential, and when people need me, I've neglected to understand how and what I can do for them. I wonder about how and when I'll accept myself fully instead of pushing for purpose, though it comes through time, patience, and persistence.

Releasing attachments to profits and what I think I *need* to do can align fragments of peace that settle like glitter. I may not be soaking in sparkling pools of mana, yet parts of my spirit lift towards hope when points of faith seep in. The night I typed this, a friend responded to a Facebook post, and we set up a meeting to relay two books to him. It pulled a layer of calm and energy over me that reminds me I'm doing some of the right things.

I fill my lungs with clean air. And then again. Between the breaths, I felt sadness in my heart and wished not to push out falsities or debris. Perhaps I need to accept I'm truthfully sacred and sharded in my wellbeing. I may not have all the answers to the problems our world faces, yet compassion and trust guide me to remember paths crisscross and weave into formations we can admire and appreciate. Honestly, and more frequently, I need to recall there is love to guide.

(Insert two days between writing sessions)

I had another thought about smoking. I learned that sometimes I smoke to give myself more time. That seems contradictory because cigarettes are said to shorten lifespans. If I want to insert a pause of thought, time, or action, I often head out for a smoke. If I instead go for a cup of water to take a break and allow myself to do that instead of pausing with a ciggie, perhaps I'll not smoke as much.

I played an episode from Lewis Howes' podcast, *The School of Greatness,* where Lewis interviewed Dr. Judson Brewer. There were a couple of ideas I heard on the show that can guide me towards being happy as a non-smoker again, and I'm tentative about cigarettes. My smoking is partly from nervousness, a lack of direction, and also wanting to do nothing as I puff.

When I grew up with my Mom, I'd often run away from situations and have a cigarette instead of facing the issues that Mom and I were discussing. Cigarettes, for me, have been an escape and an element of freedom to do what I want because I want to do it. I have thought I like, love, and loathe cigarettes and haven't forecast how and when I'll quit them.

The chapter title sourced on the topic of work, though I see now a different form of forced servitude; the fact that I smoke. As part of my nicotine addiction, I feel empty and hollow as I type this because I want to burn, yet I felt sad and pushed past the subtle craving calling me to run away.

Healthwise, I have an awful lung capacity, and though I barely ever get sick, I'm out of shape and a bit fat. I miss the part of my life when I took Taekwondo too. I was more durable, more confident, and more flexible back then, yet I remember how I didn't like working out for more than just one session a day. I'd feel weak weaselling out of a second session when I trained, though I also felt great after attending class.

It's been near a decade since I went to the dojang and exercised at a high-impact level. I can mentally recall how I felt performing patterns, and even though I was deplorably far from perfect, I appreciate the feeling, energy, and experiences I gained by training in the discipline. One strange thing about that time in my life, though, is that even if I was dramatically healthier then compared to now in my life, I still smoked.

Other than one 24-hour period in the past twenty-seven years, I've smoked every day. Estimating 20 cigarettes a day (often more) for 365 days a year, since I was fifteen, it means I've burned more than 197,100 cigarettes. If it costs a quarter for every cigarette I smoked, that's $49,275, though now ciggies are $12 for a pack of twenty.

Breathe in… Breathe out… How do I find the bigger and better thing for me other than quenching cigarette cravings? How do I assure I never smoke another cigarette again when I stop? What are the core and central roots that I need to remove that have held the addiction deep in my habits, heart, and health? When shall I feel okay being a non-smoker and not run away into clouding my lungs?

One idea to try is the water break tactic. If one wants to have a smoke, take a deep breath and have a cup of water. A question in mind is, though, why do I have the compulsion to light up? Refuelling with a clean and clear lungful of breath and having a clear glass of water is one of the first steps, according to Christy Whitman.

The next challenge and question are "what shall I do instead of taking the extra few minutes to have a cigarette." (That's also linked to the question of "how shall I quell my nervousness?")

What does it mean for me to 'do work on myself?' What is my functional purpose, and is my intuition that I need to heal myself, my heart, and my habits the central need I have at this moment? Perhaps. Breathe in and breathe out.

Learn with Love; Live for Hope.

What is the freedom we each want? Is it financial freedom? Freedom from obligations? Freedom of decision? Is it even the sometimes elusive feeling of zero restrictions and a desire there aren't consequences?

Bad habits call me. Even if I don't smoke marijuana or illegal drugs, I think I'm still a junkie of sorts. I want to guzzle cold coffee, smoke inside, and stay up to 4 AM solo at home. The ideas are self-destructive, so perhaps I need to learn to love myself more? If I believe it's great to be respectful to others, how shall I honour and respect myself too?

The tug to brew a pot of coffee called my lungs out of my chest into divulging that smoking gives me a break to stop and collect my thoughts. I brewed a pot of tea earlier instead, so I poured a glass of tea compared to having a cup of coffee. Some people believe in harm reduction, yet I'm fearful about getting to the root of this problem. Why am I afraid of my truths? I seem to share my faults openly, yet what is the core reasoning for why I do what I do? Am I an addict, or am I just scared?

The cold tea drinks like a pleasure and has substance when plain water doesn't. I've searched for outside inputs to make me feel okay when I'm not, and I distract myself with work on the computer. I've adjusted some other obsessive tendencies, like obsessively checking my bank account a dozen times a day and checking email frequently on my phone and computer. Neurochemicals triggering my pleasure centres call for mass input.

And yet I'm alone. I love my cat, though I can't converse with Zeus. I've skittered off and away from religion, and I feel compelled to find meaning in something other than a projected belief. I comprehend I need to do more inner work yet wind the keys into pleasure gained by pulling long strings of thought and plopping them out through the keyboard, filling up pages before us. I love writing, I want to do drugs, and though I remain committed to sobriety, I've stuck to other chemical addictions.

Addiction isn't just chemicals, though. Obsessions are hard to release, yet I also joke how I'm obsessively publishing my books. Even if we can lead to proactive measures about finding solutions and freedoms, it's a bit worrisome about how

I feel otherwise. Though you may read me cycling through issues, again and again, each time I pass through the loops, I get closer to understanding how to solve some of the riddles.

Thank you for reading this book and delving into my neurosis. Though I don't know what general readers shall gain, I hope this work and process can be a winning solution for people to have a home. To activate Providing Point's ideas and plans, it'll take a significant number of people to subscribe to the program, and perhaps the first dozen or so contributors do so because they believe in me.

With what I've learned, it's more than only charitable well-wishers that can and shall actualize our Freedom Solutions. Many have different motivations than money, and perhaps those who align with what I'm trying to do is because they're a fan. The idea is to provide for people, though first, we may need to believe.

THE FAN IN FANTASY

Shall I tell you of whom I'm a fan, or who my ideal fans are? When I write my books, I often write outwards to a general audience, though a few chapters had me writing directly to specific individuals. I've also written sections in the form of prayers to God, and in the first book I ever wrote, I wrote from other's perspectives.

I've recommended writing different ways, either all one wants to say to a specific person or to write anything one wants to tell every person. I've not done that so much in this set of Fountains, yet doing so can hone and focus intents.

Hearing a song or reading a book by someone we've never met in real life is a frequent occurrence, though how often is it that fans overinvest themselves into wanting to meet the creators? The fans want to know the ones read or heard. The concept of having fans is weird and wild, and it's strange to think strangers can fall in love, or as I had, become entirely infatuated with one specific person we've never even met.

I've wanted to gain a vast audience for both my music and my books, though I've marketed predominantly to people who know me already. I've shared some work with people I don't know very well, though it's because to be commercially successful with books or music, I need to reach a significant number of total strangers.

If the incentive and drive for people to read my books are because people know who I am, then it seems I want to increase exposure. In exchange for the disclosure, the hope is to gain monetary compensation for my writing and music, and though it's not entirely true I want to be famous, I do want to have more readers.

Up to now, I've shared a lot of free books and CDs with people with a sly intent of gaining interest. Perhaps, instead, I best create valuable and intriguing work instead of trying to increase awareness about me. At the very beginning of this Fountain, I asked the question, "would you prefer to be wealthy, famous, or loved?" If presented with two options, sometimes we can choose both. In this case, though, I accept all three.

I may not be seeking fame actively, though if being well known can expand my reach and assist in achieving Providing Point goals, and I can live and act ethically and clean, it may not be as dangerous as I initially thought. Regarding being wealthy, I've thought having money would cause people to be envious and want to take from me, though perhaps if I design my life correctly, the inflow of earnings and Providing Point pledges and gifts shall be ample and safe.

I realize cash and money aren't the only parts of being wealthy, though. I'm keenly aware that information, connection, and skill assets are valuable and not easily removed. The more I gain in my attitude, ethics, and morality, the safer I become to be a steward for abundance. By further learning how to love and by practicing compassion and generosity, the better our lives become.

I agree with the concept of giving before asking, though I also remember some may give without request, and not give just to receive.

English text cannot articulate every thought. I do, though, appreciate how, if we're patient enough (and remember to breathe and pause), we can slow down to be more precise. I have an acute awareness of tentative keystrokes not seen by readers. Various speeds and moments of pausing (or breaking entirely) shift a writer's context as we prepare strings of thought to share.

Slow down and check-in with your inner voice. Is the sound you hear as you process these words yours or another's? Is your mind breezing through the text, or slowly, word by word, digging into sentences and tweezing hidden agendas and beliefs. Do you hear how there's a teetering edge of what's real blending with potentially false inceptions?

Are words speaking back to you, from you, or has another

pulled sentences out from another's mind into yours? Is reading my books just an invite into a new consciousness?

Be quite careful of what you read and listen to, though. In some cases, active listening can bring people closer by resonating with a being's thoughts from their spoken voice. Yet, if we actively think and project to the world another's words, we may be amplifiers for their message. Watch the context of thoughts and feelings compared to the truth of your being.

Even if a dozen people see or hear the same thing, there may be a dozen different meanings and interpretations that are each equally valid. Just because we believe something to be accurate and absolute fact, it may not be, and some crafty minds can mix inceptive thoughts into consciousness. Some others may attempt to blame us for seeds that aren't our own.

How can we know, share, and prove our authentic ideas and identities? If mimics present a string of thought or voice to deceive, how can we confirm or disprove the accusations or assumptions? Are the words I type entirely from me, or does another guide me?

Depending on who the senders or receivers are, the messages transmitted can go through cognitive, visual, or auditory distortion. People's unique world views attribute concepts and beliefs crucial to them, even from words written with neutrality. One choice clarification can dissipate misunderstanding, though what if the sender of the message can't grant interpretation? What if concepts and ideas misconstrue because of a mix of meaning, tone, information, or inflection. What if the words aren't from their source?

I was convinced recordings I heard two decades ago were recorded specifically for me and intentionally focused on my life. I thought the music's lyrics were recorded around my thoughts, even responding and reacting to me thinking and speaking while the albums played. I heard cryptic messages, and I thought CDs released at the record store were coded discs that siphoned and ciphered from my consciousness.

The idea of recorded music made for people isn't strange.

Often artists make music for their fans, though lots of musicians also make music with zero awareness about who shall hear the recordings. With some songs, there is an intended receiver, one person. Yet, similar to my other writing, I send the music out like a wish or prayer to the world. I also babble onwards with some lyrics and don't often make sense.

When I heard Natalie's albums on the stereo, I believed that she was speaking directly to me. I thought secret technology was adapting her music and lyrics to share her messages explicitly directed to and for me, and I entirely believed she was my soulmate. Even if I was delusional and obsessed, I thought I loved her and that she was calling out to me.

Natalie may not have made any of her music for me, though I heard her loud and clear, time and time again. I believed in the message and her soul. An infatuation gripped me and led me into insanity, yet now, the enchantment wears thin.

When I've thought the entire world knows my thoughts and who I am (like when I became well known in Vancouver), and with Natalie as a tethered dream and idea, I've been confident she knows me. Yet now, in a pity-party sort of way, I believe it doesn't matter if she knows my heart, soul, and intents. If Natalie has been aware of me, I'm not the one that she wants to spend a life with together. I just don't know what the truth is.

"Trials and tribulations struggle with smiles in consecrations."

Marie Forleo sent an email a few days before this that takes viewers into a process of reviewing their past decade. The exercise guides people to reflect on the things we're most proud of from the past ten years. We also were to recall the lessons we learned in that timeframe, and though I couldn't pinpoint the specific thing I'm most proud of, the most significant experience is I'm learning how to love.

I love through sharing affection, gifts, and honest compliments when they surface, and the most significant thing I can do in the next decade is to learn how to love more. I desire to love more honestly, to love more deeply, and even on the premise of 'love more,' to enjoy having more, being more, and learning more. It also means to love more people.

I continue to develop my skills, talents, and lessons to contribute and share with others. I do this so that we can each appreciate others and the lives we live, and I want to understand and share the words "I love you" more often.

Some refer to and develop principles, yet if our intrinsic beliefs align with our actual actions, not only can we be in alignment, we can fortify and solidify our results by acting ethically. It's neat to think that love is an ethic. If love is an ethic, it shall guide our core actions to generate more, hopefully, and open pathways to mutual abundance.

> *"Part of why you love your parents is because they loved you first."*
> *— Gary Vaynerchuk*

What happens, though, when a fan craves acknowledgement and connection, though the other person is entirely unaware? What if people are aware of the desire to connect, yet shut out the fan from any chance of connecting? The fan might feel sad and disheartened. If you saw the Eminem video for *Stan*, think of how dramatically a dismissed fan may feel, even if not intentionally brushed off.

What happens if someone loves another entirely, and the other person never knows the other also exists? How much love is out there for people by strangers who they've never met? What about those people we've met, though we never knew we affected them positively? What about all the moments of love or appreciation we have for others we know that we've never voiced to them?

Some friends may think we don't want to connect or interact, or that we're too busy running our lives. What if those friends stepped out of their fear and gave us a phone call?

I've reached out often, sometimes too often, to friends that don't reply or want to talk. I adore hearing from others and have thought because no one's calling, no one wants to connect. What if we made the first contact? We often may need to message first, though don't think about the people who'd be glad to hear from us. We may forget many friends we like because we neglect and focus on other things.

If I was to send out a wish and prayer to the Contialis and the Universe, it's that people who like, love, or appreciate us would call us more often. I've sometimes not wanted to bother others with a phone call, so perhaps some people think they'd upset me if they gave me a phone call. I don't believe they would.

I have a significant amount of time to converse and connect, and I thought of two friends who I'd not called recently. I paused, called, and texted them and then checked Facebook. I'd not been on Facebook much at this point, though I saw a post from a planeswalker friend I nicknamed Tamiyo.

Tamiyo posted about a friend that passed in December 2018, and it reminded me about love. I admire and respect Tamiyo for posting a tribute to the friend, and I recalled the chapter I wrote titled *Reverence* the month he had died. That was in the 9th Fountain book, *Sand to Silt*, which also reminds me of the cycles of time and creation.

Grief is a significant feeling. It slows down one's pace and reminds us to appreciate not only the memory of the ones who've passed, though also to understand the love of those who cherished the departed. Grief also calls me to give thanks for allowing us hearts with which to love and care, and for lives living on this side of the realms of life and death, understanding we can't interact with those gone still can build resilience and reverence.

Yet when people are alive, and we don't connect with them, we can think "oh, I'll get around to giving them a call" or "if they wanted to talk, they'd call me." Remember to remind those you like and love that you do. A quick text to say hi, or even breakfast, lunch, or a random whim of meeting up, those things aren't feasible after shifting off the plane of the living.

With the psychic and symbiotic dance made with thoughts,

technology, and mental forces, we can pull consciousness into the text and speakers. When connected with ESP to prerecorded music, I've had a theory we can syphon personally directed lyrics with a flow of awareness. An extended argument is that those who've died can still communicate with us using digital and analogue channels.

We need more conversations, and not just talking or flustering up ideas. It's tricky to converse and find solutions at 1 AM when so few are up and at 'er, yet if I'm to influence our course of events, I best find myself active and engaged with people. I must not give up on my mission's premise; for all people to have a home and a life of love.

I'm a fan of love, luck, and happiness, and I'm also a fan of talking out our problems. I learn to push past my fears and concerns more often, safely, and bring forward more authentic care. It's a kind idea, yet if we can build a situation where we connect with peace, love, unity, and respect more often, we can remember others better. We may have never known some, yet their influence exists to this day.

ALLY WITH THE REASON WHY

If the objective is to find homes for everyone, instead of structuring figures to own homes, we also can work with existing organizations to ally and provide.

Chilliwack Supportive Housing is a program to contact regarding rent and apartments. At the same time, the Salvation Army, Ruth and Naomi's, Cyrus Centre, and Ann Davis Transition Society have 173 active beds, according to Chilliwack.com. There's more support than I thought, yet not enough to fill the need of everyone having a place in which they may sleep safely.

People aren't all on the same spectrum of support needs, and perhaps a blend of shelters for hardship needs and intermediate homes (multi-share places) could lead to homeownership models. That's what Chilliwack Housing Providers means to help with, and though shelter programs are appreciated, people still need support beyond homes.

My friend, nicknamed Esper, had a shared housing model idea. Esper thought about homes that have eight to ten rooms in a two-story house with a shared kitchen and cooking staff on-site. The people would share common areas and have a place within the home, though with any program to succeed, we'll need supports to allow people to achieve independent living. Sometimes it's step by step.

I want us to increase and elevate the base standard of living for people. If there are varying levels and degrees of need, do we need to support people's situations level by level? What about quantum leaps? What if a shared ownership model can activate and grant equity in homes for people who can provide $375 a month?

It doesn't just mean providing homes for homeless, PWD, or welfare people, though what if we can make affordable housing profitable? Doing so could be a giant leap for some, while a stepping stone to independence for others.

I started reading a book called *The Blockchain Revolution* by Don and Alex Tapscott. Their book shares concepts that are activated by blockchain technology. Although I couldn't yet articulate how blockchain technology works technologically, I learned more about how we can improve our situations. One concept that interests me is smart contracts, multi-signer contracts that could open up homeownership to people financially and functionally.

A partial equity share idea I have could use smart contracts for supplying and opening homeownership to people without. With 185x people giving $25/month over six years (a total of $1,800 each), a smart contract can help with an open leger to show and share ownership by tokenizing homes.

A different idea from Shanal, a person I spoke with earlier in the day, showed me a crowdsourcing site, Addyinvest.com. Addy is a program where people can sign up for shared ownership in real estate. It's similar to my idea, though different than my concept because Addy is buying the places upfront as investments and has smaller contribution limits, only one dollar. Addy also doesn't require recurring payments like my $5/week model and is for investors, and not for the cause of affordable housing.

When I breached back into writing more in this book, I'd fallen way far out and away from having any rational faith in owning and renting homes. A mentality of lack pushed me back to the original idea of Yearly Seeds, and then further away from giving because of how ludicrous it is to think I could be a player involved in a large scale Freedom Solution.

I've wanted to invest and accrue significant earnings, though, beyond landscaping, and I've felt enslaved and entwined to the keys. Believing Providing Point is my best purpose, I instinctively see myself drawing in and away in a state of flux. The late nights and chemicals stack upon each other as a process of squandered ideas and resources.

Can I be stable enough and innovative enough to evolve and produce something worthwhile? The strings of text again find me doubting and pondering my meaning based upon currently displayed results. I've discovered I'm nowhere near achieving some wishes and whims I have, and I again teeter on the boundaries of self-obsession. It's an idea to keep far away from the keyboard not to taint the streams of text, though another part of me wants to know the solutions and the truth.

If I drain and draw all of my self-defeating thoughts and behaviours and put them up on the digital table, does it link back to how if we bring issues and problems to light, we can find solutions? Regardless if Providing Point thrives and Chilliwack Housing Providers houses people, there's an entire world out there beyond Chilliwack. There are billions of people who need fresh water and a bathroom that don't have that. People all over the world need to feel loved and valued, and many may not think they are at this point.

Does the global community bound within the confines of this planet also hold lives that aren't from Earth? What about the dreamworlds and spiritual realms of those who haven't yet been born that infuse future events drawing us forward into the next decade? By 2030, some who aren't alive shall also have influenced and created for a better situation. Not just for humans, though. Think of artificial intelligence and other animals who inhabit Earth with us.

I've thought technology is a bridge between people with techno-psychic parameters. Yet, I'm not sure if the technology is being used for good, to give me the insights and awareness I need to share, or if the technology is manipulating and controlling me to keep me tiny in a shell of my being.

Even here, I thought to type "I dare not" to start the sentence, yet differ from starting with that into asking, "what if?" or "how can we?" to be more productive. Where are we in time and space right now?

I'm concerned that my obsessive tendency towards money may be a distraction luring me away from the truth. By my seeded points of want, I feel guilt and shame when I think of my gain, yet what is the subconscious belief I hold that keeps me for working directly for profit? I seem to think if I'm working for another person's benefit, it's more acceptable, even in the realms of homeownership models.

Why have I denied myself prosperity? Because of the fear of being greedy. Why have I denied myself a girlfriend? Because I don't think I deserve one. What do I think I deserve? Some moments to sit alone and contemplate. My cat reminds me I have other responsibilities than writing books, and ashamedly I pressed the next keys.

If to contribute, that's giving, not responding. I don't want to react to situations and circumstances, I'd prefer to influence, though not by direct control and command. If my books are published and processed, numerous revisions have crafted and honed the completed words, though I have next-to-nil knowledge about how others read them.

I called the 9th Fountain *Sand to Silt* because I thought future books could further refine to clay. The Wikipedia article about silt says, "silt is chemically distinct from clay" and that "pure silts are not cohesive." If that's the case, it makes me think how no matter how much I refine the sands and try to break them down, there shall be no cohesion that allows us to shape and mould a beautiful pot. Is all my writing for null, and not for a fantastic, brilliant, and beautiful future?

If I shipped off from writing and Providing Point, I feel like I'd have nothing to live for then. Zeus needs food and water, though another human could easily do that. I don't have any dependents or friends who call upon me for counsel or support, so there's not much need there. And when I've thought I'm more of a bother and nuisance instead of a liked and valued friend, contact, or support, then what is the intrinsic value I hold? Brought back to the question, "why am I here?"

I was born, yet why am I searching for my function? I've been seeking externally for value and meaning instead of developing and conveying value. My intrinsic belief is that I need to be responsible, and I know I carry such due to the past choices I've made.

I've started many things, and completion seems far away. With books, I've started and fallen away from some of them due to a lack of interest and passion. I'm confident the books I produce are an extension of my natural tendencies and obsessions, yet if the texts hold ideas worth buckets of truth, why can't I release the desire we all thrive?

Why do I feel shame for thinking of my gain? Because I've heard time and time again that I'm selfish and "it's not all about you, Robert." I feel the poison is parental. One parent assures I keep working and creating, while with the other, I feel like a taxing burden of which they don't want.

What does it matter? Why should anyone else's opinion matter? What happens, though, when another's positive opinion and encouragement lifts us? How do you respond when people build you up and support you on your path, whatever it is? Being separated and apart isn't easy, yet is it better than being in a toxic friendship, or is any form of human connection better than being alone?

When I have fewer than ten people to reach out to, I need reassess my life. I've thought of releasing Providing Point as a goal and mission, yet I don't want to quit. I don't want to give up, yet does that mean I give in? Do I give in to the pressures and pulls of other people's opinions and my fear of judgment because I'm too afraid to retract promises?

If Providing Point *is* a good idea, would it not be in a healthier and more productive state of being? Many online people say the challenges and roadblocks are there to see how badly we want something. If that's true, is it I'm devoid of passion and am accepting mediocrity passively?

I'm not sure what to fight or strive for in my life. I almost feel like I denounce everything and anything like I'm searching for nil. Finishing this book is part of what I started, yet when faith is so clearly lacking in my job, career, and professional work (landscaping, authorship, and business), how can I pursue a path that I don't know yet exists and is calling me?

For two years, I've waffled and wained with Providing Point, and if it's not a passion, is it best to let it go? Is Providing Point a sunk-cost fallacy that I've shackled myself too? Do I break the chains, or build a new course of action?

People need homes, though after two years, how many homes have we provided?

If talk is cheap, then perhaps I should ship myself off to the discount bins. I feel frustrated and agitated that these problems have been hounding me, yet it's also true if they're problems, we could and can help with the solution—that's where I like work and a challenge, even if I'm passive.

I'm shaped by elusive principles, which are clear and everyday activities for others. My focus on wanting to earn money put blinders onto my thoughts and found me chasing the days in ways in which I'm too familiar. My desire to have purpose called me into promises that seem never to occur, and yet my love for life grows. At other times, I'm riddled with psychic energy.

I've focused so much on myself, and I've over-focused on creating books for earnings and purpose. I want to finish this three-part book and clear my residual reluctance to provide value. It's not that I don't want to give, it's that I also overthink and don't always know what to share. If I focus on what I can share, my motives trip me into money-conscious thoughts, and while giving money isn't always appreciated or the best thing, it's something I wish I could do for others more often.

When my lack of income creeps in, I get concerned about how to make money. When I focus on how to make money, I reach mental blocks or twist around the same cyclical notions. Often I've found myself telling people I want to sell books, yet then winge about marketing and finding an audience. The next layer I lather on the pity-party all so often is to say how I don't know what the value proposition of my books is.

I don't understand *why* someone would want to read my books, so isn't it best to focus on that? If the books are well written, then an appreciative reader could enjoy them, and if a person would like to view something original or unique, the Fountains are such. How, though, shall a vast audience discover my words if I don't sell them?

It was December 21st, 2019, at this point in the first draft. I wanted to get back to writing for the intrinsic value it holds, and by pulling the cursor across the page and letting the words dribble out of my mind into the keys, I find a gratifying feeling. I like and love writing and creating books, even if it's challenging to complete them.

I feel active, engaged, and worthwhile when I can finish a book and release it to the world. Others may not feel or appreciate similar feelings, yet developmentally, writing a book is an extensive process with instrumental worth. Texts can be appreciated by those who see them, and though I'm not seeking validation, it'll be rad to know more people read what I write.

So if a reason (not *the* reason) I form books is I obsessively like doing so, perhaps Rudy is right; that because I ENJOY writing books, to do so, even if not yet financially rewarded.

Though my insecurities and focus on results and metrics haunt my mind, I instinctively desire to keep making these texts. If authorship is my passive career and vocation, I must actively use writing to perform and share goodness with the world. That's why there's Providing Point. I want to be a provider.

My three-point ideas bounce the ball back into the paint. Though I may be throwing bricks, hopefully, those on my team can recover the ball and make good use of it. Part of what I learn, though, is to pass the ball more often to people who have a better chance of scoring. If I'm not the one to be CEO and operator of Providing Point, then we still need to find one who believes in the ideas and has the acuity and gumption to do what I've not yet been able to do.

And yet, I can help by producing these books and plotting figures and concepts. In this Fountain, I wrote about wanting to be an idea guy, and though I may not be overflowing with fantastic ideas, another part of me wants to help support others with their ideas, work, and projects. I'm a supportive role and not the main actor.

Parts of the story require my active input, effort, and participation, yet it seems I sit passively and do nothing. That's not entirely true, though I accept the view. With the tides of the shoreline looking peaceful and calm, perhaps it's time to figure out how to lead the ship. A wayfared soul may know what to do, even if I don't.

I don't know who can operate or run Providing Point if not me, so I keep at the helm to not leave it unattended. I'm concerned the captain might not show up, which would mean I'll need to crew the vessel, yet we learn a lot on the open seas. I know bits of that from pressing the keys in the mental breeze.

A DISTANT TRAVELER

I've orbited the sun over forty-two times up to now in my life, though when I reach my fifty-second orbit, it'll be the year 2030.

Marie Forleo's Decade in Review exercise found me write down a few things. From the writing cue, "What's Next? What is my future?" the weird part is I see some of them come to fruition. As I get myself together and focus on working for my goals, one of my top three goals was only on a two-year horizon; to complete *Mosaic of Miracles*.

Gabby Bernstein is one spiritual guide I've neglected a bit. Gabby has helped me in the past, and hopefully, I remember her more in the future. On the topic of manifesting, one fundamental thing I need to know is what I want before I ease into revealing it. The Marie Forleo exercise helped me figure out some of what I'd like to do in the next decade, and Gabby and Christy Whitman's guidance reminds me I need to open awareness and acceptance, and release.

Though *Depths of Discovery* is the second book in this three-part series with *Signs of Serenity* as the next, I've thought about the next three-part book, *The Waters of Life* already too. *Depths of Discovery* and *Signs of Serenity* were supposed to form concurrently, yet my creative train jumped tracks. With two more chapters in this one, I found the course of the full-text oscillates from open hope to focused planning, and then back to open sharing and doubt. Consistently inconsistent?

Writing can be solitary, though I've been getting to be okay with that. Plotting and planning housing models seemed ludacris, especially when I started to want it to be lucrative. I may not own real estate as an investment at this time, though I appreciate real estate's value in how it translates into people having homes.

I want to supply and provide, yet I've been edgy about being the main person performing the groundwork. If Chilliwack Housing Providers operates as a company, the apartments need someone to be a property manager, and we'll need to work with tenant selection too. How do we find and choose the right people to gain the support of our programs?

If we consider our friends and families as organizational structures, there are functions and roles we play in other's lives. With friends, I'm not a high counsel, though add a bit of care and support. I've relied on some friends for contact and communication, though often it's reciprocal, and it's also true I have a few friends that are resource buddies. Perhaps those friends don't know I'm glad if they just call me to chat me up too.

I like phoning friends and adore receiving phone calls, and in the week before getting into this chapter, I also found I enjoy writing these books because of how they form. I like the personal results I accrue, and though it takes a while to appreciate my work for what it is, when it's not about sales, I reach satisfied states forming these books.

It may be a glacial pace, yet the substance and weight of my work nestle well in my mind, heart, and spirit as we continue. I'm clear now that authorship and music are my creative professions, and faith tells me my work is the right thing for the right reasons, yet a twinge still calls for them to form the right results at the right time for the right people.

I'm gratified by having something to share even if I'm not yet earning big money from writing. The significance of creating these books hold potential value for more than myself, yet the point of gratitude is how I feel positive, okay, and hopeful that the books are distributed and also sell.

In previous Fountains, I've written about the urge and feeling to stop short and rush the closing of a base text for the first draft. That feeling is here still. Though I think authorship could be my career now, I'm not sure for how long I'll write the series. I'd like to know what else I can create with the skills I've gained by producing these books.

What is transferable for us? And see that, I write the word

'us' because I know it's not me alone working on this process. Though I'm rarely conscious of other people when I write these books, I know by writing outwards, there are subvert receivers who nudge and guide me because of my thoughts and intents.

I've thought my text forms because of subtle psychic guidance; that's not all me. Zeus is here, I barely hear *his* thoughts, though knowing my cat is in our home also pulls some divine love. It's 2020 now as we traverse the distance of time.

In the Decade in Review exercise, I wrote about how I'd like to have a wife and family, though one thing I didn't write down that I want in the next decade was Natalie. Though she's where the books started, the idea of her has traced away and pushed off to a different page of my life. I've grown a lot since the first book, and though Natalie holds a corner of my guilty heart and mind, she's not the one I wish to live with forever.

The story *isn't* complete instinctively, and I'm not aching to meet Natalie as I had for years. She and I *aren't* compatible. The truth, though, is that even if I've released my yearning to meet her, I still haven't entirely. I could chalk it up to twenty years being significant in meaning, though another part isn't even the 'what if' question about talking with her. I used to want closure and to speak with her to discover the truth, yet now I seem just to want it to wash away.

Stains call deep in my heart for and from some. Releasing attachments can be healthy, yet we also need to know when to hold on. If to hold on to anyone or anything, we best understand why we want to hold on, and it's tricky to know what the potential consequences could be. I used to think if I held onto Natalie, I'd have a chance of meeting her, yet later I believed I needed to let go of her to allow us to meet. Note that one bit, though. I focused on having an outcome of meeting her in both scenarios. I didn't let go of her.

I've believed I'm set aside because I wasn't 'ready' to meet her, and now I think that even if that's true, it's been too long since the enchantment began. This past year, Natalie gave birth to a son, and I'm glad for her. If (and this is a big if) Natalie knows who I am, it's the right choice to have broken the enchantment I had for her and let her live her life the way she wants to live. I don't think that Natalie and I could bridge and bond, and that's a bit saddening to me.

Still, though, who shall travel with me into the future? We don't know what the future holds, yet I appreciate people who want to set goals and cast visions. I've shared some of mine, though I also want to connect with others who wish to connect, discuss, and develop their hopes, goals, and dreams. Assisting people with their lives is beneficial because doing so gets us out of our minds and situations. When we can set ourselves aside, we may give and share ourselves more honestly.

What do you want to build? What would you like to do? How can you do those things on your own? Do you need or want support? If yes, what is it the best support people can give you? Is it you don't know with what or how others can support you? What if you tell people what's truly on your heart?

It was Christmas Day 2019 at this point in the first draft. I wanted to complete writing the base of this text before the New Year, and I had. I was visiting my Mom and Owen at their home and felt tentative and excited about the New Year, even if it was a week away. I remember Christmas isn't celebrated by everyone, though I'm glad to report it was a calm, chill, and pleasant holiday on the island.

I feel fortunate and thankful to have made it this far into life, and in the New Year, I travelled to Australia to visit Dad and Sarah. I'm appreciative visiting with both my parents and their partners, and in two years, I'd like to know my gal and travel with her. I was single and solo when I first typed this, though, and by the point of mid-2020, I'd like to be in a relationship (as of July 2020, though I was still single).

Some say, "you'll find her when you stop looking," though I wonder if I'd not yet found her because I'd not actively sought love. Recently, I also jested, "I'm not single and looking, I'm single and wondering."

Who is my gal? Do I know her already? Is she a random stranger in the future? Will I initiate contact, or will she seek me out? Are we going to get it right the first time, or will it take a few couplings to find the right one?

Does she choose me, or shall we accidentally stumble into infinity together by fate and destiny? I'd love to and like to know, though I didn't have a clue how or who hooks up with me for a lifetime journey and life of love, luck, and commitment. It'll be kind and refreshing to know, I bet.

Yet for now, as I write this. I take a breath and revel that I'm okay and well on my own. I don't *need* someone to complete me, though I want to live with another to build and explore the next decades of life together. It excites me to think about the fact I've yet to connect with my lovestone because I can sense and intuit it'll be fantastic and rad to connect and live with her. It's also fascinating to understand that the best years of my life are yet to be lived.

The past decade included a few milestones of growth, and the next ten years are hopefully going to be impressive and worthwhile. I may not yet be selling thousands of books, though I feel proud to have completed ten books before this one. The Fountains aren't designed or expected to be successful commercially, though a weird inkling assures me they're appreciated, successful, and worthwhile as the pieces of work and thought they are.

"The right thing, at the right time, for the right reason."
— *Owen Beattie*

Thank you, Owen! It's fantastic to know you care and that you're watching out for my Mom too. The past ten years have been a trip, and near the entire time that you and I have known each other. Though we rarely speak on the phone, and we only usually connect when I visit you and Mom, I appreciate you tending the seeds and encouraging me to create and follow my heart. I'll keep chipping away at the quarries I need to manage and also learn how to be a better friend.

2020 found the revision of this Fountain at the front of the year. By August 2020, *Mosaic of Miracles* releases, and more copies of *Fragments of Intent*, *The Sands of Yesterday*, *and Shards of My Soul* shall be yearning to be read too. Mysterious forces convince me authorship is a significant profession and vocation for me and that I can, shall, and do contribute to the world.

Though Zeus was the only one I'd housed at the point of writing this, we do more. *Debris of Distance* manifests as the first Fountain in the Fountains of Flourishing, and I saw parts of that book shape when working on this one. It's not psychic or prophetic, yet rather an intuitive vision guides me to know I'm on the right track.

My music hasn't been widely known in recent years, though I think it could be a significant earnings channel too. My recordings may have been made way before their time, yet I have a hunch they're timeless in some ways.

For the next three years, I've got a lot of work to do. I have lots of skills I need to learn, acquire, and master, and though I'm open to learning and growth, if I accomplish as much as I have in the past three years in the next three years, considerable achievements and developments are rational. I don't see myself and my evolution as clearly as others, though specific feedback from friends, family, and distant contacts remind me I've made positive movements.

For the 2019 holiday season, I reconnected with my parents, faith, and intuition that I have meaning and purpose beyond money and things. I reminded myself that slugging away at the keyboard is a profitable way to live and that love is not a commodity. A few friends messaged me on Christmas Day that I admire and appreciate, and connections are valued, and sometimes more valuable than cash. Though I felt a bit of guilt for leaving some out, I messaged a few I like and love.

Thank you, Mom, for raising me right. Although some of your beliefs about earning and spending don't align with mine, I appreciate the love, care, and consideration you have for other people and me. I like how you continue to teach me life lessons on our journey through space and time, and even if I'm not living with you or am in daily contact, your grace, forgiveness, and understanding are treasures I hold. My mind, soul, and heart align to adore more for you loving me.

Zeus also is a primary traveller with me on this journey on Earth. Zeus may not have planned on us living together, though he's one who chose to stay and keep at it. In *Rings of Truth*, I wrote about the difficulty living with Zeus, though I cherish and adore my cat and wish I could hug him right now.

I love Zeus, some of my friends, and lots of my family, yet I remember that my life is my life. I'm the one who needs to tend the soil and be 100% responsible for my choices. I also need to seed and be accountable for my actions, even if I'm afraid to do so.

The Glass House holds the walls up as we peer through the windows. The dining room's west wall keeps the sunset in its frame, while the water flows on the waterfall near the kitchen. I may not yet know Aeris, though she reminds my spirit to believe and trust in fate and destiny. Aeris and her sister cue me to think about decisions affecting the timelines on Earth, while at the same time, Mooshka and Belle live both inside and outside our home. Right now, all of them were out of sight.

I can't predict the future, though I plan for it. Gathering the components of attitude, ethics, and trust, we guide the cosmological balance that reminds me of some things lived before. I learn even more to accept my trials and tribulations of acceptance and character as readers assist me in becoming who I need to be. I've yet to see the tree, though its roots hold firm and brace for the forces of life that remind me storms can teach us how to be.

The visions I've cast in my dreams tell me a few things; some bold, some sobering, and some rallying for fantasies we meet in the future. With an open heart and mind, I thank You, God, for the forces of instinct that have linked my words to readers, and I thank You too for designing me and allowing me to be kind and unwind.

The threads from the loom hold firm and set the picture well into the mesh. Some fragments and shards remind me the sands may now refresh, and I hope you have a fantastic decade from 2020 to 2030. Some of you were not yet born during those years of life, yet a few of you were and just couldn't read my books for another few years.

Most of my nieces and nephews may not read any of my books until 2025 or later, yet they (you) are essential people and sages in the saga of my journey. Chandra, her daughter, and her sister's kids are also imperative, yet not all of the next generation in their family are teenagers by 2030.

For these next ten years, we travel together, distant, close, and apart, yet the ten years before helped me learn to think of more in my heart. I feel tired, stubborn, and dragged on from the previous twenty to thirty years, yet the desired resolve I'm aware of reminds me my core purpose isn't to provide cash, yet instead, love. Like the Taco Bell girl, though, I'm inclined to think it's not one or the other, I believe we can have both and that they complement each other.

Wherever you are in your life and journey, remember you too are a traveller of Time and Space. You can look out to the stars and see all the connections, yet how those stars formed isn't something easily understood. The sad part, I think, is a lot of those stars may have died, and we can only see their light because they were shining bright before they expired.

What I wonder about is how to create new suns, and I wonder which entities on which planets shall see them. Let us heed the guidance from their placement in alien constellations.

OUR HOME

We continue living on this planet, yet our lives are sometimes separate, distinct, linked, and diverse. Some have an abundance of time and resources, while others are stressed without enough income or a moment to spare.

Beware of the false hopes and dreams that scream in your soul to burn. There's a turn of concern that helps us learn as we spurn on the text to explore Earth as a web of communities and worth. Though some pray to Jehova, Jesus, or Allah, others pray outwards to the Universe. Some others devotedly pray while claiming zero allegiance to any diverse network, figurehead, or deity.

I'm a person who's had faith in God and Jesus at times, and even then, I've wished people believing in different spiritual practices or religions be respected and allowed to act, preach, and evolve their understanding and belief. That's the R of Global PLUR; respect for every religion.

The U in global PLUR is the unity of every creed. That may not seem logical or rational, yet if all people are part of the Contialis (the society formed by an involution of all conscious thought), all creeds are united contialitically merely by existing. If any thought, idea, or belief holds in mind, it's part of our mass consciousness, and therefore part of reality and life. I used the word life there and not Earth because Earth also is only one part of the Contialis, just one point of existence.

When I lived at Simon Fraser University (SFU), I had a few interplanetary, and theoretically, intergalactic experiences. One night at the SFU pub, I was high on mushrooms and believed I teleported between parallel universes. When I got back into the bar, I thought I was interacting with different planets and entities that weren't Earth-based. The cool thing, though, was that all the people were getting along, and there was active energy of PLUR.

I write PLUR there, and not the word love because love is a part, yet not solely the only emotion linked. PLUR, in my view, is an ethic and attitude that wishes all three of love, unity, and respect with the absolute and total foundation of peace. I write my version as PLU8R (with an 8) because of multiple R-words and due to the eight linking to infinity.

In an environment where there's no struggle for survival, a dominance of ego, or disruption of being, we can more honestly work towards understanding and sharing ourselves with people. Peace is a baseline, and the link of love need not be romantic. Love can be the entire appreciation, thankfulness, and protection for another being's life. If there's no threat or danger of another harming us, when we have peace, we can attune to our core desires, intention, and intuition towards activating miracles.

By respecting people's differences and divergences, we also can enhance the diversity of belief, understanding, and communication. If we can remain in the same space as another, we can learn to accept more, and once we can entirely accept another, including ourselves, we can learn unknown parts of ourselves. I believe in communication and commitment.

Peace isn't only an environment of zero conflict, yet a non-violence protocol and ethic that can be dangerous if others don't hold the same intent to be peaceful. Sometimes high energy movement can disrupt the tranquillity of mind, spirit, or heart; think about a mirror still surface of a body of water and disruption. One small breach of the peace of the water's surface can send ripples out through the entire distance of the water, from the point of the disruption to the shoreline.

Differently, some people may find their peace, calm, or Zen amongst chaos and disorder and feel scared or unsettled in a relaxed or quiet environment. Order is a baseline and necessary starting point for some, yet inversely, respect can be the foundation for another before we find love, unity, or peace.

Some modern new-age ideas call that all of us are one; it's a concept of unity. Indeed, we're all part of the entirety of life, yet the vastness and variety of our comprehensions and nodal points (plus our consciousness) may find we're aware of so very little of the entirety of life. If you knew personally one million people, that's only one seven thousandths of how many people would be recognized by you, even if linked and part of a whole.

When we're alone, singular, and separate, we can dive into ourselves and who we are, yet even if we're the same being from birth to death, there's a multitude of contact points and shifts in our understanding and awareness. There also is a massive quantity of input points from others that can change and adjust us, who we are, and how we perceive and believe. Something imperceivable can change our viewpoints.

I am one person, just as you are one person, though every word you read in this book was selected and screened. Even if you read this entire book word for word in the same sequential order, you'll miss the full line of consciousness that made it. You don't perceive the editing and revision points of starting, pausing, and stopping, though, as I shifted my context when writing, I formed a linear text for us to see.

You didn't see Zeus jump up on the table or hear the music from the stereo as both spread my awareness into time. You didn't know I stood up to go to the bathroom, releasing a stream into the toilet, and while bathrooms are a modern-day luxury for some, and an everyday thing for many, they also are a dream for many others.

I had zero awareness of who you are and what you thought as the lines formed. The theory of One knowing every minute detail and what we've done and shall do isn't clear to me because I don't yet comprehend myself entirely. How can we even consider, understanding how we affect the Contialis on a grand scale, the concept of God that alludes ALL things are known; the One point of life containing everything and anything that ever exists?

When I wrote *Seeds of Tomorrow* and *Fields of Formation*, I was in a religious phase. Nowadays, it's still ingrained in me to give an acknowledgement of thanks to God anytime I'm about to eat food, and I say Thank You often before eating or drinking. When I'm glad or grateful for things, I know giving thanks is vital for me and who I am, though I'm not actively engaged in a religious congregation. I almost have a fear or aversion to religion now, though I want not to sway believers.

Cosmologically, I am only one person. The consequences and results of sharing my thoughts in books, music, or speech aren't in my understanding, and I've thought the Universe imploded before. If I was conscious and alive then and when I typed this, I wonder for how long this present moment extends.

What are the effects of writing and sharing Providing Point concepts and ideas with people? I don't know what the results shall be, though continue with the process. On infrequent occasions or moments, I've written that a single choice can diverge the timelines and cause significant effects like the ripples on the water's surface I told you about earlier. A friend said, 'nothing really matters' and she may believe, if left alone, the clean mirror surface returns to peace.

Even if it may take a while to calm the waters, perhaps the friend is right, and the points that cause the ripples are parts of a grand system of change and connectedness. My books may not rock the shoreline, yet I sometimes feel the rifts and sways of currents cause variations of text, idea and thought. I am only one person, and I push out, into, and away from other points of reality.

If each affects life, even if indirectly, the Contilais always shifts and holds. Those conscious in the present can remember our pasts, yet we also can dream and envision our futures. The primary point of awareness, though, is now, right where we are in time. You didn't see the twenty hours between the previous sentence and this one. You also didn't know the text during the months between the first draft and its edits. The lines of text stream and weave through the landscapes of time with letters each holding significance on their own.

Because = Be Cause. The reason is why, yet, the sai apply to the corona of my eye. Lift the sands high into the rifts and gifts from the sky.

I flew to Australia in about two weeks, and during that trip, I hoped to revise and prepare this book for release as well as see my Dad and Sarah. Zeus stayed at home for the twelve days I was gone with Arlinn looking out for him. She watered, fed, brushed, and played with Zeus when I was away, though she has a situation of her own to manage.

Though I can't claim to know what the future holds, the moulding of what I desire mixes into the breath, telling me to be true to much more than a few. I tentatively continue my journey with hope wising to be robust, sure, and stable, and perhaps the Fountains of Fortitude are the keystone that allows prosperity as we glide through Fantasy.

Though told not to get too far ahead of ourselves, I remember the importance of words and what we select. If to be accurate, we must choose the precise sounds, feelings, and messages we want to convey. Articulation and acute communication are helpful for almost anyone, and as we learn to be both informative, concise, and relevant, we can expand what we do, think, and say.

I live to relay seeds others may want for their gardens and fields. I've thought I've not much to convey, yet faith pulls to remind me I have bags of grain yet to be processed and shared. We each are seed bearers, yet who wants to share or plant, and who wants to grind them up for meal or flour? Just as money is used and handled differently, so too is truth.

The investments I've made in these books may compound with interest. The books can activate principles to assist others in need of support, and writing also allows us to see what's gone on in our minds. As the words evolve and find their place in ink on the page, their volumes nestle amongst other books held on people's shelves. We transmit thoughts, and if the fields of text are well, we reap a harvest.

For 2020-2030, I'd like to expand Providing Point and find someone to run the company. I want to continue learning and understanding money and how it works as a tool, and I want to find ways of assisting others in earning significant incomes too. I don't want to work for Providing Point full-time, though I wish to discover ways of earning an income that's solid and legit and share how to do so.

Writing is an asset, yet coupled with knowledge and coaching instincts, perhaps the intellectual equity gained can translate into trust and connection. If I can find ways of assisting others with their hopes, goals, and dreams, then I also gain the benefit of sharing time with people who are forward sighted. I'd love to work for and serve more people who want to thrive, work, and develop their Freedom Solutions while also contributing to our communities.

With an edge of new hope, I can feel the energy of prosperity poking at my skull and stirring up my mind into plots and plans for a combined future. We can find our Freedom Solutions together with my parts of solitude to allow ourselves to learn and develop our thoughts, ideas, and beings.

With three days remaining in 2019, I typed the last few bits of this chapter to lead into the next one. I felt the forward momentum and force, calling me to write and pursue my dreams. The Glass House becomes a reality, and though it's seemed near impossible, my faith and endurance help build the fantasy from yesterday.

As we move into flourishing in the 2020-2030 decade, the evolution of our work and process continues while learning what components we're best to gather. My personal drives hint I may neglect marketing and sales a bit, yet gradual advancement of the cause to provide homes and food push and pull my thoughts.

Two years ago, Providing Point was just a wishful notion, though we grow. We gave four $15/month cards to Cyrus Centre the previous week, and I reloaded the active cards earlier in the day I wrote this. Two years ago, we only had two contributors, and as we continue to learn and grow, we assist others and thrive.

What do I wish for you, the reader? I hope some of my dreams can insight you to think outwards a bit more, and I hope you can resonate with some of my fears and insecurities.

I accept we carry the baggage of the present and past, though I wish we may be glad to learn, grow, and expand. I hope you are reading this book and can develop and strengthen your abilities of understanding and sharing more universally. We all need help and support; let us learn to provide that amply.

With the next decade scuttering forth, I reverently recall the walls that hold my soul. My Mom and I put a fresh coat of paint in my living room in December, and as I see the sky blue colour in the kitchen, I remember to keep the lights down low and relish in the sounds from the computer as I type these books.

I admire, abstain, and absolve my desires to produce only for the benefit of others because I need to care for myself too. I allow myself to work and gather real love and assets that can help bring me, my friends, my family, and our communities into alignment and allyment.

Hold onto the moments you can remember of happiness and appreciation, and please give more hugs to people when you genuinely like or love them. Vocalize your dreams and fears to someone without expecting them to 'fix' your situation, and remember to breathe and slow down when you feel anxiety or nervousness. Because sometimes, we just need to stop and regather our thoughts, energy, and intents to form reset points before pushing forward with confidence.

We find moments we genuinely desire, and as we live within our own homes of spirit, mind, body, soul, and heart, we can learn to be okay in any situation. Even if we don't yet know how, let us always find ways to gather and be in moments of brilliance, beauty, and comfort more often.

THE LIGHT IN THE DARK

Chance and fate can open the gate to miracles, yet it's how we seed and respond to them that, I think, matters. For the final chapter of this Fountain, I call upon forces of light and truth that burn in my soul. Sometimes I've heeded guidance from my neurotic tendencies, yet as I write and review my books, my psyche conveys some crisp reminders.

I sometimes forget what I've written in these books, so it's good for me to go back and revisit them in time. In the middle of the holiday season between Christmas and New Year's Eve, I found myself sitting on my comfy chair in the dark because there was a power outage. I anticipated the feeling of Zeus brushing up against my legs as I sat and typed this while a cigarette called for consumption.

Naturally, I smoked the smoke, then I got two Ferrero Roche's from the kitchen, and returned to writing this. If there is one wish or hope I have, it's that I can reclaim my health again. I've thought that cigarettes assist me in knowing the truth, yet smoke clouds my mind as well as my lungs.

The countless times I've been focused and then distracted by the desire to smoke gnaws at me and my dramatic lack of productivity. With no work until late January 2020, I had an abundance of time and little motivation to work or create. The saving grace for the construction of these books happens in the night when the words flow smoothly and free.

I'd love to be a non-smoker again and also defiantly grasp at my ability to inhale the chemicals. I can't yet envision what it's like to be a non-smoker, though I know stopping smoking is one of the most significant things I can do for myself and my long term gain.

The discomfort I have about not being able to smoke amplifies the desire to smoke. It's like taking a big breath of air before diving underwater, holding my breath until the next point I can surface and light up. Rationally I know there's a multitude of detrimental consequences by being a smoker, though I also told you how I can't yet appreciate how it is to live without cigarettes.

Though ciggies might be like poisoned water, thirst calls for them to enter my lungs and body. When we're thirsty, we appreciate most any drink that quenches thirst. It's similar to cigarettes and the desire for nicotine. There is a physical and mental urge to fill up my lungs.

The desire to smoke is more frequent and sometimes more substantial than the desire to eat. I can go hours without food with little to no complaint, yet wanting a cigarette surfaces dozens of times a day. The many times I take a few minutes for a smoke during the day or night stops me from working on things, and the breaks also can be a distraction when I don't know what to do. Perhaps I need to learn to sit in peace more.

I was sitting in the dark while illuminated by the future. Is it because I wish, dream, and hope for a prosperous future that allows it to become so? Is the twisting feeling in my mind and body a vehicle spinning its wheels in the snow or mud? If I can shift to four-wheel drive and get the entire collection of my work going, can I trudge out and from the mires of lies, deceit, and misinterpretation?

I feel like I'm working for naught, yet oppositely know it's for our good. There are few people whom I can call upon, yet that's because I'd not solidified my heart and being to be secure for our future. I'm not entirely sure about the how or who, yet inklings of my past call again.

Would the cutie float down gently from above and land here in my hand? Probably not, so perhaps I should go out there to find her. Even if I can write my books and work on the computer at home, digital contact isn't the same as an in-person talk.

Psychically, I have shards attached to my brain and being, yet I want more signs to guide the way. I need to become deviously clear about what I wish in truth, and not just what I desire my purpose and meaning to be. Forcing the process might tip the structure over, so perhaps it's best I continue to build and craft supports for our future. If the foundations are damaged, we can repair them; it's just trickier when the building has started.

A lighthouse warns the boats at sea. It signals to keep ships safe, even in the calm waters holding vessels calling for some on the shore. I may not always hear them, yet, like the sea, I know they're out there in their crafts of body and soul. Spirits may align the heart to become clear and right in the mind, yet still, let us discover the shorelines during the day and not just the nights.

A lot has been kept secret from me, and when I have an idea to believe, some tell me it's my delusion, yet I cast a few pebbles into the water. Ripples radiate outwards from the source of contact between the stone and water, yet a daughter calls for fall's embrace. I do too, yet first, we must get through the summer.

My hop across the pond took me to warm weather, though I returned home after the trip. I'm not entirely fond of thinking I'll need to be in the dirt digging up weeds for a paycheque, yet unless I find another way, I may have to. What I'd like to see is people interested enough in my books to buy copies and read them.

The principles of giving hold real, and I honour the earnings commitments I've made up to now. I continue with Providing Point as an idea planted in the soil and gardens of our life, yet I'm one who needs to remember to tend the seeds and not just leave them be. Some people may be best left alone, yet I hope we find me as a person we like to know.

With more conversations and communication, we can hear and share more of our core desires, and when we find the people that want to work with us to activate those desires, we move closer into finding more frequent miracles. It probably is a good idea to connect with more people who believe in the missions of these texts. Providing homes for people is not a one-person job.

If to activate any giving program, it requires communities

to gather and work together. We find ways to allow each to have a home, and as I'm glad and thankful to have an apartment to live within, it may not be where I live five years from now. Living in my suite has been beneficial and helpful for me on my journey, yet I build and move into a new house in four to five years.

I've lived in the same home for more than a decade, and I don't fully understand that. How can I be so close to the same spot I was in a decade ago without a girlfriend, profession, or vocation? I'm sure I don't want to go another decade alone without a female companion, yet who shall she be?

Deep in Wonder is another title to use for a future book. I've also thought of writing a book titled *Freedom Solution*, though I'm not ready to write a self-help book sharing with people how to live. I have a few tidbits or points of recommendation, yet to write an entire book with the intent to improve people's lives didn't seem to be in my cards again at this point. It's bizarre to think about how life will be a decade from now, as lots of change comes within the next years.

The Fountains have been so much about what I want. Sure, my books hold ideas for sharing with others and improving general life, though I've not tuned into thoughts about what other people hope we can do with these books. I've gleaned barely any input or opinion about what others want to read and have created purely on the premise of what I want to make. If I can shift a bit, and listen more, perhaps I can heed guidance about the right ideas to share.

It's true, though, I'm glad I've written what I have up to now. I've also written a bit about what I don't have, yet that may be a sly joke. I've written twelve individual books and have three three-part books available for sale as of typing this. Though few of the books have sold, I believe in their merit and worth for that they are. I remember I've learned a lot by writing the Fountains, so perhaps some of the skills and awareness I've acquired can benefit others in tow.

From Rory Vaden on an episode of *The School of Greatness*, reputation precedes revenue, and results times reach equals reputation. I think I must cultivate my character to have a positive reputation, and then expand my reach by activating results with that foundation.

For a few years, I was doing all sorts of things that were not positive, and as I shift and change my attitudes and behaviours, it can have a positive impact on how people see me. Perhaps my reach and results improve too, and that'd be fantastic. I know I haven't lived life the way the majority of the population does, yet I also hope I'm doing the right things.

I write, and I work. I reach out, and I respond. I learn to love, and I learn to live. I tend the seeds of needs met to let us each reach the points of our highest divinity, and though that may be a bold or arrogant statement, if I can do so for myself, perhaps I can convey wisdom and guidance so more may reach their goals and objectives.

Lifting people to higher points may not be what I yet do with these books, though is that because I'm still building my own life? Can't we create and level up *with* people and not only for ourselves and others? After this book, I have a lot of work to do; to keep tending and seeding for our lives, continue with this series and, with assistance, we'll find some miraculous things happen in 2020 and beyond.

The first draft of this Fountain completed on December 31st, 2019, and I felt hopeful and excited about the next year and decade. I realize that by writing these books, I can elevate the baselines of not only my life, though also that of others who want to thrive and excel. With fortitude shifted into fantasy, we reach the point of flourishing. Doing so takes bases of yesterday and faith into this, and with some shards in mind, we've played in those fields already.

With a secure home, people can do amazing things. If I'm allowed to have what I have and do what I do, then I atone. To the courses of life and work, we provide homes for others, yet the work of the next book, *Signs of Serenity*, had already started as I leaned into the plow. I may not teach by direct example or command, yet as I evolve and grow, we can sow the seeds of future yields.

Glean perception and the mention of sands that again turn to polished stone. Though I've been alone at home, other than Zeus, I realize the fragments and shards also combine into the lines you see. As the seeds sprout and start to creep out of the soil, the saplings reach up towards the sky and sun and become sure and reliable trees.

The text presumes a few things, yet as strings hold up the lattice, it's with this idea that everyone can thrive with the support that draws me to gather the components required. Fires hold a kindred flame and share the warmth, yet if we can learn to control ourselves and our light, we can focus and share our gifts and abilities to assist others.

Some may not want to give their light away, though, for those that don't, I guess the rest of us must shed a bit more of our illumination. I hope we may give our love and trust to friendly folk who assist and support us to carry the communal yolk. My parents have guided me well, and though nestled into the shell, the Spirit helps unfold the sombre cold. With an edge of curious certainty, I thank the forces of God, life, and the Universe for allowing me to see that I shall always know the world is a part of me that holds the key.

With an edge of devious delusion, the dark signs that share my mind shall not eclipse the sun that shines in our hearts. And, with a trip of defiant dismay, I wish, yearn, and pray we can continue our journeys into the next decade. With an abundance of hope, resources, and absolute love, we press into our futures, dear.

I got to visit and share New Year's Eve with Chandra, the gal I wrote to in the first book, *Finding Natalie*. She's been a great friend through the course of these books, and though not the one I settle down with and move into the Glass House with, I'm dearly and meekly thankful she is part of my life.

Chandra and her family have treated me very well through the years and have included me in their celebratory days. Birthdays, Thanksgivings, and Christmases have found me with her family appreciating the truth that we may gather.

Without being in connection with people that matter to us,

we can neglect to remember that people can love and appreciate us. Do not keep yourself away from the world. Please bring yourself out of the dark and be a light in another's life so they can see, feel, and know PLU8R too.

The first name I ever mentioned in this series of books also has been shielded and set aside. I hope he can endure and provide a tide of thought, reminding us that we can't buy friends. We may not yet see the gifts relayed from afar, and it may take some courage and faith to trust another to see deep into your soul, eyes, and heart.

Lies can be robust and prevent the trust from being there, so open a corner of your mind and heart to the idea that you can be and are loved. There's a sad fact that some people shall never love or trust, yet you can choose not to be one of those people. Open your spirit to chance and dance with the starlight to remember, for yourself, what is right.

I cannot change your life. That's the work of you, the Universe, and God. What I can do, though, is to remind you that you are one who has given me a fantastic gift to remember that people are out here on the same planet pushing and pulling for something better.

Even if I can't wave my Mom's magic wand and give people love, a home, and hope not yet known, I can be the seed planted in the soil pushing and bursting forth with the wish to be a tree.

As I ask God and the Universe what they want to tell me, I press the keys to find a bit less fear and deceit, greeting me into the next moment. Though I went away for the trip to visit Dad and Sarah, it was that month I formed the Revised version of this text. After that, the Unlimited version formed, and then the Finally Found version. I may not have 'found' Natalie, though in writing this book, I've found my resolve to continue living and dreaming.

I know I can't tell you who you are. I also can't share with you the exact desires of another's being. What I can do, though, is assist you in seeing the whims and wants of a stellar child who shall gather the components of our Freedom

Solutions. We then share them in the gardens that want and permit us to be there.

The wares of the next text shift into the gift of perception. From what I hear, to what I see, and then what I feel, I moved into what I want to understand. I listen to her speak to my mind into our shared heart and soul. When we can clear the web of lies and understand each other, then, with truth, we can share our lives with the world.

It's not always easy to presume we know what's right, even if we think we have the absolute truth. What we promise may not yet be given, yet still, my Shivan helps decide how and where we'll reside.

By reading this book, you've given me much more than I yet know. It was only an idea and wish at the start, though, as the grains of truth settle into now, I remember the world of Earth may need to desire we learn to hone and love our craft like we've learned to treat fire.

(Here is the close of the 11th Fountain)

LOOKING OUT TO IN

From what I've heard, it's a good thing I hold some doubt. I've been told that God loves me, yet what I hear from the world too is no one wants to hear. If we ask a question, we may not receive an immediate answer, yet it could be a good thing to make some requests.

Even if we've not met some, we've heard from media or social that some understand the world clearly in their hearts. Do you trust the tones you sense, or do you still need to see to believe? Some speak lies and deceit while trying to make it so sweet that they wish we'll never meet.

There's a twist in the lines carrying the current. Magnetism orbits the wires that allow us to hear *Fable* from the stereo. I've based much belief on sound, and, if what I've thought is right has deceived me time and time again, this text may be far more to explore before I can guarantee it's You.

Some speak to vast audiences, hundreds, thousands, or even millions of people. Those audience members hear every choice word spoken while forming different comprehensions. If it's the same message spoken to a multitude, each person has a different worldview and perception that can glean a different lesson or meaning.

Variations of syntax are also audible points of input; it's not only the tone spoken that can hint to what mayhap be hidden or subvert knowledge. We can hear or read a message, song, or recording over and over, continuously gleaning varied insights from it, yet if there's such a variety of understanding from linear and static sources, how can a person's message be accurately conveyed? How can the exact message be precisely understood the same by thousands, or even millions of people?

Every distinct view cannot be the same. And yet we've heard absolute things can't deviate from precisely what they are. If something has explicitly one, and only one, meaning, then how and why could any disagree with what that thing means?

Each person is unique and held as a single entity and node, and if there's variation in how others hear that person, that person is still the same being. We may distinctly understand and interpret different ideas and beliefs, yet dare the choice meanings of words cause diverse views and understanding, how can we be sure to know what another means?

There may be alternate opinions about an issue, and beliefs can shift and evolve. Some hold fast to what they've heard without confirmation, yet do not stay fixed and static in your view. If what we believe doesn't cross-reference with what the truth is, there can be distortion and deception.

If what we cross-reference as truth isn't fact, then a different form of misguiding occurs. We need to know what the truth is as a reliable baseline, and not just because it could be a widespread belief. Just because a majority believes it doesn't mean it's right.

At times, it seems every sound I hear outside directly references to my thoughts. I smoke on the patio at night, and I hear voices from people that seem to be reading my mind. I can't always discern whether it's my imagination playing tricks on me, or if I'm part of a psychic network that puts me as a focal point. It's disconcerting to think every thought links to a conscious mind, and even that many of our thoughts aren't our own ideas. Groupthink is a mental thing, yet this section focuses on sounds that we hear.

When we talk, we hear our voice, yet can a projected reference of our innermost thoughts be amplified and vocalized back to us too? Are some points and beliefs echoed back to us and aren't from others? Sometimes a neurotic and timid self intends to disrupt, and some of the voices I hear, even if real audible channels of sound, link telepathically to myself. There are hints that some people demean to share hate and animosity, and though I can't always tell what's real, I hope I'm wrong.

As you see every letter, word, line, and paragraph in this book, I too have seen them, though from a different perspective. You may see a digital or printed version of the full text, yet I saw the words form, shape, and evolve with separate and distinct temporal points of input.

When we see a piece of art or the face of another person, it's often taken many years, layers, and moments to allow that vision to be. Things may seem instantaneous and absolute, yet eons too help shape some ideas. With art, there can be a static picture, a completed form, something seen as a final result, yet its creation came from fluid and evolved time. We often don't know the stages, processes, and developments of art as if forms.

People may be the same beings from birth to death, yet changes morph parts of them also as we evolve and progress. Faces have similar qualities; eyes, ears, mouths, noses; those building blocks are almost universal. The quality of sight can be focused or restricted yet stimulated by similar tangible rays of light, and we can see shared inputs, yet vision may be deceptive. If actors or illusions make us believe one thing, the opposite may be the truth.

We can't rely purely on sight for the validity of belief, even if we think it's a sure thing. If I believed in love at first sight, how could it be true of her? Seeing may not always be believing, yet instead a pathway of confusion.

From Viktor E. Frankl's book *Man's Search for Meaning*, I gleaned a gem. Viktor was a concentration camp survivor, and his work camp group helped prison mates from committing suicide. Viktor and his friends did so for one of them by reminding the mate about a primary reason for living. The person needed to finish a set of books that he alone could write, and they encouraged him to endure and persevere past his situation to bring the books to fruition.

When someone shows us or tells us something, they're sometimes intentionally putting a fresh idea into our awareness. We're often conscious of what we see or hear, and we can't always un-know or un-see something, yet if we search for something on the Internet, are we actively seeking to behold such?

We must continue to learn and discern what we allow into our eyes and ears to protect our psyches from corruption. I also must mentally clean myself as I want the waters of these books to flow unobstructed. Some of my books start like mud, yet I work to purify them and remove some of the contaminants.

Crystal clear words on a page can be more far more permanent than sound, and when we read terms from a page, if we think we misread the text, a simple pause to rewind and go back can almost always clarify. We often can verify the certainty of our comprehension, and if we see a word we don't yet know, we can pause and look it up. Afterwards, we can return to where we were reading.

And yet videos are a different layer altogether. We may not see all the words we hear in a video, though the graphics, colours, shapes, and people we see are sometimes vivid and influential. Video is often pre-recorded, not live, and maybe where my mom gets her term 'mindless television'.

If a video is (or isn't) a replay, I can sometimes sense pre-reflexive responses to my thought as if the people on screen can hear my mind. I heard a long while ago that if a person looks to the left, it means they're lying, so because of that, I cross-reference what I hear and see from people while changing my line of sight.

If I think an idea is right or not, I will put my eyes in one direction or the other. In-person, I deflect eye contact and shift my eyes, yet with video, it's much more natural just to stare at the screen. My beliefs and perceptions skew how I behave, yet I'm sure others also regulate their responses in line with their truths. If we've based on fact or opinion, we'll each probably act differently.

We continue to learn and understand the elements of serenity. I know we can feel sad, yet I mustn't deflect or distract from that emotion. Some experiences aren't pleasant, though allowing the feelings to pass like waves of water can let us clean some of our pain. My aunt Judy explained to me years ago the *emotion* of peace. She told me it's how we can feel sad, though keep above the waterline, to be hopeful or optimistic while acknowledging sadness and not being overwhelmed by it.

The feeling or idea of peace can link to silence and stillness as we're alive and well here on Earth. Some are deep in their woes, losses, and disparaging truths while cold air surrounds. Movement and activity can allude to energy and high vibrations, yet oppositely, I have a concern of people freezing and turning cold. Stillness is not always peaceful and kind.

Our bold stare against the screen can take us into a trance. Moments of thought and language attempt to explain my desperation of light, yet a plight calls me to remember the sensed saddened waves of aggression. I recall moments of tension and fear, yet how can I return to defiant hope again?

We assist people to live, love, and thrive, and with a desire to create as a way to learn, play and pray, I place a pace of text into the fray of words. Here, they say, forever and a day doesn't always mean it'll be tomorrow.

We mustn't lend, steal, or borrow some grains and seeds of truth. It may be best to share and procure positive manifestations and ramifications of complexity into welcome things. My metaphysical pain trips (MPTs) in Vancouver were not pleasant, though they're part of my experience. My MPTs included waves of electrocuting energy coursing over my body, something that I believed to be a punishment.

I felt hundreds of MPTs and warrior lashes in the year 2001 on Pender Street. That was all before I went through electroshock therapy in the psych ward, though both base on electrical input.

When I went through electroshock therapy in 2001-2002, I was brought me into a room where they performed the operation. They laid me out on a gurney and strapped me in. The doctors gave me an Oxygen mask, and then, while lying down on the table with the mask on, I was injected with a cold liquid. The doctors told me to breathe deeply, and a few moments later, with the cold fluid in my arm, there was a strange taste, and then I went unconscious.

The MPTs were not clinical electroshock therapy, though they affected me significantly. During the MPTs, I would feel like I had electrodes in every pore of my face and parts of my upper body, and then it would feel like I was being electrocuted in each of those pores. I've heard of others calling these feelings zaps, and those people experienced them when going through withdrawal from psychiatric medication. I was on a drug called Paxil at one time in my life, yet I was off that drug months before my MPTs.

Yet there are different feelings I've experienced that are beautiful, feelings and memories of serenity. On K'Gari, what is called Fraser Island in Queensland, Australia, I remember feeling and hearing deep peace within the forest. The trees hung peacefully, and the stream we slowly walked beside trickled with deep stillness. I adore my memory of K'Gari and wish to go back again in the future. I'd love to go with my future girlfriend or wife, yet I don't yet know who she is. I understand, resonate, honour, and appreciate the tranquillity.

When we can vividly remember and feel serenity, like what I found in the island forest two years before typing this, signs of life churn peaceful waves in the soul of our spirit. Though I sense only a rare few tranquil memories from my past, I also hold many that are not positive.

I want to and must hold my being with attunement and deep alignments of peace. Love carries in some of my memories, yet a unified field of recollection is still piecing itself together. I have lots of blocked trauma and experience to unearth, and I'm sure knowing such can be beneficial as raw recollections of my core meaning and purpose.

I can feel the energy in my body remembering mixed emotions at Christmas Eve church meetings too. One Christmas Eve was absolute solitude and peace I felt when in a holy moment, yet many Christmases held deep sadness and longing for Natalie. I remembered sobbing both beautiful and woeful tears, thinking of how Natalie and I have been kept apart for so many years, yet my natural reflexes remind me if I meet her in real life, she'd probably leave me alone again. Would she?

Wonder, I guess, is the feeling. The fanciful whims of hope and love call me to dream, and the lure of lucrative lunacy reminds me to tether to the moment of now. I understand and accept the feelings I've had, and even if not rational or transparent, sadness is a form of honouring the truth of ones we've loved who we can never seem to know.

I accept that just because we love another, we aren't entitled or owed reciprocation for the depths of feeling we have. One thing I'd like for myself is to learn how to feel relaxed and let myself let go and slow down. I'm not often overly high-strung, yet I obsessively distract myself from processing some of what I don't want to think or feel. I've denied myself the experience of feeling beautiful states of being too when I've become fearful or angry. Yet, I can appreciate now how I can shift nervousness or fear into a feeling of excitement and aliveness.

Is accepting the unknown a healthy, conscious choice? I want to feel healthier, primarily in my respiratory system, though I've fouled my lungs with twenty-seven years of smoking. I'd like to harmonize my breath with slower energy settling well into my heart, and fewer clouds of contaminants.

I miss my Taekwondo training and how it felt to perform some of the patterns. There were parts of one Poomsae (pattern) I loved because of the feeling of power combined with the movement itself and a kiup, the loud sound made at the close one specific Poomsae. Even though I was a smoker when I trained, my health was significantly better than it's been these past few years.

I want to feel safe, loved, and sure. I want to feel close to my lovestone and hold her in my arms. I want to feel confident that what I say is true, right, and just, and that my actions harmonize with my body, soul, spirit, heart, and mind. I prefer warmth compared to cold, I like comfortable hoodies and jeans compared to dress pants, suits, and ties, and I also like the feeling one can get by stretching far back in one's chair with tingles in the brain, and then sitting upright, feeling light and soberly high.

I want to feel secure in my truths as they are. When I wrote *Depths of Discovery*, I remembered more feelings I wish to reencounter and experience. The energy felt in some of my most loving or tranquil moments may not be immediately replicated, yet lead to how I faithfully know I can have more peaceful and passionate moments in the future.

Another prime thing I've heard and read is we can choose how we want to feel. Conscious choices and trusting feelings compel me to move forward in faith. The holy opinions of being in a divine state are sensations of freedom, yet I also desire feelings of movement and aliveness—happy and excited to experience moments of bliss.

I realize a lot of what I've written about in this section are solitary feelings or, more-so, non-relational feelings. If I think of how I want to feel with other beings, the first one I thought of is Zeus.

Dear Yang, from the January 2020 flight from Shanghai to Brisbane, weirdly and strangely, it seemed like you were interested. I sensed a kiss or a hug would have been super bold, though also welcome. Am I as delusional as I told you I am? Energetically, you enticed me, yet I honour your kindness and conversation with this brief mention. You reminded me high-quality gals might like me, and I want to put in a better effort to connect and communicate with other women.

Dear Chandra, from the left out and not forgotten chapter of the book that started this series, I'm glad we talk, and I value you as a friend. On my 2020 Australia trip, hearing your voice and how we interact made me tell you it's an idea for us to travel. I appreciate your attitude and ethics and hope what I see and hear from you is accurate and not a delusion. Thank you for welcoming this year and this decade together, and I hope we're still connected when it's 2030. Thank you.

Dear forces of life that allow me to write this book, thank you for the grace and compassion that enable us to live and thrive. I hope I may honour the worlds and Earth together in the dismay of how I seem to want to go away. I ask we may learn to stay right and just without being trodden on by others. Thank you for allowing me to be where I am now, even if part of my penance is to hold the keys in an ironic and symbiotic freeze. There are years locked in days like these, yet still, let the moments of peace and serenity ease into our lives.

ROBERT KOYICH

ADJUSTING PROMISES

Mentally pacing with a desire to smoke, I hold on and wait. There must be more to do than sit around and wait. My 2020 trip to Australia brought me back to Chilliwack and what goes on there. Though I'd not been thinking so much about Providing Point during the journey, that shard of intent is ingrained in my psyche.

Going on holidays can be rad, refreshing, and fun, yet the tug of knowing I have work to do also calls me with a slight nudge and reminder to write. The thought drills me with a propensity to tool away with the words, and I returned to writing this book after going a week without my computer.

My Dad transferred all that was on my previous laptop to a new hand-me-down one that works like a charm. I can again put YouTube videos together and write, and though I paused for a moment, I let myself sink back down to Earth.

Sometimes being high up in the clouds is irrational, and I appreciate the stability of heart. Breathing in and out, the cycle of my breath soaks in the drum 'n' bass playing on the computer. While I adore music, I hadn't been playing much when away from home. I create more music, yet I'm also sometimes tired of hearing my own voice.

Writing gives us a chance to break away from my nattering, yet my text is a different form of rambling. I appreciate it, yet who else enjoys taking cruises along the rivers that meander? We wander through the landscape of my spirit and soul with my dear kitten-cat Zeus. He was an ocean away, and I missed him and felt sad that he's often alone.

When I tell people that I think Zeus is lonely, some say that cats are okay to be alone, yet I don't think that's entirely true. My previous two cats seemed abysmally sad and lonely when it was finally time to put them down. Winks and Boots had contracted kitty leukemia, and even if a legitimate disease, I wonder how much of their condition was from feeling neglected.

If and when I'm a parent to a live human being, I want to keep in daily contact with them, even after they've moved out. I don't want to create an emotional dependence, yet as my parents have with me, we can place boundaries and rules to guide towards independence. How we give gifts of appreciation, connection, or time abundantly can share how there's a point where we may not be in contact.

I have been highly dependent upon my parents and their partners for much, yet my emotional drive to connect with them may come from a point of lack. How can I generate and share more genuine care and appreciation for them? I felt full in heart full here. I came to Australia to visit my Dad and his wife, and while I appreciate the trip significantly, I also had my poor me side chirp in wanting to disappear. I don't always connect well.

I love my Dad a lot, though it's a group of three when there with him and his wife. I want to connect with both, yet there's sadness when I think of Dad, and a desire to distance when I think of Sarah. My Dad's wife and I have different values and expectations, and that leads to conflict with her when I visit.

I want my Dad's wife to be happy and feel okay with her life, yet me visiting disrupts their usual business. Due to such, I adapt and adjust how and what I do. If setting myself aside after travelling half-way around the world is something I need to do, I accept it, and I'm glad to have my ciggies to get away from the situation. I don't want to use cigarettes as a coping mechanism, yet remember some things aren't worth money. I also remember my ciggies in Australia during the trip weren't entirely on my bill.

Weirdly, the news of Harry and Meghan was at the front of the press. Harry and Meghan wanted out of the monarchy, and in a twisted parallel, I wanted out of having to meet up with my Dad's wife because we trigger each other with our behaviours. It may mean giving up trips to see my Dad, which I don't want, though I'll find a way of paying my way and not relying on Dad and Sarah for financial support. I want to be self-sufficient, so perhaps that can be motivation for me to live better.

As I told you that, I felt a wave of positivity and inspiration. I won't be subservient to a human who's so critical of me, and it saddens me that letting go may mean I won't see my Dad so often. I could hear his wife giggling at the idea, because, and I could be projecting, she doesn't seem to like me there in their home.

I guess I lose Australia trips, yet it may be better than gaining financial support and living with negativity and waves of aggression. It's a tricky situation, and time fluxed between when I was on the trip, and then, months later, editing this book. With the three days remaining on my journey, Dad was in the other room watching TV, and his wife was in her office. I chose to sit with Dad.

After Dad and I watched two interviews on TV, he went back to work, and I went for a smoke. When I got back upstairs, I opened my laptop, put some music on, and got back to my work and process. I put on an audio file I recorded in 2017 as background in my headphones, and I set back into writing this book.

Finding financial independence may require these books as a product, so if you bought this book, thank you! You are contributing to providing charitably for others, while also helping me earn. I'd not yet set the earnings commitment for this individual Fountain or *Mosaic of Miracles*, the three-part compilation. However, I inevitably chose to put the earnings to Providing Point for *Signs of Serenity*, and 51% of Mosaic's to Chilliwack Housing Providers. It was January 2020 when I first wrote this part, though the official release was in August.

Do I return to Australia? It wasn't yet clear to me. In the preceding days, it seemed a big 'no,' yet the night I put my hands on the keyboard to write, I was a 'maybe.' It's distinctly clear I waffle on things, and this seemed to be no exception. The next two days led to the day after when I returned home. It seemed like I was away for a month, and though there are things I missed back home (like my cat and my friends) for the two weeks away, I didn't regret not landscaping or shovelling all of the snow.

It was ten days after leaving Australia when I came back to this document. In retrospect, it was an excellent trip to see Dad and Sarah, and, indeed, my home hadn't felt filled with love and happiness. It had been a bit drab, and I understand that I'm definitely in a rut with my set patterns of cigarettes. You know I've brought smoking up a lot, yet I'd still not found a resolution or adjustment of the base behaviour.

My job landscaping seemed like a light out of the abundance of time, though I've lacked drive and motivation. It had been more than a month off from gardening, and while I thought I wanted entirely open days to work on the computer and be creative, I felt lazy and unmotivated to create.

If we guide ourselves, positively or negatively, there needs to be an impetus of change, and if I've committed to a task or promise, I honour such. That's part of my process. I keep my landscaping job for the year 2020, and even if I've bitched and moaned about it, I made a promise to do so. My job is also an income-generating asset, and sadly, it's also because I didn't know what else to do with myself.

I find clarity about my core desires, and though I've written a lot and cycled through ideas and plans frequently, I see how I'd narrowed down my actions and activities by the choices I've made. I feel and fear I may be too passive when I want to feel fired up and energized! I want to remember to breathe and hold onto clean air, and as I keep writing these books, it's part of the process of pushing the keys and accepting I can choose how to live.

If you, as a reader, see me cycle within circles of self-doubt, complaining, and apathy, it must be annoying, though imagine being the person who's had these issues surface and repeat time and time again. I'd been working myself a bit mad from this process, and I guess my cat's not been on about it either. I neglect to speak to him sometimes.

Then I remind myself these are the Fountains of Fantasy! Let's get back to dreaming!

I wish for fantastic and seemingly impossible things, yet I also learn how to write them into life. I've covered a few things in the previous two books that link this volume, and one thing I want to help thrive aside from me is the Providing Point program. I want to help own homes to rent to people for $375 a month, and I'd like to hook up with a fantastic gal and live with her for life.

We sometimes need to know our function and purpose before moving forward, though what if I just need to align? How can we spend more time with friends and family? How can we find the time and place to interact with other positive, forward-thinking people to activate our miracles? What do I do to have our financial needs covered and allow myself to be a car friend again?

Who do you like, appreciate, and admire? Am I over-focused on what's instead of how's and why? *My* core why is that I want to be a loving, well-integrated, active, prosperous, and respectful human being for decades further into the future, and by sharing resources and building programs or concepts to let others live a great life too, I hope to give the world more than I yet have for myself.

I want people to like, love, and live with each other, and I also wish we attain the core desires of our hearts and souls. The way I've attempted to do so isn't so clear, though we learn how and why we work together in our lives. We must remember that if we don't like life, it's our responsibility to change and build what we do want., and if we genuinely wish to contact people and actively work on friendships, projects, and our attitudes, then we must take action and do so.

I need to learn how to successfully market my books, Providing Point, and my music, and by creating more music and videos as a start, I also follow through with gleaning pledges and preparing texts. With a few breaks from writing the base text of this book, I took myself through many points of experience.

After not adding much to this book for a while, I spoke at Toastmasters. I talked about the Fountains and my written journey, though the main thing I mentioned is that we need to start something if we want anything to go anywhere. We often land far away from where we first started (like how, with these books, it was Natalie who began them), yet in *Mosaic of Miracles*, I may have returned home.

The love and life I've lost and denied time and time again call me up not to ask if, yet instead, when? When shall we sit, meet, greet, and take a seat? When shall the one I love amongst the many others on Earth wind her hand into mine? How shall we sip drinks of wine in our shared home? When shall Zeus and I have our leading partner live with us?

I see I don't know who she is yet, though I can feel the hope, faith, and truth that tell me she knows who she is. I didn't know when she'll be here, though the energy of the music and the psychic feel of a smile creeping up onto my face spoke these words as I typed them. She knows of me, and I realize we both hold the key. To mix in a fun rhyme, "remember, it's a Zed, not a Zee."

I'd love to share more of the story about how these books manifest, and during the construction of the base versions of these works, I see the cart before the horse all so often. I spin back to carry the weight of my words, and though I've written how all the lines are like train tracks guiding people along my pathways, switches, twists, and turns, we draw the thoughts into a linear form. With you as an engine, perhaps we can travel with ease.

It's a fact I sense there are many attached to these pages and journey. Although *Mosaic of Miracles* started as a wishful idea to complete another three-part book, I could detect how we're activating miracles. Calling forth the Fountains of Fantasy, if I understand my process well enough, perhaps I learn further how to articulate my reasoning for things. I want not only to tell you what I want to do, though also how we can work to do so. These words and paths matter.

In the Toastmasters program, the pathway I was on is called Team Collaboration. I presented speeches on leadership, mentorship, and also learned more about how to tell a story. I practiced working with audience awareness, I learned much about speaking to a group, and the skills gained spill from an overflowing cup into saucers, sometimes.

I don't want to feed people crumbs or a tipped drink, though. Getting to the meat and potatoes of my message isn't always crisp and clear, and I obfuscate the truth sometimes. I can make things complex or convoluted, and though I don't do so intentionally, we get to the heart of the matter.

From my desire to live, love, and thrive, I extend with the Introversial prerogative to allow us to learn, create, play, and pray. I'm hesitant about the prayer part, yet it holds fast to my mind. We learn to share paths with people, yet another thing we learn is how to gather people to walk and see those paths together.

It's nice to go for a walk outside, and I prefer walking even better when I can talk with someone on a stroll. If Robert Frost wrote of the two divergent paths in *The Road Not Taken,* I wonder if I'm blazing trails or want to walk the trails to get blazed. I feel comfort in knowing I've already travelled the drug path, even if I don't ever go back to it.

The signs call tempests to chill, and while the walls call temptations of the pill, I know what I miss about the drugs. I appreciate serenity knowing I don't chase Natalie or a high, and I used to believe drugs were love. I also used to believe in love like a drug, and though it's kind to know I can remember such things, I keep the scrabbled lessons. I'm meekly and wholly grateful I don't have to sacrifice my soul again.

Shackled to the debris of lost claims, I shift my aims towards the future. If I consider flourishing, it's still in formation, and while *Debris of Distance* is an idea to explore, perhaps the foundation is also a concept to work on. Fountains provide yet need replenishing to hold enough water for others to drink. However, some flow eternal and infinite.

I sip from the streams of tomorrow, yet I want to draw from the depths of yesterday piece by piece, bit by bit, and grain by grain as we form how the mosaic melds. I don't know how to tell you how this resolves, though it's because I didn't know where it's going.

If we start something, we often don't know where it will go, though if we want to go anywhere, we need to start. I started six years ago wishing and wanting to meet that one specific gal whom I thought was my soulmate. I realize that even if Natalie is a part of me, there's a multitude of others that matter to me too. No one can never replace the dreams we've held and seen.

In the centre of the riddle, one point of truth holds fast. Though I can't cast out demons or devils on my own accord, some others step in and push them out and forever away. I thank the forces of life and death for keeping us here orbiting around our sun.

If we think of all things as one, I realize that I, as one, can't comprehend how my thoughts are all. It takes a different form of energy to let me know I hold my life in my hands, and I wish, hope, and pray that none shall take it away.

SHIFTING SANDS

Magic: The Gathering has been an obsessive part of my life in the past decade. I've played a lot, I've owned a vast collection of cards, sold them all later, and I visited the local shops frequently when I had a car. The obsessive concerning point, though, was around the topic of money and imaginary funds.

I had thousands of dollars of cards I bought on eBay and from the stores. The issue, though, is that I'd purchased almost all of them with credit, which was debt and not actual cash. My irresponsible spending resulted in high-five-figures of debt, and in 2015 I sold my entire collection and had to declare bankruptcy.

I've grieved the loss of the cards and still feel a twinge of regret about selling all of them. I had more than forty dual lands and also two Moxes plus another few thousand cards that would be worth more than $30-$40k total in today's market. That said, I console myself by reminding myself I cleared my entire line of credit and credit card debt to zero when I went bankrupt. It was my credit that paid for the cards.

I'm not yet exceptionally successful in many areas of my life, though lessons rise from the results and solutions of my poor actions. "Take my advice, I'm not using it" is one quote I like. With my credit abuse and my explicit drug use as two examples, I can tell others about the consequences of bad decisions.

I want to break past hard lessons and lean into shared wisdom and success, by helping people know what to do, and showing them how to do it. The previous Fountain talked a bit about Providing Point and my charitable giving, yet this one was meant to be more about me for me. I've not yet gathered a high-income skill set to teach, and honestly, I need to learn more so we can work and achieve exceptional results.

Copywriting is a skill to develop, and I also need to learn more about selling and marketing. If I'm going to accomplish the goals I've set out in these books, I need to level up and quick. I'm fortunate I have some qualities required for success—perseverance, some empathy, earned experience, and good motives—yet I need and want to develop my interpersonal skills further.

I want to interact with a diverse range of people, and I want to increase my abilities to communicate and understand others. I want to learn how to share and show more genuine appreciation, and if I want to help more of Earth, I need to be ethical, stable, and sure in myself.

Confidence is an asset to cultivate, and so is an openness to learn, grow, and expand. Those skills are vital for our success, and as I evolve, change, and restructure, I also remember to hold fast to what I've learned to be right and just. I align my intents accordingly—choices about what we do and don't do matter.

As we move forward, more right choices make sure we also have something left to share. I like the pun there, did you catch it? Or were you left right out?

In the week before continuing this chapter, I started writing a book called *I Need to Tell You*. I set the book as a preorder for May 5th, 2020, which gave me a deadline to work towards, though I cancelled the project because of my motivations. I was writing a book to earn, not to convey value. Instead, a week after that, I began a different publication, *A Year in Change*. *I Need to Tell You* is a book of recommendations for people who want to live by working a creative profession and vocation, while *A Year in Change* is a journal tracking my life and process in a one-year timeframe.

The ability to learn something can come from the point of interest or accidental acquisition, and by learning, then doing, and then teaching, skills can fortify and secure. Though I've been cart before the horse person often, writing *I Need to Tell You* could bundle lessons I learn about how to activate success in life with a creative profession and vocation.

As awareness falls into my consciousness, I adapt, learn, share, and create. The process of building on the fly is a skill

I've used with the Fountains, though I've been hesitant in other fields. It's inspiring to know my skillsets are developing, and by sharing what I know with others, it can improve our situations.

The Fountains and Providing Point intend to gather and share abundantly with people, and with the creative guidebook, it's more about teaching and letting people find their hope and live a life they'll love. I want to help others who aren't trapped in poverty, too, because I wish to assist many people and not only one demographic.

People buying a book is a way to give to me and the causes I support monetarily, though I'd prefer it's because they believe in me and want to assist with supporting the objectives. It'd also be fantastic that people want to read my books as these books mean to help people to activate their Freedom Solutions. There is more value in them than just monetary support.

It's a neat thing to have multiple projects on the go, and because I value creative diversity, having open and concurrent plans assist when my interest wains or I meet a wall. I can go back to chipping away in a different quarry, yet structurally, I allow myself to ease up on the OCD parts of the Fountains and my writing style.

It's here I remember others have undiagnosed illnesses too. People riddled with profound anxiety, or people who are authentically depressed, may not have a psychologist or psychiatrist and are living undiagnosed. People's experiences best not be diminished or minimized, though, so I hope we can find ways to help those who are battling with symptoms and situations. Some diagnosed receive treatment, while those undiagnosed often don't.

I've had some crazy times, yet the medication I take assists me to be 'normal,' even if I think I'm still kind of weird. Differently, some think I'm entirely reasonable, and that *they're* the ones who are messed up. I don't believe we're incurable or ruined humans who don't deserve to live, I believe in wellness recovery and mental plasticity.

I've thought lots of negative things about myself at times, which might be why I'm occasionally paranoid; sometimes, I hate who I am. My books help me with my self-worth issues, and by becoming more explicit about who I am, my work improves and surfaces more of my intrinsic characteristics, values, and beliefs.

These books seem to be more resource-based as part of my long-term process and vision, and though a lot of what I've written may take many years to activate, by sharing my books and my hopes, goals, and dreams, there are some key lessons. I'm not teaching specific skills with the Fountains as far as I can tell, though perhaps there's some wisdom trickling within the streams of text.

People say we shouldn't compare ourselves to others, and I believe and understand the merit of that. Some people also minimize or normalize others' experiences by saying, "We all go through that" when some things are entirely messed up and not okay. Even if our experience is unique to us, minimizing or normalizing issues can seem to discount our validity. Condoning questionable behaviour because someone's labelled or diagnosed with a mental illness isn't right either, though.

With my mental issues, health, and capacity, I've thought I'm psychic, and telepathy is a common thing. Others think I'm entirely delusional because it's not in their realm of understanding or comprehension. I've often held ideas or beliefs about things others can't fathom, and though some may write me off as delusional (or attribute it to my drug history and use), it's difficult to discern what's real and legitimate when people tell me it's all a hallucination or fantasy.

Just because one idea doesn't gel or jive, though, it doesn't mean a project should be written off. Passion projects and processing journals may not seem to have a viable audience, yet I believe if we can get someone hooked on our work and give an interesting read, writing can be a win/win for reader and author. I hint to myself to keep working on my books because, eventually, one of them will sink into someone's heart, and another's, and then many more too.

I don't want to approach books as texts telling people to create for money, but I do want to write a document for those who create. I'd like to help people learn how to make money, though if I'm the one to tell people how to earn with their work, how can I do that if I've not done so myself? I may not yet know, though, with what I've learned, I activate valid success principles in my life too. It'd seem paradoxical to write a successful book about how to earn when I've not done so myself.

Is the Magic in the gathering? Can I form a knowledge product to earn sales and share content worth far more than the purchase price of a book? I think I can and shall, though a nagging pinch of doubt creeps into my shoulders. I try to push the feeling off and away, yet I felt it dig in a little more. That may be a section to write; how to build confidence in ourselves and our abilities so we can endure past all of our lingering fears, doubts, and limiting feelings.

And by the process of digging myself up and out of my situation, I learn how to thrive. Not just live, though, to thrive! Although I allude to my addictions and emotional wreckage, people who have persistent mental health issues understand some feelings feel like they'll never go away. There are fleeting moments of wish, hope, and faith, yet there are also parts of feeling awful and that no one cares or wants to communicate. I've felt that, and it's not nice.

New beginnings are a choice, yet with life, we have our entire existence before that moment. If we choose to make a fresh start, we've experienced so much before that moment of beginning. We've heard the saying 'forget not the past,' and while my past doesn't always haunt me, I know it's stuck in my subconscious. We build layers of time, day by day, creating the foundations of which we've set our lives upon.

I hope it's worth others joining me in the text to follow a path towards happiness and success. It's taken a considerable amount of effort and dedication, and I won't just leave it up for naught. This work matters to me, and I believe.

A week later, I thought of the idea of 'getting back on the horse' if we fall off. I noticed sometimes we might need to walk with the horse because it doesn't want to carry us. Who is the horse, who is the rider, and more importantly, where do we want to go? Without knowing a destination or objective, how can we proactively move towards success?

Bit by bit, grain by grain, and seed by seed, I learn and teach. Getting more definite about what I want to do is essential on my journey, and I need to see and experience progress and forward motion to help me feel worthwhile and be okay. A challenge is not only being okay, though also helping others to be all right. If others aren't, I can be a support and open ear for them to talk to, and just as my Mom can't 'fix' my situation, I can't fix others magically.

I can, though, be loyal, honourable, and trustworthy support and friend. I'm getting closer to finding my peace. Earlier in the day, I learned more about how I am as a human and friend on this planet. I honoured a female friend who is in a relationship by not attempting to sway her one way or the other. She's a marvellous human being, though I want her to make her own choices without tempting fate by speaking what I think is best. If I don't always know what's best for me, though, how could I tell her what's best for her?

Even if I think a person must follow their heart and make their own choices, I want to help other people learn more about themselves and how to make good choices. As I learn more about what is right for me, I find and share how people can act with integrity in line with principles that guide us to believe.

I find a gal who has similar intents and ethics as me, one who wants to work together, and we form a mutually loving and respectful relationship. With the next ten years of my life, I move forward into my fifties, and I don't want to do it alone.

I heard somewhere our forties are where we solidify the pillars of who we are, and I was also told we learn who we are in our thirties. Perhaps I'm a bit behind on the learning curve because I'm still learning things about myself that I'd not known before. I hope to continue to surprise myself by finding out more parts of myself that I like and admire.

I'd like to advance my financial position by clearing all of my debts and forming a buffer fund for emergencies. This year (2020) needs to be a year of solidifying a few things beyond completing *Mosaic of Miracles*. I wanted to have the base text of this book written by my birthday, May 2nd, and then revise it to a finished version. Alluding to the saying I've heard time and time again, I need to get my Oxygen mask on first, and quick.

With broken commitments and promises, I allude to the fuel of the duals and how it correctly stands that I've pissed away the sands. Yesterday was a decent day, and with a deep breath, I let out a yawn.

It was 3:57 AM March 4th when I had written this much, and I was ready to go to bed. I don't like going to bed for the nights where I don't landscape the next day, though I can, on rare occasions, make profitable use of my time as I learn how to sell myself on my dreams.

I wonder about 2021's releases. Before finishing the *Debris of Distance* project, I needed to complete this book. My hesitant and rushed beliefs cross-sect and redirected me into gaining my footing and setting my feet back upon a stone. We've only three years to go to 2023, where my five-year future self had written to me in *Seeds of Tomorrow*.

Although my faith holds a variant concern, I wonder if the cigarettes must continue to burn. I feel a bit of guilt and shame for my nicotine abuse and addiction, as I don't want to damage myself. I want to secure my faith and trust in myself, God, and the Universe, and even if I've messed up the order of the words, the worlds that we mix within hold a thin layer of a shell. I trust myself enough to know I won't toss or puff because there has been enough of both already.

And so, as I steady myself and get ready for the next day, I send a wish and hope to pray that we live forever past today. I cannot claim the aim or name of the one who held me up against the wall, yet I think it's time to get ready to work and enjoy the summer and find a lovestone for fall.

I may crawl into bed late on my open evenings, yet streams of ideas and dreams remember tribes hold fast and compete together, functioning as unified teams.

Let yourself soak in the calm and warm waters, daughter. You may not recall I went away to find your mother, yet please remind your brother that we forget not about Celest. Some people tell us we can be better than the best, and I hope my audacity helps me climb the wall. Because, as far as I can tell, there may not yet be footings to grip and hold us up.

Remember, your mother loves your children and you. Forward to their birth year in two thousand fifty-two.

DIPPING IN THE WATER

I started the *A Year in Change* project near the end of February, beginning from a place of *not* being okay. I found myself feeling useless and hopeless, and with the project, I turn myself into determined, hopeful, and successful.

What success is for each of us is also different for each of us. Some find family life and a happy and healthy core family unit as the ultimate objective, while others see fame and fortune as the optimal goal or situation. I've wanted a family and wealth, though not fame. It seems I'm a long way from either, though.

I didn't have a girlfriend to start a family beyond Zeus and me when this book released, and my bank accounts we certainly lacking. I'm wealthy in some ways compared to others by having my apartment, a job I like, and access to food, water, and a bathroom, and fortunately, I also have late nights and open days to dive into work when I find I want to focus.

My health is decent even if I smoke ciggies, I barely ever get sick, and I also have great potential for social and spiritual wellness. Continuing with gratitude and thankfulness, I have my cat, a cup of coffee, and this book to form too.

Additionally, I've learned a lot in the past few months and have an openness to connection and communication with friends and family. I love the phone, and I believe in being honest and making mistakes so I can continue to develop and learn. I've wished to have more in my financial accounts, yet I'm glad and thankful to have what I have.

My desires aren't always on the forefront, yet it's true I've been all right and well supported by a few sources and people. My Mom has helped in a few ways, and I'd like to return her favours. Mom sent me grocery cards with a brief note for quite a while, and I kept most of the letters she sent. I want to return the full value of the food given to me by Mom, yet I'm not sure when I'll have enough money to do so. She may not accept the offer, though if she does, I hope it'll be a welcome return she can use well.

I learn how to earn my way in life, and I begin to afford much more than Mom told me I could. One of the parental beliefs stuffed at me has been the saying, "you can't afford that," and I break from such programming.

My friend Arlinn and I talked about how I'd been since I came home from my 2020 Australia trip. I'd not been well, and Arlinn's recommendation is to use positive affirmations. She means well, and I know that she cares, though I'm not going to deceive myself and speak lies. I'm a pretty kind, unique, and forthgoing person, yet often when I get stressed out at things, the first words out of my mouth are cursive and demeaning. It's terrible when I start swearing at myself.

I live life differently than many, and although some issues are similar to others, the way we handle and deal with our problems needs to work well for us to thrive. My lessons may not yet be fantastically clear, yet I gain enough wisdom to assist inspiration. I'm a loyal friend, and though I want to be radically open and honest, as a communicator, I also don't want to home in on and focus on faults.

I'm not so easy on myself, though it's worth it.; I think it helps guide me to do better. I'd pondered if I wanted to continue with Toastmasters, and even with a reluctance to quit, I left the Wednesday night club. There are all sorts of pros and cons, yet my feelings and intuition are what I need to heed as authentic guidance. Toastmasters helped me a lot with my ability to speak, though I wasn't gaining much joy from the program near the close.

Many Toastmaster nights resulted in late nights writing much of the Fountains books, though, yet I didn't know if the creative nudge was worth it. I won't act from a point of defiance, yet perhaps I need to strengthen my backbone and ability to make choices. I quit, and if I find I want to go back, I can. Making prepared speeches didn't enthuse me at all, though, as time evolved, I learned how to talk to an audience.

I started writing this chapter in early March 2020 before continuing. Back then, there wasn't the practice of social distancing, and the idea of quarantining ourselves wasn't even a thought, and when I resumed, it was April 3rd, 2020. It was quite different with pandemic restrictions and allowances. The stock market had crashed, getting groceries wasn't such an easy task, and brick and mortar businesses (and other large corporations) were in jeopardy of closing down in a global crisis.

I put this book on the sidelines because I was landscaping a lot and also because I didn't feel inspired to create it. The goal was to complete this book and combine it with the previous two before November this year (2020), yet I enrolled in a course that helped me set a release for July 31st, 2020. With the project *A Year in Change*, I attempt and succeed in building positive habits such as reading every day, focusing on learning and connection, and also cleaning my home. That book is very much my journal.

I'd not tended to the Fountains barely at all, and what I wrote before COVID-19 seemed old. Freedom is a high value, and I want to do things that enliven me and excite me. It had been a terrible feeling speaking at Toastmasters sometimes, and while some love being called to talk at the meetings, I wasn't thrilled to do so.

It's good to expand and extend our comfort zones, though, and I realize I've complained and made a lot of excuses. I'm not part of the Toastmasters group due to disliking the obligation to speak, and in April, it was my last month with the club.

Some say we need to do things we don't like to grow and expand, and I agree with that. Doing difficult things expands our capacity to do other things, and some argue attending a meeting is also a social event. I'd barely talk to people during the breaks, though, and it became more of an obligation than a pleasure.

Another thing I've complained about is how few seem to *want* to connect with me. Barely anyone calls, I've been ghosted by some, and I'm certainly not popular. Other than Arlinn and a couple of other friends, hardly anyone was calling me other than my parents. Even if I reached out to some here and there, an exceptional few would seek me out for conversations.

A lesson I learned near this point of the text is that a core desire I hold is to be valuable. I feel compelled to provide more for people, and though it's appreciated that people are kind, love can be the better offer. Is that a reversal? Is it people think I don't care, like, or love them?

When I get wrapped up in books and daily tasks, I focus so much on myself, my needs, and my wants, and even with Zeus, I love him dearly, though I have neglected him because I've been too busy working on the computer. When I'm out of the house landscaping, Zeus at also home alone then.

When I stop to pause for Zeus, I've felt awful for returning to the computer because I know I don't give him enough attention. We can choose to adjust our actions, though, so I don't fall into the trap of feeling guilty. Let's bring back the discussion to positive things.

Work is an excellent thing for me. During spring 2020, many people lost their jobs and had no idea what to do for income. I kept my landscaping job, and my friend Elspeth also joined the landscaping team. Elspeth can drive the truck and trailer, and honestly, she's a much better worker than I am. She demonstrates a fantastic work ethic and skill, yet add to that fact she's often had a marvellous attitude, bright and cheery energy, and a sweet tone of voice; she also helps Zeus and me out a lot with our life.

I meekly understand and accept that I have a fortunate situation, and I'm dearly glad about it. Having a job and home are crucial variables, though liking and appreciating both of them causes me to be grateful. My cat has been excellent and kind, and with the global recession and market conditions, I know I'm lucky not to be as severely affected as some others have been.

Even if I don't have lots of money, I'm thankful to have an

income where I can set aside some money and invest a bit as of now. Considering how I am at the point of this recession, I know I'll be set and ready to capitalize on the next one.

I filed my 2019 taxes and found I drew in one and a half times as much money in 2019 than 2018. Although I'm not sure how I believe I'll earn even more this year, I've been positively money-focused sometimes and make good choices. When I focus too much on money and calculations, though, I realize that it takes my attention away from other activities and people I'd like to connect with and enjoy.

Though working on books keeps me separate and apart, it'd be nice to know about who I'm writing to before I type things on the computer. I guess with social media, I have an idea of who *could* read what I write or post, though to have absolute confirmation would be helpful.

I recorded a brief video at the close of the day for about a week, and though I didn't continue, I thought it something I'd do consistently in the future. I wonder how we evolve in the next years. Shall there be heaps of online activity? How shall we thrive and support others and ourselves in the future?

Have I been wise, or am I foolishly putting money into things that will not net a return? If I get over-focused on funds and investing instead of people, will I continue to be alone at home alone with Zeus as I ponder what to do?

Shall I reach out to more people with my books and music? I rationally cannot predict the future, yet I can build and plan for it. The Fountains seemed like they were running dry because I wasn't clear about the books sharing the kind clear waters I hope them to be.

Perhaps it's time to find alternate sources of life and water and not rely so much on these texts? As the world was on hold and near lockdown from COVID-19, it became another challenge to overcome to allow me to thrive. I felt chemical feelings pushing from behind my eyes like I'd been swimming in a chlorinated pool. I needed to break.

(And then a few days later, I resumed)

On April 8th, 2020, I spoke with a dear friend, Ruth, who used to manage the group home I lived in during 2002-2004. When talking with Ruth, I thought again about using Providing Point pledges to buy homes. Previous figures calculated we'd need 200x people to give $25/month to purchase homes in under 3 ½ years, though with adjustments from the call, a different plan arose due to the difficulty of gathering 200 people.

If the purchase price of a home is $200k, we could, instead, put the house or apartment on a 30-year mortgage when we have *fifty* people contributing $25/month. Fifty is a quarter of the number of people as an initial idea, yet it's not only about adjusting the number of people to give, it also is about ways to own more homes sooner.

Fifty units of $25/month are $1,250 a month, which could repay a 4.5% interest loan in 20 ½ years. That's not faster, though it's quicker acquisition because it requires fewer people per home. Ideally, I'd love to pay the mortgages down faster, though finding the crucial people and variables to kick start the housing program was the challenge when I wrote this.

If we aimed for fifty people to pledge $25/month, then as we gather more people, we could pay down the debt sooner and reduce interest costs. The hurdle of gathering people to buy the first home is a daunting challenge, though to quote Keiran Fitzpatrick, "I have a plan!" Keiran also told us plans don't always work out how we intended, yet and he recommends we keep making plans and adjust and recalculate our endeavours. I can. I do. I shall.

Crunching the figures and numbers to plot and plan is one thing I can do. For every $25/month pledge past the first fifty in the idea shared in this chapter could put $10/month towards the first mortgage, and $15/month aside into Providing Point's account to pool up our resources. I say *our* resources, because this is a collective effort and not only me.

Each person that pledges to Providing Point matters, and if I confer with them for our purchasing decisions, we can use democratic leadership for our work. When I wrote this, we had fewer than ten patrons, though we gather more.

Providing Point is my initiative, and it's an extension of my book work and commitment to giving and sharing. I understand anyone who pledges as a patron or housing contributor for CHP allows us to do what we do, and it's my responsibility to operate and expand the programs. Because it's others who enable us to give and let us thrive as we do, I owe much to those who give pledges in the cause of providing for people. Many need and want additional support, and we're a valuable group of people who become more to produce.

With the figures shared in this chapter about $25/month from fifty people, by adding $10/month from pledges beyond the first fifty to the outstanding debt for our first home, we could accelerate the payments. If we set aside the other $15/month for future purchases past those first fifty people, we also could build a buffer in case people withdraw.

According to the plan, for the first home, we'd need a down payment and fifty Seed Contributors. A Seed Contributor is someone who pledges $25/month to Providing Point, though this model was not the final answer. People wouldn't receive an equity share like an idea I share later in this book. It also became Chilliwack Housing Providers to own the homes, while Providing Point focuses with grocery card support.

Another idea was that for the first 100 people to sign up as a Seed Contributor, Providing Point could grant a 1% equity stake in our first home. What about dropouts, though? It wouldn't be rational to consider people donating for five or ten years, would it? What if someone bought into the idea and then scooped later?

Fifty units of $25/month could allow us to have enough to mortgage a place when we have 50 patrons, yet the liability of the mortgage would be a significant risk. If we had one hundred contributors for the first home, we'd be closer to acquiring a second home, yet the debt of the first would be lingering. 20 ½ years is a long time, and I can't expect patrons to pledge for such a duration. It'd be nice, yet nowhere near rational to believe most would.

I've not talked much about blockchain technology or cryptocurrencies in this book yet. It may seem askew, yet I've learned a bit about blockchains and crypto and from what I've learned, smart contracts can tokenize resources. Micropayments and multi-signature contracts can facilitate fractionalized ownership, and the idea impels me.

Multiple people could share in owning $200k homes, and as we expand our capacity to buy and own homes to rent to people for $375/month, the figure of $375 is one thing I set in stone. That's because income assistance allows that much for the monthly shelter portion on recipients' cheques, though can we also create investment opportunities?

The plan is to enable people access to affordable housing within the governmentally allocated amount, yet the big crux and limitation are me. These plans to provide homes require money, and I need to build the program.

I've been attempting to find lures for people to give. Yet, as I persevere with shaping these ideas, plots, and plans, perhaps I inevitably stumble on the right blend of tact, value, and calls to heart and action that allow Providing Point and Chilliwack Housing Providers to thrive. It takes far more than one kid and his books, though. It requires people like you.

DIVING IN THE POOL

Okay, it's time to reclaim my life and grab hold of the future. I invest in a combined yield for those who've revealed You and us to be true. (That includes many more than a few).

Anyone who buys and reads one of my books may be interested in me and what I have to say, so thank you! I hope we may entice others to look into my heart and text. I appreciate the value people give me by buying and reading my books, playing my music, or, as I've found in the past two weeks, watching my videos.

I started recording nightly Facebook live videos on April 1st, 2020. Although I barely saw any activity from people on the videos in the comments, a few of the nightly videos went well. A walker friend (Xenegos), a patron (Godo), and another Magic friend (dear Ben) hopped online, watched, and interacted with me as I recorded. The night before, dear Miss Ashley and my cousin typed in their comments while I sat on my patio speaking to the screen.

I realize if I want to gain followers and a mass audience, I can broadcast openly on Facebook, and post publicly on groups. I can record on Instagram and put myself out to the world of strangers, yet I've been hesitant to do so. I want to deepen my connections with those I like, love, and admire already, while also finding more readers.

I accept meeting new people is an opportunity, though I have horrendous trust issues from my spotted and tainted past. It could mean playing small, though, and even if I appreciate and enjoy my tiny, monotonous, and super-kind life, I'm not sure I want millions of followers. What, though, about leaning into the fear of being well-known?

Realizing I prefer connecting with people, I still can be selective and cultivate a kind and peaceful garden. I tend the fields by keeping Providing Point open, yet even with that project, I believe that it'll be a great work of a many, instead of a mass supplement by the majority.

The Providing Point premise of having every person give $5/month to house the entire homeless population isn't rational, yet I may not be reasonable. Others have told me that providing just a few grocery cards is beneficial and also more than others give, and yet that may be true, some shards improve the meld. I want to expand our groups and find ways to provide much more than we yet have, and though I have a home, a job, and my cat, giving food, homes, and connection, let me know we grow.

I'll confer with people on big-spending decisions for the company, though the program is operating as an extension of me as of July 2020. Because *I've* received support, I'm inclined to give more back. If I didn't receive income assistance and support from my parents, I'd have a dramatically different life.

Because I have many blessings, and what seems to be the absolute luxury of a job and home, I can do far more than I would be able to without those supports. With gratitude for abundant sources, I understand I'm fortunate, and I want others to have such fantastic things for themselves, too. That's an R-word, reciprocity, in PLU8R.

I've written that I wish to earn like the 1% and share 99%, and as of *Mosaic of Miracles'* release, I contribute $150/month to Providing Point. With the support of less than a dozen other people, we're sharing seventeen $15/month reloadable grocery cards, though that's our what. What I'm telling you in this chapter is more about my why, reciprocation.

What I'd like to know is why *other* people would want to give to Providing Point. What can we do to tend the needs and desire to let us expand? If my intuition is correct, people believe in me and give contributions because of what I work for and believe in and want to support such. How may I find more people to read and pledge?

I believe in a Universal Basic Income. If *every* person received $1,260 per month free, then we would have Full Seed. Full Seed is a concept I wrote about first in Fountain four. It's when *all* people have their food, shelter, and necessary transportation provided for them. Locally, it requires $15,128/year ($1,260/month) per person to allow Full Seed to manifest.

Many people receive and earn more than $1,260/month, yet the $5 idea of Providing Point is to provide Yearly Seeds (one person's coverage) one by one until we can care for everyone. The $5 plan is a concept stipulating that if *every* person in the Fraser Valley gave $5/month, we could house *all* the people who need and want a home, yet don't have one at this time.

I moved forward with the $5 idea with Providing Point gathering via Patreon, though I ran into hurdles. I chose to message all of my Facebook friends, yet when I messaged a year or so ago, I was directly going for the hook, to ask for a pledge. Although we gained a couple of patrons, I changed most of my friends into contacts.

Contacts are people we know that know us. There's usually a catch as to why one would message the other, and in my case, I was attempting to gather pledges and sell books. I was treating my friends as customers. I made money my focus, and it was in those times I lost a lot of friends. It was similar to when my attention was buying, selling, and trading Magic cards. The result of those actions was Bankruptcy in 2015.

I've not worked on my book *Nodal Input* for a long while. I remember that book because it includes my codes and subvert knowledge, yet the title tweaked in here because of the Magic reference of Moxes. I blend in an Emerald to slag a Tic Tok link and how I thought to get another drink.

I've sipped sad and slow from the entire union of woe, yet how can people slink into the wink brought up to sup with a risen cup? I dive into the pool after filling it up. A pledge may mean it's in between the line to straighten my spine, yet if I don't have to landscape, I can tape up the poster of how these things started to host PLU8R.

Before speaking signs of lines to meld and weld, I'm held by those who've gelled and spelled the son of Ron to be a swan over moonlit dawn. If my books are for me, the people who like me, love me, or those who support me and believe in my causes, I need and share kindness, love, and compassion abundantly.

I may be doing the right things for the right reasons, yet the trippy part is knowing when it's right, and also how to connect with the correct people. I'm glad, grateful, and thankful to continue this journey of text, time, and trust, and though I might lust a bit now and then, the pad and pen keep hands in the bands for dual lands.

It was thirty-eight minutes past ten on April 18th, 2020, when I continued to add to this book. It had been a trippy past couple of weeks, yet clarity hones as I receive grace and gladness. The gladness reminds me that my work is for our community and not only for me.

In the next week, I may only have one landscaping shift, yet that excites me because I can get back to working on my relationships and creative projects. I dearly appreciate my boss and his job, yet I need to get past working for a wage and focusing so much on hourly earnings and what I want just for myself.

Here, I think of two types of wants. One, our selfish focal desires, wanting things only for our own lives, and two, outwards and openly seeking our core desires to benefit society and the world at large. When I'm landscaping, I think narrowly of the landscaping team. Yet, when I get myself in front of the computer writing, I work to activate substantial dreams for our more extensive and expansive future.

Since I don't fantasize or imagine well, I trust my impulsions and conscience to make this for us. It also was only in the past year that I learned the term trust fund baby. I didn't know or understand the concept that some people have never had to work. They've had anything they've wanted given to them, and I think, in some ways, I've been like that a bit too.

Even if I have a job, I have received a vast amount of time, money, resources and connection because of a fortunate birth and situation I couldn't forecast for myself. With things happening in the United States, I know some of it is due to the tone of my skin, and I'm not sure how I got into this situation in life. I'm also not yet sure how to allow others such fortuitous circumstances.

Where I mentioned I want to give due to reciprocity, I can't comprehend how I landed my home. With the concept of taking 100% responsibility for our life, I couldn't ever (as far as I'm aware) forecast or have planned many of the parameters of my life. I attribute my situation due to extraordinary circumstances that I never chose for myself, and even if I'm fantastically glad for such, why can't other people have such fortune and luck for themselves too?

And yet the 100% responsibility point reminds me it's my responsibility to do the best that I can with my circumstances. I don't understand how yet, though I accept and appreciate my gratefulness and atone well by doing what I need to do. Since it's my choice as to how I respond, act, and behave, I admit that I didn't know, think, or understand how I could be like a trust fund baby without knowing about it sooner.

Why do I have such an easy life compared to some others who've had to fight, bleed, and struggle for everything they have? Why would people need to suffer so much to have their life honoured and respected by care and support of society? Why do people need to struggle? I have difficulty understanding or accepting that the choices I've made about how I live and behave could assist me in having such a healthy and brilliant life, yet it's not all due to a blend of wise choices.

I've fluxed between denial and grasping my fate as one due to a life of contribution. Is it because I do what I do that allows me magnificent blessings, or am I fed massive fortuitous abundance without my consent? It finds me baffled about my situation. The fact I'm actively thriving isn't only because of my choices, is it?

My life may be rigged, aiding my optimistic outlook, and I may show the result of having it easy. Can people adjust their perspective always to be positive? I think we may, though it takes consecrated effort and action. Writing these books evolves my attitudes and ethics, yet the Fountains started by wishing to meet a famous singer.

As I wrote, the books moved me through time. From a relationship that was a no-go, I shifted with the singer still lingering in my conscience and soul. I pushed out and past that into working for the world and not only for meeting Natalie. It's bizarre to think in rare moments that by denying her, I urged myself to work for others beyond myself, yet people have been pushing and pulling strings of the loom to allow us to resume.

Instead of being her groom, it's so amazingly clear to me that she might want me to live for the world instead. I've been one to ask the world, "why can't we love?" when twelve books find me shunting away from dreams again. All the while, I see I fell back into an acidic pathway. Why does the name Natalie pass my mind when it seems the only way I can ever understand her is when all the threads unwind?

"I still don't know."

I see how the Fountains are entirely a different form of writing than *A Year in Change*. The Fountains twist and pull my heart and soul across the landscapes of above and below, while the other book is just a way to let us know.

I get cryptic riddles woven in with these words, yet the feelings I experience are entirely different than just telling you about my life. Fountain books are not easy to write. The work torques my being and seems to turn me inwards to guilds as a defence.

I want each to thrive, and when I'm one to have a great situation, I don't always understand how I can share such luck. Some say our lives are our own doing, yet I don't often think about how others make their life too. When others have difficult or troubling experiences or have all sorts of misfortune happen to them, it's disturbing to me to consider others have a primary role in creating that for themselves.

If I'm living so kindly, is it honestly, indeed, and entirely because I live right and well? Gabby Bernstein says her friend

Joel has a steady, secure, and stable life because he made many little right choices. I hope that's what I can do with my life, yet I know I've made thousands of poor decisions. Where is the grace that others can also have that allows us to move forward?

For what I do and receive, can there not be a balance to assure others may gain without having another give in or lose? *Shards of My Soul* is a book I'm afraid hadn't yet found its place, though perhaps the mosaic can repent. If sands pass one after the next, is the hourglass nailed down, or can we spin it back and invert upon itself, resetting the timeline?

I need to stop here. I feel too much pressing on my skull with the energy of tentative certainty.

It was 11:27 PM, April 18th, 2020, then.
I came back to this near 11 PM on April 21st.

With a link from my aunt Lori, her idea is that life is just a bunch of paragraphs. Who shall be in the next one I write? Is it amazingly accurate to see the view of how I'm explicitly not You?

Capital letters called the underlining I used to mind when I lived at SFU. Back then, when Microsoft Word underlined a bit of text in the blue squiggles, I thought it was Natalie talking to me; hence I called her QBlue. If emphasized in red (a spelling mistake), I called it NRed and also thought it was her. Both those interpretations were my mind hinting for me to believe she was communicating with me, yet I was delusional according to rational thought.

When one is delusional, he or she may believe the falsities are the absolute truth. The difficulty teaching, showing, or telling a person what the truth is, without calling them down for imagination, is that if we denounce another's belief, there can be layers of shame, anger, and denial in the flux. The radical views another hold may be clutched to as gospel truth when the facts claimed are hogwash. I still don't know if Natalie is a delusion or reality, yet I've learned a lot this year.

I bet I was delusional about Natalie, yet some spiritual

guidance and contialitic (conscious) awareness, plus absolute feelings in my body, allure me to believe in hope. As much as I think, I find myself wishing it wasn't real; my heart and soul claw at fate for a reversal that could manifest it as such. I don't know who she is, and I can't claim any knowledge of a solution. Other than what I think or believe, by understanding, I *don't* know, and it doesn't mean she doesn't know either.

Celest? Are the previous generations above or below us? Are we climbing upward, or releasing others to the sky? What if Elspeth is right and the atmosphere is an abyss and not the heavens? What if, when we look up to the sky, we're peering into a bottomless pit of time and space? Could we be looking and falling away into infinity?

Do the dare few drops of habitual water pool and gather well enough to form a sip of new divinity? If the water stops, does it again flow for us? Perhaps, my dear kitten. Yet remember there is always a bowl of water from which you may drink, Zeus.

You don't need me to turn on the water to quench your thirst, yet I wish you an excellent clean drink of water. I need to give up on crying out in dire desperation for the waters to flow when I cannot demand them. Instead, please drink that put out for you with a reminder; this human doesn't have it out for you. The waters of life are placed there for us when we choose to drink like the others. I accept what's there.

I don't need to drink the waters of Natalie as I thought I needed. I wish I could sip a drink with her, yet as the years progress, perhaps she wants that I drank from a different cup. Maybe she knows of my desires, yet the fires call over the coals of our souls. We may quench our thirst with most clean water, yet the desired streams need appreciation, attention, and protection compared to thinking we drink from only one. Thank you for taking a sip.

FORK THE COUNTER

The chapter title is a Magic reference. I realize I'm addicted to a few things other than cigarettes, and some of those addictions have hankered on me for a few years. A few of them have for more than a decade, though two big ones I think of are spending money on things, yet more recently, my technological dependencies have been an issue.

Constantly checking email accounts, bank accounts, prices, and also Facebook notifications have become a psychological leash to me and my daily activities in life. Writing, reforming, and producing these books is a fuse of chemical and cosmological energy, yet I don't like how substances have been the fuel for me and my identity either.

I've often bragged and proclaimed when I'm going to over caffeinate and put myself to the plow. I've so often written about my vices, yet some of them hide behind the curtain. Some spells require a point of green mana, yet the X cost is something that could easily be Mana Drained. That might not make sense to non-Magic people, though.

I want to be honest and share my secrets. My Dad would recommend for me not to do so, and in the past, he's told me to keep my tainted history and wrong actions from the discussion. With my Mom and my Dad, I want to be fully open and honest, yet there are a couple of things I want to share with them that I fear Mom and Dad would react negatively. One is my investment choices, and those link to my spending habits. Mom hates foolish surprises. Dad, too.

A friend and I talked about a potential deal at this point in the first draft. The friend had a 2009 Mazda 3 that we were considering leasing to me. The sale wasn't in writing yet, though I was to share the proposal with my Dad. I wanted to see and hear what he thought. The numbers would be $200 a month for insurance, $150-$200 a month gas, and $100 for a lease payment. Those figures were almost within bounds of my current budget, yet it'd be $450-$500 I could invest or put towards my mortgage debt instead. The choice was not to follow through with the deal.

Talking about having a car again is maybe contradictory to Providing Point ideas, yet I want to have a better life than I've had up to now. I want to provide for people (the grocery cards and homes), yet I also want good things for me too.

People's desires are different, yet is it a universal or prevalent thing for people to want more? Some, I guess, want less or as little as possible, yet I'm more a person who wants to evolve, grow, and shift further into abundance. I would be glad to have a few things of which I've yet to acquire, and I hope people don't get mad at me for that.

I humbly wish and thank God and other forces of life for allowing me what I have. I'm exceptionally fortunate, and though I mention it a lot, it's from a form of gratitude and reverence. I know some don't have a home or food, and I'm writing to you about wanting to have a car!?

It's not easy, and I can't tell you if it should or shouldn't be. I realize I have it *a lot* easier than some others, and I accept I have more than some, and though I appreciate what I have and gain, I also wish for balance and abundance to progress and evolve further.

The Glass House is something I mentioned in *The Sands of Yesterday (The Second Three Fountains)*, yet feedback from a reader said she didn't understand what I meant. The home builds in 2024-2025, yet I don't know how yet. I can see the entire inside of the house, and I'm baffled how I push and pull it to manifest it five years from now.

If these are the Fountains of Fantasy, I encourage you to fantasize and dream too. If you can envision fantastic and marvellous things for your future, I remind you some visions and daydreams may become a reality. We may not yet know how we get to those moments, yet imaginations can manifest in our living world.

Dream of good things, have fantastic hopes for the future,

and also actively admit if those dreams are what you want. If they are, make it so.

A basic dream I hold is to have enough money to afford the new and beautiful home; I wish to have a positive net worth, zero debt, and to have more than enough to provide for a family of five plus three cats. I want to live with a woman until she and I are well into our eighties or older, and I've thought to produce grandkids for Mom and Dad. I want to be able to fly anywhere in the world to visit family and friends, and also to be able to fly loved family and friends to my home to visit for a few days or weeks.

I want to have a profession and vocation based on communication and connection where I can teach others the required and needed skills for success. I want to work with people so we can thrive and find our Freedom Solutions, and I also want to work on my book projects and record a track every now or then. I don't want too much attention or to be super-famous, though that may be a consequence.

I want to earn and gather money for my projects and programs, and I also want to generate and earn royalties from my books and music. It's not entirely irrational, either. If I ease up on myself and my projected need to have meaning and value, I also hope to lighten up on the smoking and lose the fat around my belly. Having healthy lungs and a strong heart can let me go on adventures that few would ever have the chance to experience.

My wishes, wants, and dreams call me into the future, and though I don't want to force or open the Akashic Records, I'd like to have some signs that tell me how the dreams I hold come to be in life.

As admissions of love crawl into the dove, we find a kind threat. The difference is it's a beautiful remission that winds the loom that calls the cross aside. I reside in and develop how I weave the thread about how the difference between T and D might see lines and sing signs. I've enclosed myself in yields of text, yet does the context remind me how to keep the peace?

Some wish to pull the fleece, yet it may be geese to renew

227

how we use a cue. If I'm to generate a message, it must hold integrity, and I must communicate it to necessary people. We, hopefully, align a beneficial result for much more than only me.

Telling the truth can be easy, yet to also have value and meaning, I think, is the pursuit. Kate Tempest mentioned, "happiness, the brand' in her recording *Hold Your Own*, and though I don't think I'm searching for happiness primarily, I'm seeking to feel and be okay. Maybe the way I find that is by ensuring I cure my faults held clear in the vaults.

If I slow down and press the keys at a different pace, I hear the rhymes lace each press of space. As if I had a clue of grace, there may be another place to live, yet as far as I sieve the time and text, the next climb into the pit is where I hope we may sit. It is not Hell, yet rather a place where we may tell each other about how Aeris has a brother, and her mother is one I know.

I can't yet hear them say and agree it to be so, yet the spin of kin and kind wind my sins awkwardly within the mind. Let us design the line to share the trine.

Can I ask her for a drink? Would she let the slow sip tip the cup into the graduated cylinder of PLU8R? This reminds me of another who isn't her, yet can I slant the fur into a full-court press? Do we yet make the oil for those who toil and task?

Remind me to ask the olive skin of how I barely recall we can and do relevate in this life. It's a drop within an ocean, yet the smile struggle potion sips a notion of crossed devotion. It's sometimes how we know grandmas drive too slow.

If my purpose is to love and provide, and my mission is always to be okay, does it mean the late nights are working towards that, or just tossing it all away? I adore my cat, and while I've not thought of him so often at work, I often want to pick him up and give him massive hugs. Zeus doesn't always like that so much, yet one big way I show affection is through physical touch. Thankfully COVID doesn't apply to my cat and the few rare people that I can see and know.

And yet, who's there in my arms when it's time to sleep in my bed? Some nights Zeus curls up on the corner of my bed, yet I've not laid in the same bed as a gal for more than a decade.

It's been twenty years since I've had sex, yet it's also a weird thought that some people have never had intercourse before. It's doubly strange that some people never have sex until married, and if that was true for me, I might have been a virgin my entire existence into the age I am now, forty-two.

There's a movie, *The 40-Year-Old-Virgin*. There's also a movie called *The 40 Year Version*. The first is clearly understood, though the other is about an artist starting a rap career when she's forty. I'm not mimicking either starring role, yet they seem oddly aligned. In one case, I've been without sex for decades, and for the other, I want to succeed with sharing my voice via online distribution. The critical point is, perhaps I should work on finding my voice, and not often 'finding' myself.

Anyhow, the world is weird, wild, and beautiful. It was near the start of May 2020 when writing the first draft of this chapter, and I received feedback about my book *The Sands of Yesterday*. The feedback rings true with this book also; there isn't a formal proposed opening, middle, and conclusion, and I talk a lot about my thought process, of which few have an interest. I remember that the feedback also encouraged me to continue writing for therapy and the intrinsic value, not commercial viability.

What business would you like to run? Would you approach business from the point of what product or service you want to sell, and would you see the company purely as a vehicle to earn money? Would it be not to have a boss, or to work from home or abroad? Would you run a business from the viewpoint of achieving a particular result from your work that isn't financial?

With my work, I've approached the point of view that it's best is to create for and from a purpose. A vital part of our businesses is remembering we may not start our companies for the same reasons we endure with them. Providing Point is what I started, and yet it's an extension of myself and what I do, I've not, however, gathered many stakeholders that want to contribute and work alongside me up to now. With the few patrons we have, I appreciate the support, although a large share of what we gathered up to release was coming from me.

I want to be one contributor amongst a multitude, not a single person carrying a big part of the weight. With a shared equity model and numbers, a new parameter was two hundred people giving $5/week to own a 0.5% of a $200k home completely in near four years. The difference when I mentioned it this time is that I found the first person who would potentially sign up beyond me. I relayed the concept to the friend on the telephone, and he said if we can gather more people, he'd consider contributing.

A difference in that phone call, too, was how I didn't feel guilt and shame talking about gathering for the program. I've often felt grimy and sly anytime I even say "Providing Point" to people. When I mentioned the program's name in casual conversation to people, I'd often irk myself by shifting to a propositional notion.

To expand, I removed my limiting fears and concerns of judgment, and I also remind myself there is profound value in what we can do; to provide for people collectively. We're part of a local community, yet I need to build conversations about Providing Point more often and trust it's for our good.

It's taken a long while to get to being okay with talking about my hopes, goals, and dreams verbally. Because I've had a few legitimate friends who call or reach out to me, I see it as a sign that I had pushed people away from me. That's from where the grimy feeling came. I tried to sell, propose deals, or ask for Providing Point support without giving, and I pushed the vast majority of my friends and contacts away.

It's now my process and commitment to make a garden out of the desert. If other attempts to counterspell the years I've put into these books and foundational building persist, I may have to tap double red and Fork their counter. Back to Magic terms, if running in a Jund shell, I may not have access to blue for my counterspells, though I know Red Elemental Blasts would work well too, and Mindbreak traps are a thing.

Something I needed to keep in mind is to work on and

release *Mosaic of Miracles*. To do so, I needed to finish the first draft of this Fountain, revise and edit it, and release the Unlimited version. After that, I bundled the three individual books into the three-part compilation and reviewed it again.

By the point of the final edit, it was only a couple of months away from when I wrote this chapter, yet hopefully, the results of this book resound. Where shall we all be by then? Perhaps we'll be able to revisit other people's homes. Maybe, if we're allowed to visit, I'll have a home where people can gather for focus sessions again. Will people allow me the opportunity and privilege to work with them towards achieving their hopes, goals, and dreams?

I mean to be vital support, yet it requires trust and a willingness for others to share. If I'm allowed to talk about and help build other people's futures, I think it'd be fantastic for us all, and by being supportive of others, I gain a benefit of having function and purpose. When it's someone else's desires I'm tending to, it gives them a chance to excel and extrapolate their wishes into life while giving me a break.

By exploring dreams and fantasies, if we trust and allow ourselves to do so, we can activate miracles. It's by working together with people where the magic happens, and by being restricted to our homes, limited about who and where we can connect, it makes it difficult. Yet difficulty, when overcome, can result in beautiful things. A kind tap on my shoulder reminds me that I may be on the right track.

Let's examine the course of fate and destiny we're on. Are you at home alone because you needed to recalibrate and rebuild? Do pages, words, and visuals create your future? I hope we honour life when we're again allowed to bridge and bond, and I want us to move beyond the online and digital communications on which we've relied. A hug seems lucrative, yet that may be the wrong word. Perhaps not?

How will it feel to wrap your arms around them and feel them squeeze love back into you? That question may seem a weird question for some, yet many people have zero people to give a hug to these days. I can hug my cat, though he just tolerates me. What will it feel like to give and receive a genuine hug from someone who loves me thoroughly and entirely? It seems like a myth, a dream, or dare we, a fantasy.

How appropriate is it that these are the Fountains we're within? Something else that seemed a fantasy when I wrote this was not staying up super late on the nights before open or free days. It was 12:10 AM, though I'd stayed up until 3-4 AM or later most of my previous weekends.

I feel heavy in my feet planted on the floor as I push out the closing blocks of text for this section. Time, rhyme, and the climb give and aid my continuance, and if we're reading this book, it may be time to turn the page and read the next chapter. How you *could* respond at the end of this chapter is to stop and reach for the phone and call someone you like or love.

If you asked me what to choose between reading more or connecting with respect, I'd say we can do so with both. Honestly, though, save the book for now and have a conversation. Ask the person what they're plotting and planning. Or, you could ask them a different question, "What is your biggest fantasy today?" The results may surprise you, yet if you ask them that today, check in with them a week later (or even the next day) and see what changes in their response.

Dreams can shift like sands along the shoreline. Sometimes the tides of life dredge the shore, yet there also are fantasies shipwrecked on the coastline. Those vessels may not be able to return to the ocean waters right now, though remember, even if painful, some dreams may restore our craft and the meaning of life itself.

FORCES OF INSTINCT AND DIVINITY

For a couple of years, I was quite religious, yet the past year or so has found me lacking quite a few things, including spiritual guidance. Since I've not been praying to God in the past months beyond saying prayers of thanks, I wonder if I hone my intents by speaking to Him in text.

Right there, though, I find that capitalizing the H in Him is from social influence, something pulled from me because of a guilt complex. I've not been giving authentic or true worship to any deity, and I feel or fear I've lost my ability to ask the Universe for what I want with my thoughts.

The idea of sharing more of what I want from the world cues narcissistic thoughts about thinking I deserve more than I'm worth. Religious views would say anything we receive is fortuitous blessings from the Creator and also that we can't earn salvation or our freedom. How true is that? Other people and books assure we can have it all and that if we do, it's 100% our responsibility.

When describing prayer to others, I've sometimes said that prayer is us sending a wish out to the Universe or God and that an answered prayer is the granting of those wishes. When I wish for things, I remember the adage of "you get what you wish for" and also "be careful what you wish for." With a subtle hesitancy, I wonder what wishes I've made in the past and if parts of my life are manifest from wishes made many years ago? Wishes like, "I wish everyone would leave me alone!"

Well, I am alone, and recently I've wished for more conversations. I'd love more meaningful conversations, yet almost any communication seems to be appreciated. By enduring social isolation, I understand the value of having people call or reach out, and I bet some famous people may get overloaded. We may not fully appreciate the wealth held in their social capital, yet, then again, some famous people know it, honour it, and use it for great things. Where I seemed bankrupt and in debt, I know now I also can tend friends and speak with more of them.

It's easy not to be right all the time and still be glad to live. I don't necessarily deserve love, attention, and respect, though they're desires I hold. From the past months, I know if someone calls me and wants to talk, I'm not going to shut them out. I'll return their call. That applies to *almost* everyone, as there are a few I wish I never have to interact with again because of their malicious intent.

With people, I can't always discern who a friend is, and with the book about professional creative vocations, I also could write a book about how to be an excellent communicator and friend. The two different books source from being awful at either, yet by trying and failing so many times, I've picked up some skills, abilities, and knowledge in both fields.

Due to my social failures, I barely have anyone to talk to, yet perhaps by rejuvenating some of my friendships with new behaviours, people can find me socially prosperous again. Is that a fantasy too? What happens when I breach past the element of just being alive and step into a life and role of being an active, engaged, and productive member of society?

This year, I've been working landscaping, which doesn't provide so much for others, yet I get to earn some cash. Having money allows me to buy things and invest, yet making substantial social and communal contributions is a core desire for me too. I want to do more for others, yet when shut out or ignored, it's tough to do alone.

I suppose others feel ignored and disregarded too. Many people who Providing Point means to help and support are marginalized people, and those people can use and appreciate our extra love, support, and assistance. I understand I have a home and job, yet I think now how some without either also may be lacking basic human decency and connection too.

If someone is neglected and not allowed a home and meaningful work, how much worse is it that they may not have any love or respect? Giving people food is a thing, yet what a lot of people need isn't money or resources; what's required is safety, kindness, and genuine warmth. How do we provide that?

I admit I'm hesitant about interacting with random street people because of safety concerns, though many without a home are thoroughly decent humans who've just had a rough go. Recently, I've been thinking a bit more about our disparity and class battles. It's not easy at all.

Where I have an abundance of some things, I'm also aware of where I'm lacking. That's okay, though, because I persevere and endure, and I have enough gumption to rectify my points of lack by putting in a solid effort.

I don't give up, yet some have, and that doesn't leave them in a perfect place. If holding some character assets, perseverance, stubbornness, and my obsessive devotion are three things. Hopefully, I can entice people to give and share.

I want people to give to the causes I believe in, such as a UBI (Universal Basic Income), as each person, I think, should have access to more than enough for themselves. Criminal activity and bad actors are a concern, yet I also believe in just punishment and reward. In line with religious principles, I believe in forgiveness and letting people atone for their mistakes, yet I don't think we should punish people for circumstances beyond their control. I hope we can be grateful for what we have, and I hope we can be generous with others who don't have as much.

I saw a post about billion-dollar earners. The post said that billionaires should share everything earned past the billion-dollar mark. Someone's comment in the post's comments argued people *shouldn't* receive equal treatment and freedom; that people should be treated equitably for their contributions. What about basic human decency? Don't all people deserve support?

Regarding money, some share heaps of cash and give abundantly, and I wish there are more people to do that in the future. I want to be one of those people. Part of *my* argument and premise is that the baseline, the *minimum* allowed for people, needs to be increased and put at a decent and well level.

If *every* person had enough for their home, food, necessary transportation, and utilities (the concept I call Full Seed), then our world would be drastically different. People could still earn significantly more, and though it may not be a solo mission, my cause stems from the concept of all people having enough.

A base part of Providing Point isn't that people *should* contribute to the cause, yet instead that I wish people *would* and *want* to give to people. The $5 concept holds that if every person gave $5/month towards another's basic needs, we could house every person who is homeless locally. The idea started in the town I live in, yet if we expand the concept globally, there are millions of people who live on less than $2 a day. If we shift the numbers a bit, the $5 idea is one to pursue.

Some have advocated for redistribution of wealth by taxing only the wealthy, yet what about sharing the burden collectively? What form of redistribution could we perform if people considered it their responsibility as citizens of Earth to care for the wellbeing of all? It's quite dreamy, because some don't care, though for those of us who do, what amount do you see fit to give to assist another? Would you contribute a dollar? A hundred? A thousand dollars? Should it be a percentage of your earnings?

Logistically, it's tricky to find how to bring resources to the people who need it. In the book *Blockchain Revolution*, one concept is remittance payments through the blockchain. Billions of people who have mobile phones can gain access to money via cryptocurrencies and blockchain networks with ease. Ignoring currency rates and conversion, if Earth has the potential of transferring money to people digitally all across the world, could we do that for everyone?

Some against cryptocurrencies are against them because of volatility. The fear is crypto investments could go to zero and that people would lose everything. You may not know that there are also stable currencies that remain non-volatile to price fluctuations. It sounds like we're getting into One World theory, yet what if we could use mobile phones and the blockchain networks to have a stable currency that all people could access and use together?

Money is a powerful tool that can help balance justice— global issues of some having money and others not, cue me with social responsibility and ethical behaviour. If we can gather wealthy proponents to help adjust the disparity, I wish and hope we may assist with a balance.

Projects and businesses can address how to fund those with next to nothing, and we can rally people towards giving to those in need. If Providing Point is local now, I don't forget the rest of Earth either as I continue, and with the audacious goal of providing homes for every person without one, and gathering enough to provide groceries for a multitude, how can we move even wider? If we want to assure people have not only food and a home, what of others with even more basic needs like needing water and a bathroom?

Many NGOs and non-profits or for-purposes are doing the work, and a few people have told me to give to them. If I can provide only a bit, what if I can also encourage others to give to those in need through me? I'm not yet great with for-profit work or book sales, yet I'm willing to give it a go with Providing Point and the expansion of my audience.

I need to share the concept with more people I don't know, and it takes a lot of courage to break out of wishing and wanting and stepping up and acting instead. I feel the urge and compulsion to do so, and even if I'm not religious, I believe some are called to do things.

Although we don't *always* have to finish what we start, I started this process. By making my motivation to see the results and consequences of providing, even if the financial metrics show less than $100/month gathered from others at the point of this draft, I give multiple hours and efforts into the Providing Point program. I'm willing to give years to it.

Since the fourth book, I've been writing, waffling, and waving, yet I step forward and step true to make something worthwhile for our group. It takes a lot more than one kid and his books, yet the books are where this sprouted; it's my responsibility to water, nurture, and fertilize the seeds.

If you could wave a magic wand and change anything in the world, what would it be? The question is similar to another one I've asked before; if you had a billion dollars, what would you do with it? Is a magic wand more powerful? Perhaps, because money is not always the solution.

We can't change a person's heart with money, yet magic can cast spells of instantaneous inversions of love and hate. Money can cause greed, jealousy, or envy, though it also can be instrumental in funding things required for our cohesion. I've heard people criticizing and complaining about people who are billionaires calling them greedy or saying they do nothing to deserve that much money. I've also heard people complain about the poor and saying they don't do anything either.

I don't know right yet what it's like to be super-rich, yet I don't have hate, negativity, or disdain towards those who are. Wealthy people are fortunate, yes, yet why would we pin the wealthy as the enemies to humanity, when such levels of wealth also can be a powerful force to assist in bridging humankind together?

Most who earn $2,000 a month don't have access to the same resources or connections that millionaires or billionaires do. Seed can have a significant impact, so if we set our objectives to be wealthy or well-off and allocate part of our resources to providing and producing, we find some surprising things. If a generous person has $250/month to give, think of how much more he or she could provide if they had a billion?

J.K. Rowling is one of the world givers. She said, "You have a moral responsibility when you've been given far more than you need, to do wise things with it and give intelligently." How can we maximize decades of wise choices and investments of time and thought? Wealth can be a signal of fortuitous mass circumstances, and I believe we can use it for the betterment of our planet.

The more we earn, the more we can share. The founder of

Duty-Free shoppers knew that entirely too. He gave significantly to charitable causes, and he didn't seek recognition for his gifts either. From my wishes, hopes, and dreams, I have an obscure objective; to earn, gather, and generate millions, yet also share 99% of what I procure.

If we go dream case scenario with Providing Point, say we gather $5/month from 300,000 people (the total population of the Fraser Valley area), that's 18 million dollars per year. We could house every person who's on the street that needs and wants a home, we could amply provide grocery money for them too, and we would still have *half* of the $18 million to share with others who need additional support.

Nine million dollars isn't a massive amount of money, though it can do quite a lot. I need to know some of these figures for when I call people about Providing Point. $5, $10, or $25/month to me seems like a challenge to gather because I don't yet know how to convince people to sign up. Why would people give to my cause to provide? Should I ask for more, and expect fewer signups? How can I build up the audacity to ask for $250/month or even $1,500? One person giving $1,500 per month is as much as *three hundred* people chipping in $5 a month. Should I aim for an even higher number of pledges and a high value per promise?

One point I note here is that while I've been in motion, I've not been taking massive action. I've been talking, wavering, and delaying the process of picking up the phone and calling people about Providing Point. I set up a call page to plan for cold calls. I'd like to ask three main questions; what do people think or feel about the homeless situation, what do people think we can do as individuals and community, and, most vitally, what contributions will people make or give?

I feel trepidation, yet I remind myself that we'll go nowhere really quickly if I don't try to move us all forward. I want the base level of monthly income and support to level up for all people. Those that don't have an income need at least $1,260 a month, yet lots on government support receive that much and still don't have enough. I think the base should be $2,000.

What would happen if every person had $2,000 a month, and it wasn't only a three-month COVID coverage? What if everyone had $2,000 a month continuously, and could earn more if they wanted to do so? Canada's GDP was USD$1.713 trillion in 2018, with 37.59 million people living in Canada. If we multiply the population by $2,000, we have 75.18 billion dollars per month. Times that by twelve, we find 902.16 billion dollars per year would be needed to provide full coverage of $2,000 per person per month.

If more than one person lives in a home, it could be significantly liberating to give people a constant $2,000 per month. *"So far, $146-billion in spending has been announced by the federal government to help Canadians stay afloat during the [COVID-19] pandemic. More fiscal measures may be required to support the economy in the coming months, the analysis adds."* wrote Monika Gul in a City News website article published on April 30th, 2020.

If our government can't pay for UBI, then from where shall the money come? There are additional costs by not yet having a UBI, yet how can we afford to have one for all people? Even if finding a way to provide $1,000 a month for all people, the baseline lift would be substantial.

How can we facilitate all people to have a home? How would having zero people homeless affect your community? How different would your life be if you had $1,000 extra a month? For some, it would mean never having to worry about having food. For others, it would mean being able to afford a car. And for yet other people, it could mean taking professional courses, levelling up their skills, and advancing professionally.

For me, it would mean always having an abundance of food, having the option to pay for car rides, I could invest more for my future, and I could pay my mortgage off in fewer years. Courses and learning cost money, though taking them can improve my abilities to earn and contribute. I want to learn too.

$1,000 a month is only $12,000 per year, though that much money extra per year per person would affect us all. It could mean that all people have access to a place to live, some would lift their standard of living substantially, and by sharing that much with everyone, it could cause significant shifts in every life that lives.

If our government can't provide Yearly Seeds to people, perhaps Providing Point can. It'd require collective input to do so, yet the math speaks a possibility. A tiny bit from everyone towards those who need it most can dramatically shift the balance. Providing Point may not be able to cover $1,000 a month for every person, yet 253x $5/month pledges can provide a Yearly Seed for one person. That person's life would be well changed.

DEVELOPING CONTINUITY

Some people need to be heard, though they may not feel like anyone will ever heed them and what they want. At other points, some could be afraid to listen to others. I've had concerns about others' wishes and fear malicious intent, yet faith shifts into assuring people have a voice and are respected.

The world of Earth can be a weird, wild, and beautiful place. There are billions of humans, yet we're not the only species. There are one to two million animal species, yet rhymes put me back to a concern at my home about Zeus. Zeus hadn't been defecating in the litterbox for a few days, so we went to the vet to have a doctor look at him.

The vet took an x-ray and found his insides were mainly okay, just backed up, and the doctor gave us some meds to take twice a day. With a few deposits in the past days, slowly, we return to stasis and let the hands of the hourglass pass the grains of our truth.

I'm quite thankful to have my pet at home. Though I've often complained Zeus doesn't speak English or other human languages, it's nice to know there's another living being in my suite. A couple of years ago, invasive energies were diddling me when I went to bed, and since Zeus has lived here, the spirits have stayed away. I'm not sure if it's because of Zeus, though it's a comforting thought to know I don't have to deal with metaphysical molestation like I used to.

With Zeus, I am over-affectionate. I give him lots of hugs and kisses and squeeze good love into him. I wonder how much of my touch isn't entirely welcome or embarrassing to Zeus, though. No one else witnesses my overt displays of affection, though we don't always need another to see what we're going through to feel embarrassed. I love my cat, yet I can't talk with him and ask him questions that require an in-depth and vocalized response past meows.

Money-wise, after four vet visits, the cost was more than a thousand dollars. I was working fewer hours than the weeks before because of missing a shift due to a holiday, and also because another was hired onto the landscaping team. I continued working in 2020, keeping active and productive, and though I prefer free and open days, I also like earning money.

Providing Point gained $60 May 17th, from a dearly appreciated friend, and we had $809.23 in our account. With $210/month worth of grocery support going out each month, we were spending slightly more than we were gathering per month, yet we had enough money for four months of grocery card support.

I cold-called only a bare few people from the phone book to talk about the program up to this release. It's not easy or comfortable to cold call people, though doing so can be a way to expand our exposure and reach. Asking people for money isn't something I like, yet fundraising is imperative so that we can share more cards and also more per card. We had less than ten providers, yet I started messaging my Facebook friends and contacts about a newsletter idea.

I messaged 64 people on May 24th, 2020, to ask who I can include in our monthly newsletter, and twenty-three people said yes! I've written about how I don't want to treat my friends like customers or money sources, and I won't, yet I wish to share my books, our programs, and include people in the process.

I'd lost a lot of connections with people by promoting or selling things in the past, yet when I make cold calls, it's often to total strangers. It's also about gathering information about what people think we can do for our community, both together and alone. I'd barely worked on Providing Point and expansion beyond writing these books, and though the Patreon page is live, I'd not been consistent with it.

My copywriting ability is developing, and I hope to learn and develop it further. I think the best marketing strategies are subtle, ethical, and non-intrusive, and I'm learning to share what I'd like; more pledges, more book sales, and more conversations. Go back to Gary Vaynerchuk, though, and his book *Jab, Jab, Jab, Right Hook.* Don't just go for the ask, remember to give abundantly and share open and honest care with people!

As my soft skills improve, I learn how to earn trust, connection, and respect, and I remember providing for others holds value. Sometimes my connection and input are valuable to others too, yet my worth isn't just pushing and pulling to mooch money from people. I learn to provide more beyond cash and things, and reciprocation occurs.

Zeus reminds me of how I've not tended him well. I've thought Zeus was on poop-strike intentionally and wanted to go to the vet. I wasn't as concerned about financial costs as much as I thought, and I wish Zeus and I could have a real dialogue. I'd love to hear him explicitly, by verbal speech, tell me his concerns, grievances, and joys. I'm awful with those who can speak to me sometimes, so guessing my cat's thoughts is a challenging thing.

As is, we went to the vet the next day. From the *Rings of Truth* chapter *Give In or Give Up*, we know I have a defiantly strong-willed cat, and I like that about him in some ways. I can learn much about how to get what I want using the correct tactics, and I won't goad or manipulate with subversive intents, ethics, or energy. I learn how to control myself and my thoughts, and as we align with the collective will, we also honour multiple points of activation.

Zeus knows that he can do whatever he wants, yet sometimes he's triggered me and negative consequences. The cat is deftly smart, and though I don't like what he's sometimes doing, he's attempting to get his way too. If he wanted to make us go to the vet to drain my money, or if he made me mad by not drinking when I turned on the tap on his request, he may also do what he does. We gather real, honest, and ethical support and love assuring we do far more together in cooperation than individually self-driven wills.

If I yield to forces of faith, I also ally with our conscription of trust. I honour others' preferences and desires, and I even waver not from procuring a plan that's stronger than a plot. We may not be able to force others to do what we want them to do, yet I can manage and control my reactions, choices, and responses. I think it's right to align with the betterment of my own and other's lives, and I hope to be a seed to heed from the wise without having to disguise the text.

It's weird with Zeus, because he seemed to be acting alive and okay, yet also refused to use the litterbox. I guess it's better than him crapping on the floor, yet what was the issue? Zeus has telepathic powers, so when he's siphoning my voice or thoughts, I remember using words can speak an unspoken voice. How much can we do that with our text?

During the week, I'd learned a bunch from Grant Cardone and his book *The 10X Rule*. It was because of Grant's book that I started doing more for Providing Point, and it was because of my cousin Tyler's advice that I messaged most of my Facebook friends for the newsletter. It's also because of my psychodrama with Zeus that these books gain acuity in both thought, sight, and sound.

I accept I'm not a standard human, and I understand that Zeus is no ordinary cat. We're a magnificent combination of multiple lives and mental points, or, perhaps, Zeus is just a regular cat, and I'm delusional. Are all the other cat humans deceived by the feline species linked to God and the cosmos' core? Our mind is wild, weird, and beautiful, and I can see how humans can be considered familiar to our indoor cats.

A friend names Josie gave me the feedback about an earlier book and commented on how I organize my books, by sections, not in a standard format. There's often no introduction, body, or conclusion, and even in the chapters, there are various strewn topics of consciousness. Like life, the text can be sort of ADD with recurring themes and strings, although the body of this work also holds a finite, solidified, and correlated series of ideas and words.

I cycle and jive between points that peripherally may not have crystal clarity, though as the ripples of thought, text, and energy ensues, this is what courses through my mind. Like direct injections of chemicals, the super-late nights of coffee or tea and cigarettes blend with the enduring premise of forging new paragraphs.

The endearing and enduring process of finding what matters fuses my obsessive exercise of crafting new lines of thought; it helps better my psychological outlook. I may not have so many crisp or direct lessons to share, yet I hope to form these paragraphs into pages, chapters, individual books, and compilations that are distilling into *The Waters of Life*. These books are a combined and consecrated series of thoughts we may share with others.

Providing Point is my primary business, yet I don't earn a wage from it. As I sell more books and garner understanding and awareness for the program, we open pathways that can harness a collective ideal. We can supply people with more than we yet think or need, and though that may sound arrogant, if you've woven even ten minutes into the future, another block has been formed that shall never be changed.

The immutable ledger of what someone does or doesn't do can't take away the fact we've shared more than I could have ever expected. When my cousin signed up as the first pledge for Providing Point, I didn't know how far this program would expand, yet with the right attitudes and influence, we find it become a global movement.

If we're supposed to think ten times what we think is reasonable, then I'll keep multiplying the figures and concepts exponentially expanding possibility. And, by assuring I do, the right things, the right people, and also, crucially, the right reasons develop at the right time.

If I focused only on profit and financial security for myself, that would be playing small. As I instead push and pull myself to fixate upon solutions, generosity, and accomplishments to adhere to and improve other's situations, we all can win. Life is a team sport, yet the gains and ideas off the field also are necessary to think of the next move. I'm not so great with planning, yet vital, valid, and voraciously aligned proponents of the Providing Point project assure we thrive.

I work landscaping, and I also learn how to increase my efforts, actions, and efficiency when I didn't believe I ever could. I humbly, gladly, and meekly remind myself how fortunate I am to have people who believe in me, some that mean to be 100% out of my conscious awareness. When I intuit or think they're there, some may flash a deluded thought into my mind like smoke. Some of them also allow me to nestle into the comfort that I forgot they're there the entire time.

And though I entirely neglected them, I shift to an R-word, Repentance, and another R-word, Reverence. In addition to those two, there's also Resilience. You may not have known the term PLUR, or what I've written, PLU8R, though the ninth Fountain book's chapter titles are all R-words from the PLU8R philosophy, even if not all of them.

I've so often neglected my philosophies and prerogatives. They're central premises, yet I return and build with and upon them. Representation of the sands of time pass through the hourglass, yet I entrust it's not glued to the table. We can stop and pause, turn the glass upside down, and recalibrate.

As we cycle back and forth, twisting and turning, I also see how I've let so many grains pass without knowing who's meddling with my mind. I think about the doubt of the grout, yet a sprout grows up old and wise into our creative reprise to disguise.

"I still don't know."

I'd not yet started to put in the real work for Providing Point, and though selling books is tough, and in some cases a dream, we can find it as our lifeblood and driving force compelling us to write, craft, and draw more. I see the meld and can't tell you how they cast the spell, and as she passes by the corona of my eye, I cannot say how high or low the soul shall vie.

With three-point one four, the myth of nine more also calls a wish I make. I cannot take back the past and change it, yet I hope for faith and nourish our future. Here in the present, we land with my book in hand. When these words formed, it couldn't be right, even for myself, yet as this work resolves appropriately, these words enter into your sight.

Hold on, says, dear Ron. This is a sign of Serenity to open the doors to suite four's two friends. Cali is one who lived there, yet on the other side of the air, the waters hold their mast to tend the future cast. I cannot yet outwit, outplay, or outlast, yet have I already? Is this a Power Nine card of the blue and two that hold me onto you?

Shuffle the deck, roll to see who goes first, and then drink in all of the mana that the spells tell you to counter. Just have this dispersed so that I need not exert love's thirst.

People have wanted me to think with my heart, yet my mind gets in the way all so often. If our body tells the truth, I need to drink more clean air and brush the rust off of my soul. Though the pressure is on control, I hope they cast another bowl and enjoy the full inhalation. I won't, though, even if I love green.

I shouldn't tell a friend who to trust when Jund is on or off the scene. I don't know what movie it is, yet something tells me it's linked to deep trust. If it's true, the Emerald Loverock is squiggling amazing and kind energies and things into the thread wound around the sound. A spool found us to be tender, calm, and cool to resound with MindSound.

I find myself when I write these books, yet I also find inner truth and think of random things. I'm not one of the kings, and I, sure as anything, am not a pawn or queen. I remember I can't step forward out of myself, and I also remember that some people have tried to take me from behind. It's not a kind thing, and I wish it wouldn't happen.

So, with the myth of who I'm meant to be with, I call Elspeth, Chandra, and Liliana. I remember thinking I'd like to couple well with all three, and yet Kaya knows me well, I tell her many things. I hope our truth is known.

I choose not to hear the fear that creeps under from below, yet tow along the raft across the river to remind into whose heart cupid did deliver his entire quiver. It's hard not to shiver when I think of the past, yet again, it's me to outwit, outplay, outlast. We can win the game of Survivor without lying, and we also can succeed without abusing confusion and collaboration.

Cooperation of love strengthens and holds more than the three winners in the fold. I hope Michelle, Natalie, and Tony can talk openly and have a conversation, yet they're not the only ones who've won and played again. Forget never the other seventeen who put Fiji's story into the way we play and hold. Metaphors we've yet to comprehend and grasp find it's a form of life they let us lend, so told.

I tend to *The Sands of Yesterday* and the *Fragments of Intent*. It was *Shards of My Soul* that seeded the fields of future yields, yet it's this *Mosaic of Miracles* the rekindles my spirit. I merely ask myself, also, to remember that it's not my role, function, or purpose to assure that everyone else *needs* to hear it.

By the forces of instinct that link our thought with the truth, I dive deep into our world to remind us we live decades past and beyond our youth. Of decades, perhaps we explore another five or four? Yes, yet not within a war.

A DISCERNABLE DIFFERENCE

What is the truth of the matter? My cat was at the vet when I typed this, and it was an awful feeling to think that he was sick. He refused or couldn't poop for quite a few days before going to the vet, and I wanted him here at home again. His condition held so much inside his intestines, and because he couldn't poop, I felt brimming with anxiety. I wasn't well or happy.

I felt angry, pissed off, and sad that Zeus' status was out of my control, and I had to wait to hear from the vet. I didn't know if he'd be okay, and the wish, hope, and prayer were that the vet could clear his insides, and he'd come home. I want to stay on Earth for, at least, another decade with Zeus and note the permanency of our work sticks by having these books published and released.

Although I've not sold much up to this book's formation, by release, we shared a few more copies. Selling books helps allow me to thrive financially, something I need, as I wasn't entirely thrilled landscaping. I almost wished to be fired and not allowed to continue working for my boss.

I have meaningful work to perform outside of ripping out weeds and mowing people's lawns, and another could smoothly perform my landscaping job, probably far better than I can. They also could do so with a significantly better attitude.

My books, the Fountains, are purposeful and beneficial as we allow them to fuse, and as my boss is fantastic support, care, and provider, and I honour him and his family. The greater-good benefits I seek have me forge my path forward, and though I know that landscaping isn't my preferred career, profession, and vocation, I'm glad and thankful my boss was okay with me working less for him.

I may make less money from digging in the dirt, yet I have other things into which I want to invest my time, effort, attention, and energy. Providing Point has called my heart, mind, spirit, and soul to work for our collective communities, and I'm glad, thankful, and honoured to have the program and my books as my work.

I appreciate the people who buy and read my books, and I also am dearly glad and kindly thankful for every person who's signed up as a patron for our giving programs. I accept tons of people don't understand or consider the street and homeless populations, yet those people on the street are vital community members too.

Zeus is one of my most pivotal friends, and though I don't know how to thank Zeus right now, he's one of my best and wholly loved companions. From Fountain ten's chapter *Give In or Give Up*, I'm thankful Zeus quit scratching on the furniture so often and wish, hope, and pray we can live here together peacefully. I was projecting that we may not.

I thought Zeus didn't want to live with me anymore and that that was why he didn't use the litterbox. The hope is it was just a medical issue, and not due to me, though one big thing I gained from Zeus's vet time is I remembered more about who and how some people are friends. I found the truth about some I like, know, and love.

If I had one superpower beyond eternal health, it would be to be more loving for a vastly more significant number of people. Love is a core value, and when socially deprived by distance, time, connection, or space, it's hard to remember how to love others when not allowed to connect.

If Grant Cardone's book *The 10X Rule* has any influence, I remember to put massive action into effect into life beyond the pursuit of money or financial success. A successful family, career, and profitable giving program are what I work for, and I seek to be glad, thankful, and hopeful.

Energetically, I felt tingling and alive with a vast range of feelings and emotions the day I wrote this. I was shivering with an edge of fear, excitement, and terror about not working a primary job. The aliveness reminds me some things aren't suitable for me and my wellbeing and that I want to work and strive for multitudes of people and not only me.

I've often not known where to put my effort, attention, and energy, yet having time at home to create feels beautiful. I've been nervous about the future as it's uncertain, and I want to talk with my Dad again. We speak often, yet for right now, I need to forge new text to spend the energy coursing through my body.

I felt highly insecure and wanted to lay down and rest for a bit, and though it's always a great option to have a nap, I want to be productive and use myself fully and thoroughly for the good of our planet. I'm not entirely sure how to tell you these books are good for Earth, yet I know that they are.

If you're reading this book, a horrendous amount of love and luck guide us on this journey. Though you may not often be aware of people's love and care for you, I wish and hope many and much may work for you. It's a miracle we're alive and on this planet, and it's scary to think that some have zero belief in our futures and loves.

I wish, hope, and pray you to know who you can connect with and who you may trust. I hope when you need to connect, others are open to talking, and with our life and our work, these books, Providing Point, and Chilliwack Housing Providers, and a bit of loved Magic are also at my core.

I need to comprehend what I can do for others beyond money and love, and when I find people open to conversations and communication, it's a kind and glad thing. It seeps into my heart, soul, and self-worth that there are beautiful people out there, even if, throughout the past couple of months, we've not been allowed to have friends and family close due to COVID and social distancing.

Even on the good days, there may be edgy feelings. Some always deal with anxiety and fear, though as we evolve and learn to be okay and not have to run or hide, we can openly share how we feel and what's right for ourselves. I talk and write a lot about my feelings, and different people draw separate forces and topics out of my voice and text.

Some of what I share is overtly known, yet a lot of it is cloaked because I haven't always trusted people. My Dad is the person I trust the most on this planet, and yesterday I talked with three of the most important friends I have in my life. It's bonus points that I like, love, and appreciate them even if there's an edge of caution with one, a boundary of honour and decency with another, and an acceptance I don't know yet who *I'll* partner with for our long-term relationship.

It's not easy being solo, even when living with Zeus. Zeus wasn't here the day I typed this, and he helps me speak up and ground out with someone to love. I don't like being entirely alone, and my neurosis and mental health felt so fragile that I wanted to just disappear from consciousness.

While we're alive on Earth, we have ourselves to deal with daily. The grounding support of another being is crucial, vital, and, for me, the cornerstone of emotional, mental, and social wellbeing and health. I don't know how people can live entirely alone and remain even remotely sane or okay without another. Am I overly dependent on some? Perhaps a bit.

Knowing I am sometimes, and that I'm not always okay on my own, I learn what to do to be okay and feel grounded and secure. The phone is a beautiful thing and also a psychic disruption, yet it's also a cognitive ballast that keeps me tethered to positive sides of energy.

If the person I speak with is grounded, secure, and stable, then I'm more inclined to talk about the future and build. If the other is in crisis or needs to vent about their life, I can help be stable and grounded support for them.

Dear Elspeth! You called! Elspeth is a kind, refreshing, and healthy friend in my life. We were to go to the vet later to bring Zeus back home, and I'm glad Elspeth had a free/open day today too. She's been overworked and stretched thin with multiple commitments, and I worry about her and her emotional wellbeing.

A 10-15 minutes conversation with Elspeth shared how I hoped my boss lets me go from work, and it's a terrifying notion, to think about being without a job. Amazon sales weren't yet a full-time income, yet I'd seen tiny starts in the right direction. If a non-profit is my main focus and work, though, it's not an income source for me. Book sales are a crucial and pinnacle part of allowing me to do what I do charitably without having to keep a job, so I advocate for them too.

My Mom and Dad wouldn't be happy to know I wanted to quit my job. Sometimes things like jobs aren't worth the money they allow, yet my most recent paycheque enabled me to pay for Zeus' vet bills. I'm pushing towards absolute certainty that garden work is *not* my preferred long-term path, yet telling you this in isn't so much to convince you. It's to let me know what is right for myself by mentioning it to another.

Humans are weird, wild, and wonderful, while cats are amazing and fantastic companions. When living in the Glass House, we adopt two calico kittens I mentioned before; Mooshka and Belle. The Glass House builds in 2023-2025, and it's a considerable task to activate. To construct the home, we'll need significant earnings and additional income from coaching and counselling. That's my work in the future, yet bit by bit, grain by grain, seed by seed.

How do we find more people to work together to develop our futures and families? How can we help others beyond food and shelter? Can we help them with their relationships, work, and dreams too? Who would like additional support and guidance? Who honestly wants to work with and alongside me?

What skills or ideas can we share to benefit other's lives? Can we be knowledgeable and resourceful enough to assist people to better their lives with a profitable and paid position in the future? Is it the right choice to continue landscaping as I inevitably chose?

The uncertain and edgy feelings of emotional and mental stress I had from Zeus's situation fused. The senses also coupled with too much coffee, and with my uncertainty about work and desire to scoop from landscaping found, not all of these things had resolved at the point of the release. It all cleared and refined by the completion of the next three Fountains, ten to twelve mean to be about fantasy and dreams;

reality pushed my being into text.

Although *Mosaic of Miracles* was supposed to be in its final version by November 2020, it was done sooner due to my commitment to release the book by August 1st, 2020. With the next three books slated as The Fountains of Flourishing, I think we're getting there expediently. Thank you for reading this!

I appreciate the attention, kindness, and support we receive. I'm not explicitly clear how *you* benefit from reading this, though the deep-dive insight into the world of a star-crossed child can entice us to work cohesively. I'm glad, fortunate, and thankful these books form, and though it takes a multitude of readers and contributors to assist Providing Point to thrive, the connections and supports manifest.

Be sure to tell someone what you need and want. Also, be sure to recommend this book if you liked it. If you need a friend, it may seem daunting to call out to people to have a conversation, though, as I said on the first day in the book *A Year in Change*, we need to build our lives ourselves; no one is going to do it for us.

I use these books for a variety of reasons. I write to sort out my thoughts, I write to share my ideas and intents, and I write to gather money for people I can't yet alone afford to support. I write for our generalized wellbeing, our shared situation, and I'm a conduit for a new life, new thought, and new experiences.

While we each can be a channel for the things we need to know, no human being may be able to tell you what your solution is. Be open, honest, and transparent, yet also be a person of truth, hope, and love. Have faith in yourself and your core desires.

I've often demeaned myself by being vulgar and cursive, yet these books also remind me of the crisp and bright points of goodness that can reside in my heart, mind, and soul. Hopefully, the spirit of our text can convey some value and worth to others, and I wish, hope, and pray that each of us may have an abundance of what is right for ourselves. In our lives and our world, I don't always know what's best for people, yet I endure, progress, and develop for life.

My Mom may tell me I'm not able to afford things in life, and my Dad may be critical about my spending, appearance, and perceived foolery. However, I also don't think either of them knows or appreciates how fully I understand my future is so much better than we could even believe. I may not have yet lived up to my parent's expectations, yet my potential, momentum, and force of instinct believe we shape a future better than the one I'm working to build.

It's for our communities and wasn't yet in your awareness, though I meekly and thankfully ask Zeus can be okay and love our life here at home. I wistfully recall being over-obsessed, and I also wish to atone for my neglect. By not stepping up to the responsibility of success much before 2020, I thank the Universe, God, and the frolicking forces of fate for fusing sanity and security in my being.

We endure and entrust what we need to do for more than now. I can't take away the memories you hold that you wish not to have, yet we hopefully can build and share more positive experiences, feelings, and ideas in our hearts and world. Decisions and choices already made can help fuel your determination to live, love, and thrive, and if you're not having an easy go at life and feel you're putting in a solid effort, stop, step back, see where you've come from and where you want to go.

Ask others what you can do for them, and though I may not like the feelings I was going through the day that I wrote this chapter, the experiences are foundations upon which to recall and build. I gained clarity and insight into how I am, how some others are, and what matters to me in my life during May 2020. I'd not yet gathered all the components of my Freedom Solution, yet I can guide, assist, and teach.

We also grow, build, endure, and trust. Thank you again for reading these books. The Fountains take me through some challenging experiences and times, and if you've read all my books up to now, I'm baffled and wondering how and why. I often forget what I've written after I've done so, yet a printed book is a long-standing testament of what an author wanted to say or share. I think more people should make a go at writing a book at some point in their lives, and if you've started one, please finish it.

We're on Earth as a collective and group of individuals alone, together, and apart, yet the divine also bridges and bonds parts of ourselves that we don't yet know. Sometimes our truths are identified by a vast number of people to keep the secrets safe in our hearts and minds.

If you have a chance to assist another in their life or journey, do so. It can open you up to the fact there is brilliance and beauty in each of us, including yourself, and the worlds in which we live.

HOW DO YOU WANT TO WORK?

Do you want to work by function, mission, or desire? What if you can combine all three? For me, the purpose of landscaping has been to get out of the house, earn some money, and interact with people I like. Is that a trinal (three-part) order of the function, mission, and desire?

I want to interact more with people, preferably on the phone or, better yet, in person. I've made financial prosperity a mission, both with the book work and Providing Point, and I believe we can do some fantastic things. The books and the program matter.

In the past days, I've put in more effort, though I'm not yet at 10X levels. I've messaged about 180 people asking about joining the Providing Point newsletter with 55 email addresses gathered, and that's far more people than the previous time I had an email list. It's nowhere near what we need for Full Seed, yet I've set goals that are way out there for our program.

Chilliwack Housing Providers and Providing Point started here in the Fraser Valley in Chilliwack, B.C., and since we're in a fantasy Fountain, it's best to cast the lines and concepts far out and plan for massive success. When we gather $5 million a month, we can buy twenty $200,000 apartments every month to lease for $375/month. For every home we own that we rent for that much, we also want to provide groceries. The target set for grocery support was adjusted recently to $100/week per person for 10,000 people requiring about $4.5 million per month.

I realize we need to prepare for how to control the cards and their distribution, and we were still near the start. When we have $5,000 per month gathered, we can share $50/month with one hundred people and work towards increasing the number of cards provided to two hundred. Chilliwack Housing Providers' next target is $35,000 a month to buy the first home, yet with 10X levels, the goal should be enough to own and care for at least ten people's homes. The longer-term goal is to provide ten thousand people with a home.

With Grant Cardone's advice, books, and programs, our plans can expand further. Since working for Providing Point isn't yet providing me with an income (I mentioned a 1-10% idea in *Rings of Truth* though hadn't activated it), I need to cover myself and how I'll also achieve my prosperity, wealth, and wellbeing.

The number of people needed per home has shifted a lot in this compilatoin, yet there are also static variables from which I won't waver. For the affordable housing rentals, the rent shall remain the shelter portion granted by the B.C. government for PWD or welfare recipients, $375/month.

For every home owned and leased for affordable housing, we can expand and gather more to cover future homes' mortgages. A principle and objective are to buy the homes outright on a twenty-month horizon, so we don't need to have twenty or thirty-year mortgages as a liability. In the shared homeownership model, we also don't want to pay years of interest and instead aspire for complete ownership.

Five dollars is a kind and cool gift, and it's also an entirely reasonable amount for someone to give with little concern or thought. If I need to be wholly rational to succeed, I remember there are lots of people who may not provide even $1 a month because they have money issues. Yet, others may have and want to contribute more significant amounts. For some people, $1,500 a month to charity is a pittance.

At the point of this chapter's conception, all gathered through Patreon was declared on my taxes each year because we weren't yet a legally bound charity. The programs are an extension of me as much as my books are, yet I remind us people are trusting me with their pledges, not a legally bound non-profit at the point of this book's release. As we gather more and prepare to house people, we can lead to incorporation.

To have Providing Point as a legal non-profit, we require at least three people on the board of directors. When we legally register as a non-profit, we'll also be allowed to share tax receipts for pledges and donations to the program. There are a couple of people I think of for being a bookkeeper or accountant, yet I wonder what other jobs and roles we'll need to fill.

Knowing there's so much work to do for the program is seeping into my mind, and instead of fear and doubt, I feel excited, inspired, and hopeful. I can run Providing Point as a company and not need to be out ripping up weeds and mowing lawns. Even if I don't receive a salary or compensation for running Providing Point at this time, I adore the premise that it's something I helped start.

We can carry forward for the benefit of much more than a few and share our life. Advertising and marketing are required, and writing these books as long-running process journals helps mill the seeds gathered into a meal we can use to bake. I set my issues aside and work for solving problems, yet I also love hearing from friends and family when they call.

Since, as I seem to think, feel, and see, I have an abundance of time, I can make great use of it and do fantastic things for this planet. As long as I'm alive, if I do things right, we'll see me keep at the plow to rejuvenate, renew, and reseed with harvests continually. By doing so, we may be able to help supply the globe, yet boldness and audacity are required. The contialitic and psychic bubbles and baubles cycle and cipher me allow us to continue to dream, fantasize, and activate miracles.

As we manifest our world, I'm not Jesus or a Messiah. I'm just one life force that refuses to submit to the idea that we can't work together. I may have a narrow mind, focus, or view sometimes, yet dispersing thoughts about how to escape traps, turmoil, deception, and abuse, forges our grace, kindness, and respect. I'm compelled to create new text, new solutions, and new concepts to better our worlds.

Expansion is apparent, appreciated, and necessary to allow us to gather, guild, and build to lift and increase the baseline of what people may have and receive. Every one of us can live a life where we're glad and thankful. Though some may not believe in gratitude principles, when a person not focused on gratitude finds themselves given something, it can lift their spirit and energy anyways.

Hope instills recognition as a natural reaction, and though some people may not want or have much need for money, it can quench with the waters of life. If we all are allowed space and time to breathe and be thankful we are who we are and have what we have, there may be a stronger desire to thrive, and when allowed to succeed, we may feel better putting in hours, days, and years of our life into shared objectives to better our world.

A profit generated motive, a foundation or cause, or an hourly paycheque can inspire, yet would you prefer to see how much you can build, give, and improve? For quality wellbeing and life, I do that, and for as long as possible.

Since I'm not devoutly religious and a bit of a skeptic, I don't want to rush to Heaven to see if it's there. I prefer to excel, learn, and thrive on Earth. Grant Cardone says in his book *The 10X Rule* that "Success is a journey, not a destination" is a "cute" saying.

In Grant's context, he was dismissing the saying because it meant people thought they didn't need to be successful to be okay and secure; that plodding along was entirely okay. I see the saying as vital and crucial to me in the way how Gary Vaynerchuk says, "Love the process and the grind more than the payoff." I remember that working also has a payoff that's more significant than money, and not just for me.

If to succeed, though, we need to activate results. It's fantastic, pleasant, and dreamy to fantasize and imagine, and even if I believe that we can thrive in The Glass House in the next couple of years, I set audacious goals for my books and programs. I admit, though, that I anticipate secondary and significant gains.

It's a multi-win as I do this. From a self-focused viewpoint, I get to live, love, and thrive, while I also get to learn, create, play, and pray. The play and pray parts are my weakest points, though I firmly believe playing and praying are vital. Why do I need to play? I don't *need* to, do I? Perhaps, as there are tremendous numbers of things we can do for our own soulful and spiritual enjoyment. We may need to play to allow ourselves to thrive by having some fun too.

I think, here, that if we keep ourselves playful, we may find more happiness and satisfaction. I love the deep dives into wishing and fantasy, yet the deeper dives into the grit and grind required to thrive are what I'm starting to create. It'll take horrendous amounts of work to do, yet I relish in the process. What shall be our results?

When I'm working on these books, it's often gladly. I find enjoyment and growth by forming these texts, and if the secondary benefits of the book's formation result in sales and pledges, how will we see our programs expand? If I excel and write these books *and* actively seed for our futures, I also want to have more moments of joy and happiness.

Working for double benefits is kind, and it reminds me how much I like this process compared to mowing lawns and weeding. My job seemed more like an income source and not so much love, and I could feel a contraction in my spirit and soul, thinking about landscaping.

That's such a big sign because fear and lack mentalities can focus on meagre earnings as a need. I don't want to *need* a basic income; I desire to excel and thrive! If I worked landscaping tomorrow, none of this chapter would have formed, and I'd be feeling bad and bitching and moaning at work. What I want and need is book sales and a team leader for Brad and also Providing Point so we can expand our companies actively.

My books are my channel and challenge for myself and the world to step up and contribute life. From the Fountains of Fantasy, we shift into the Fountains of Flourishing to find how I learn and excel with these dreams and wishes. The three Fountains of Flourishing compile into the next three-part text titled *The Waters of Life*.

We slowly and surely develop and tend the seeds planted

decades ago. Some of them seemed dormant and dead, yet there's still so much life to live. We've not encountered many moments or people yet, though each is part of the Universe as I call forth sanity and truth. I hope we may provide for each in love.

Expand, neutron star, expand! Blackhole, explore, expose, extrapolate, and extend! A trustworthy friend is a dependable ally, and also someone I hope we each may tend. Some may attempt to bend us to their will yet hold fast and recall the points of love we have that never fail or betray. Those people may be few, yet those that challenge or contradict us can be indispensable to fortify our sanity, truth, and resolve.

"Be amazing, slightly better than perfect"

And yet, Grammarly almost always tells me to change the word amazing to the word fantastic. I understand I'll never reach perfection, though I don't need to do so, right?

If what I do, say, or make were considered perfect, it would be a high compliment, yet I know with my efforts, actions, and behaviours I can and could always be better. The way I want to be better, though, is in comparison to myself and how I have been.

I remember that sounds may found fortunes of fate, and how we speak, think, and act is crucial. What we say, think, and show also affects life, an if how we choose to behave and communicate is an essential factor, please let us understand our intents, values, and beliefs before assuming we know what's best. *I* still need to clarify more of my reasons for performing some actions and tasks and must check-in morally.

I've had challenges with principled thinking and behaviours, and I'm still changing things I need to prune and trim. Even if I think I've overcome a habit, the remembrance of it can trigger the craving to do so again. Forward motion is necessary, and momentum can help hold it together, yet commitment to ourselves and our principles is what we need to allow ourselves to flourish.

If we start from yesterday with faith, we can develop our fantasies from the point of fortitude, though what happens when we begin to flourish? Do we meet *The Waters of Life*? What comprises such? To what causes and missions will you devote yourself?

Where do you want to be or go to get your hands and soul, and heart deep into worlds of work? Perhaps you just want to stay at home to love and cherish your family and friends. That's okay. Do so. Maybe you enjoy working a job you have and would never want to do anything else. That's okay too.

Perhaps you desire to do more, yet don't know where the time or money will come from to do those things. That's where we may need to develop and be creative to find and activate our Freedom Solutions. Time holds each grain of truth and every required moment, and I'm thankful to know we continue to grow and sprout new seeds. As an Emerald nudges links of wages from pages, our evolution of being can help foster new varieties of formation.

Even if my writing isn't teaching specific skills in the Fountains, there is impeccable merit and worth in what the work assists us in becoming. *Depths of Discovery* wasn't long ago in the series and process, yet much has transpired and mulled within foundational blocks of this text and craft.

I'm thankful to form these books, and I'm also grateful to have access to people and places for which others would only wish. It's my responsibility to make good of this work, and it's my duty and promise to allow us to prosper and thrive.

No one is going to magically wave a wand and make my desires come to fruition, though as I hone and shape my visions, so too, I share with those who read my books. This is the journey of The Seed, and I wish this seed produces seed of its own to be sown time and time again.

Dear Aeris, Celest, and Paradox, I have not forgotten you. You remained dormant for a couple of decades, yet you sprout and flourish too. Thank you for your guidance and patience while we floated as distant glimmers in my mind. We come to know our home as a place to thrive and share, and though no one is telling you, right now, how we came to live in the situation we have, I hope we may appreciate our journeys of life as this unfolds. Thank you for waiting.

THE CONCEPT

This chapter formed the same day as the previous one, though I felt compelled to write it. I thought more about expanding my ideas with 10X philosophy and added to that a name. It was here where we had the concept. The concept is Chilliwack Housing Providers (CHP).

CHP stemmed from Providing Point ideas in this and the previous two books, yet this chapter is where I share the premise. I didn't know what a Ponzi scheme was, so I looked it up in fear and found that the basis of this idea *isn't* one of those.

I was thinking about Providing Point's Patreon page and potential pledge levels for the grocery card program. While the maximum someone may pledge via Providing Point's Patreon page is $100, I wondered about a one-thousand-dollar pledge level. With that one-thousand-dollar number in my mind, it cued me to recall the homeownership idea.

I got my Providing Point notebook out and started to write down figures for a potential plan. The numbers base on the premise of new homes costing $200k, though if we're going to fund future homes with pledges, the money given by patrons plus my contributions, we'd also need long-term commitments from people. For the uncompleted concept, patrons would need to contribute for a minimum of 18 months for the idea to work.

I shifted the idea from having long-term patrons into a fractionalized ownership model. The contribution levels are high, yet the equity shares are more top too. In this Fountain and the previous ones, the equity stakes were, at best, only up to 2% per person. With Chilliwack Housing Providers, the now second branch of Introversial (Providing Point being the first), I started a separate Patreon page for the homes.

The previous model depended on hundreds of providers

per home, yet the final model bases on monetary gives that range from $250-$1,500 per month. For a 1%-10% equity stake in the suites, we can purchase the places within a shorter time horizon while also maintaining the commitment of $375/month rents. I reversed the math from homes purchased over a two-year timeline, and when I calculated monthly requirements, I accounted for the overage. After shifting and adjusting the figures, a $1,500 a month pledge over 20 months will result in a 10% equity stake in a $200,000 home.

Patreon takes near 5%, and PayPal makes a bit too, though the Patreon commitments are in US dollars. The currency exchange, at this point, adds a significant buffer that allows us to buy more expensive homes, yet $200,000 is a decent number to work with. By thinking of people potentially dropping out of the program, the monthly pledges are for shares in the homes, each home being 2,000 shares.

For $1,500/month providers, they get ten shares per month of the 2,000 total. Over twenty months, they'll own 200 shares, which is 10% of the home. $250/month providers receive one share per month for 20 shares or 1% of the unit over twenty months. The idea isn't for profitable investment, yet instead to facilitate affordable housing with equity stakes as a reward.

We'll need to cover property taxes and home insurance for the residences, yet the guiding motive is providing homes, and not making profits on the investment. A hesitancy guides me to hold the program as a legally bound company, and not personally under my name. Incorporating the company is due to higher contribution levels and potential monetary overage, so we find Chilliwack Housing Providers to be a separate legal entity when we gather $25,000/month.

If we have only $250/month providers and reach funding, we'll have a significant excess of funds, yet that can allow us to buy more homes in the future and also build an expense buffer. We'll need to hire one property manager per ten suites, and the overage can help pay for them and other supports for tenants.

We purchase our first home when we reach $35k/month or 100 patrons and have six months of active support. We can keep the holdings within CHP, yet procure share certificates for the contributors. As we own more homes, the more people we can rent to, assisting the challenge and objective of sheltering people. With the previous housing models, we'd need $20k as a downpayment, yet with this model, we could soon buy the first unit outright. We also can use a bank statement loan to purchase when we gather enough in CHP's bank account.

Six hundred and six people were homeless in the Fraser Valley in 2017. When I multiplied earnings goals beyond limited thinking, we can consider $5 million a month gathered by 20,000 patrons to purchase 20 homes a month. At $5 million gathered a month, we can buy enough homes to cover all homeless people in less than five years.

Bit by bit, grain by grain, seed by seed.

If pledges to the grocery card program are likely to be $25 or less per month, we'd need, at minimum, 200,000 Seed Contributors to fund the goal of $5 million per month. With the highest CHP contribution of $1,500, it's under 5,000 contributors to reach the 20 homes per month goal. Providing Point can handle and care for people's food needs, while CHP can provide homes for people.

It may be useful to have separate programs for a few reasons. Providing Point is an easy program to give to with a $5-$25/month pledge, yet for people who want to give more, Chilliwack Housing Providers can reward with incentives. Shared equity stakes are for CHP pledges, and a more substantial monthly commitment may be suitable for people or companies that think a $5-$25 chip in is tiny. To share food is a great thing, though some may wish to have a more substantial impact with a $250-$1,500 pledge.

Providing Point is open to accepting significant one-time contributions too, and not only monthly contributions. You can send one time donations via e-transfer to **ProvidingPoint@Gmail.com** for groceries, and

ChilliwackHousingProviders@Gmail.com for housing. Up to now, the most considerable one-time contributions are $200, $60, and $50 though if you'd like to give, please use either address according to what you'd like to provide.

It was 2:43 in the morning when I typed this. I didn't have to landscape the next day, and with the things I did for Providing Point and my books in the previous days, I wondered how and why I'd want to keep landscaping. I committed to working in 2020, though, and with work on Monday, I was okay to do so. When I start pooling and upward cycling with these plots and plans, I wonder why to continue with the job, beyond helping my boss and getting paid. I kept my 2020 position is because I said I would.

My boss has been fantastic to me, though, and as I may have said before, I want him to have staff that *want* to landscape, preferably on a long-term horizon. He needs a team leader who can drive the truck and trailer and also operate machinery, and that's not me. I'm glad Brad kept me for 2020 as someone to help him out, and though mental and physical limitations became apparent, I also didn't want Brad to keep me on as a charitable donation of a job. It makes me think of how some people on the street also don't want charity, though they'd love to rent a place for $375/month. What happens if we buy the homes they rent?

We sort out concerns about Providing Point and the grocery cards, and currently, there aren't many restrictions on the cards. We can replace one, and only up to one lost card. If a card is lost or reported stolen, we cancel the first card, issue a new one, and then buy back the lost or stolen card from the program. As we expand, though, how can we assure people don't trade their cards away or hoard more than one for themselves?

If someone gives or trades their card away and doesn't report it lost or stolen, if used each month, the card's funding continues. If someone gives a card away and then asks for a new one, we cancel the replaced card and repurchase it from the program. The consequences for people who trade their card away in barter or a deal with another is legitimate, and though it's an integrity issue that needed solving, I didn't yet know the answer.

I'm not a street person, though I seem to think it could cause issues if people trade cards, and perhaps for the program too. If Providing Point and CHP are going to become successful and thrive, we'll need to think of potential issues and also find the solutions. One way to curtail the traded card stipulation is to give one and only one card to people, and by not replacing cards, people could be more likely to hold onto them and not abuse the grace of a replacement.

We were in our infant stages, and we needed to gather and retrace a few things to ensure a stable path. I realized how it'll require a massive input from myself and others and that I committed and recommitted to the program for us once again.

There were times where I was ready to quit and give up, though I'm glad I didn't. Zeus was lying comfortably beside me my bed when I typed this. He'd gone to the vet *again* because he wasn't pooping, and he came home two days before after two nights at the vet. My pet is a fantastic friend, and I've counted him as the first person for whom I help provide a home. The litterbox issues were in May and early June, and by the close of July, we seemed to be out of the woods.

For Chilliwack Housing Providers, I'd love to know how and when we gather the components to buy and hold the first rental property. It'll be easier for the second and third and beyond, yet Providing Point is also a good idea. Having two programs for different levels of giving is helpful, and finding how to share the worth and values of the plan is a challenge. That's one thing these books assist.

I'm eager to complete this book. Even if the individual books don't sell well, I trust the three-part compilations can have a substantial positive effect. As the books form, all the $5+/month patrons gain access to the PDFs of these texts through www.Patreon.com/Introversial. If you're one of them, thank you so much! If it wasn't for all of the patrons, we couldn't share as much as we do!

It's been a long journey to reach the 12th Fountain book and *Mosaic of Miracles*. I'm thrilled to think there are more books to write after this one, and I began Fountain thirteen during the first edit of this book. I chose the title *Debris of Distance*, and though I'd not thought of all the titles for the following books, bit by bit, grain by grain, seed by seed, a teetering balance creates the right things, at the right time, for the right reasons.

2020's summer season is in the past when most of you read this. When I wrote this part of the first draft, we were just about to enter June. By the final edit, it was near the middle of August. There had been some hot days, a bit of rain, and I'd seen flies start buzzing about my living room and kitchen. By the time you read this, we're possibly in the fall or winter season approaching 2021's New Year's Day.

What has happened with Providing Point and Chilliwack Housing Providers by then? How many people shall have signed up for either program? Will dear Zeus have another feline companion living at home? Shall we have a female companion living with us too? Will I have worked through the year, or will I have quit my job to pursue my creative projects full-time?

Will COVID have had another wave? What will be the result of the U.S. election? How shall Margaret and Elizabeth, two elders in my family, be faring in their homes? What happens within the next five to six months shall be crucial in a few different ways.

With an entirely different shift in the text (because it was the next day when I continued), I wonder how much manipulation and devious behaviour I'll need to deal with and counteract through the following years. Hopefully, not much, yet it's a definite possibility that people could attempt to control and drift me away from my primary prerogatives.

The plots and plans held tentative thoughts about Zeus and our issues, and while I was brimming with nervousness and edgy energy, sparked psychic anxiety wound profound uncertainty in me during these pages. If my thoughts aren't delusional, for my mental health and sanity, I'm delighted the

Zeus lives with me and assists this work and process. I pursue my creative and communication work to refract and rebalance with our world, and I'm thankful we continue.

Since it's clear I didn't know what to do for the micro realm of my home at times, it might be helpful to shift to macro ideas again. I put a bit of faith, trust, and confidence into Zeus and the Universe that we'll be all right, and we won't need to sting an operation. I spoke with my Dad earlier in the day, and he reminded me to stay calm and not panic.

Where this chapter started with the topic of Chilliwack Housing Providers, with the turn of 12 hours, it reverted to what these books have, at times, been for me, a coping mechanism for when I'm not okay. I remember others have their battles and issues that are prevalent and at the forefront of their consciousness too, and I'm not an exception.

I've not had so many emergencies or crises in the past months, yet I also acknowledge and recall uncertain feelings were building. When we go through uncomfortable feelings or situations, we have a massive opportunity for growth and learning, though gratitude spun me into this. I miss the moments of life I lived before I ever psychosed, and new ways, days, and rays of hope bring peace to our home like a dove.

Though the Fountains of Fortitude formed, and the Fountains of Fantasy are almost complete, I put my consciousness into the consecrated effort that allows these books to flourish.

"What you wish on me, on thee in three, with alien transmutancy."

I feel a bit calmer now. I can slowly ease back and slow down. Sometimes we need to step back and pull ourselves out of the rivers of our thoughts and emotions. I'm still learning how to do so for us because when my thoughts have run rampant like torrents of braided context, fractionalized divinity is part of the shard I carry. I remember it's wise to keep away from dangerous drugs like meth, acid, and coke. It's because I didn't stay away from them when I was younger that my mental issues

273

surface, disrupted, and changed me

Meth loaded my mind with corrupted data, acid opened up channels of consciousness I would never have imagined existed, and coke? It's a hell of a drug. Nowadays, it's coffee, rare cola, and cigarettes that I obsess over. Caffeine and nicotine aren't as damaging as hard drugs in theory; however, I could feel the chemical cycles of addiction attempting to derail me from an entirely proper and positive existence.

Our issues resolve into peace with the sign of the dove. I don't consider myself above reproach, yet it seems, sometimes, the world treats me as if I think I am. I'm not clear how to explain all of what I believe and do, though these books are a way to help tell people how and what I think we can do for each other, ourselves, our communities. I and my books are for the benefit of our shared PLU8R.

BACK AT HOME

This closing chapter is a wish, a hope, and a prayer. Let this book be read by people who live in a home that Chilliwack Housing Providers purchased.

I wish and also pray that Zeus is living with me, here, at home, no matter if my house is where I wrote this, or if my dreams, fantasy, and diligence manifest. I crave for us to work together, and I thank the forces of life, light, and luck again for allowing us to accomplish a *Mosaic of Miracles* to better lives.

Dreams hint I may have forgotten some things, yet the crucial, vital, and needed people, ideas, and pets adhere to our situations. We need not let them go. The town in which I live has had troubles, as many communities have, yet, we remember to bridge and bond our loved and appreciated connections to strengthen the fabric of society.

Our choices matter, and just as I feared a slip of consciousness, a lark cued the dove to fly free and share with others too. I cannot work alone. I also must not quit on others or our dreams.

I won't manipulate or control others and their behaviours, yet I wish and desire each person can make wise and kind choices. Death is not an option for some, and as much as they may want to leave Earth, it's here in the living world where we now reside. Sometimes we can't talk with people when we wish that we could, yet never give up on the hope that we can learn to understand spirits too.

Honour each other in the ways we can and administer layers of love and protection around the lives that need it most. Some may not think we do, though our experience, our soul, and our spirits entwine the wishes, hopes, and prayers of others. If we can improve our outlooks and share abundant compassion, forgiveness, and kindness, please let us bolster and fortify the bonds of truth, sincerity, and faith too.

Just because another doesn't believe in you, it doesn't mean I don't. Dashes of sunlight filter the visions we see, yet so too, the rains may fall, call, and wash away. The bolts of lightning and the rumbling of thunder may scare some, yet storms also revitalize and rekindle the hopes of strength. Sometimes you may need to cry out and yell; a good scream, for the right reasons, can cleanse the harmful residue others have stuffed into your psyche. Just because something is in your mind, it doesn't mean it's you.

We can sever our negative influences from others, and if, sometimes, someone's opinion and advice contradict us and who we are, we must keep our truth and good intentions. Heeding other's help or misgiven guidance can ruin our being, so don't be tainted by the wrong of others' minds.

People may not seek or want to destroy us, yet beware of other's control dramas and misinformation. Don't let people infect our rational mind, as there may be attempted disruptions of our best courses of life and allyment. I'm glad, thankful, and appreciative that my books come to fruition, yet there is much more than caring for the text and seeding fields required.

Insights, connections, consciousness, and lessons allow this work to hold firm. A devoted instinct, a developed set of ethics, and a continuous evolutionary attitude nestle in my mind when I write these books. It may be a cast of thousands, yet I'm probably not the director. If to be the playwright, though, can I tend to the entire cast and crew? We must manage the seeds of lost needs in the fields of hope, so people may love and excel, and not just wish to cope.

Living on wishes and prayers is not a sure way to be, though. I must plan and take action and refuse to submit to the manipulative and wavering notions that wish to control our choices. We may need to shed some people and concepts to allow us to work and live with peace, love, unity, and respect, and I remember having a focus is valuable.

I've had pushed premises and beliefs stuffed into me by people who wish to be behind me. Other supports give a counteraction to forces of life that don't want to allow us to be or thrive. Though I've gotten tired, exhausted, and done with the malnourished relationships I've held, I learn to seed good food, true love, and authentic care for those who reciprocate.

Instead of destroying or inciting hate, I shall attempt not to misrepresent or deceive. Some are amazing people we don't know, yet so am I to many others. We forge the future together in this home, and with Zeus, even if not human or part of my DNA, he's family and nudges me to remember peace. Peace can be when we're not okay or all right, and when we can finally speak our truth and denounce any of the negative or not preferred feelings or thoughts. We may have peace, a sign of serenity that allows us to return to our natural selves.

Sometimes people may require a reset point, a moment of pushing out and away from all conscious awareness or belief. We can reclaim our actual beings and accurately speak what we want and need to say, and sometimes what we need to say is absolutely nothing.

Though we don't end our own or other's lives, we may wish others to stay out and away from our thoughts and mind. One way we can share peace and love with someone is to let them be exactly how they are or want to be. No recommendations, no thoughts, no attention, and absolutely no interference (unless there is a significant danger). If you wish to share incredible wellness, one of the best things to provide some is separate and distant love and regard without pushing at them.

And yet, sometimes, we may need to push out against boundaries and beliefs another holds us too. I wasn't happy with how the previous weeks had been, though I made forward motion on a few things that matter; I wrote the last four chapters of this book, I honed and sealed concepts regarding Providing Point and Chilliwack Housing Providers, and I also can more distinctly see and think where things can and shall go.

And it's not Heaven or Hell. It's not even a physical location anywhere globally. It's into the moments of truth and guidance that seep into my mind, noting that that moment is now. When we become clear and concise about who, why, and what we're thinking, perhaps we can seed some grace and forgiveness without neglecting other's reasons and intents.

Though some speak love, act love, and preach love, there are points in time when I thought some wished for death.

I believe in Life.

Some cannot give or take away the feelings and experiences any of us have had. Our influences are occasionally subverted and unknown, yet when you become aware of what is a fact, you can change and hone your responses to interact with that truth.

I know my parents have tried to criticize and control me for a long time, and I also remember my cat is the best point of love I have. Although I fear there will be a time that I won't be able to hold any of the three of them, I wish, I hope, and I pray that appreciated energies course through our beings. I want to assist in radiating hope from the fantasy that we all may flourish.

Although we may not yet know *The Waters of Life*, the work assists in restoring a state of wellbeing of which we've never known up to now. The tones of thought and flesh mingle and meld, yet according to PLU8R with additional reciprocity, I'm just one human being. I recognize and accept my actions affect others in a reciprocal effect that extends cosmologically, and though I wish I could change parts of the past, similar to blockchains, the actions and behaviours of the past are immutable and held in some people's conscious awareness always.

Even if we've entirely forgotten, people can remember us in different ways and from entirely different perspectives. I shouldn't attempt to tell you what you should or shouldn't believe. It's your life, your choices, your truth. What I can share with you, though, are my choices of life and the reality I see and share.

We don't forget about love. It's too central to who we are and who we need to be. It's not simple to think the world will magically change, and we'll be able to pick and choose what to believe as the absolute truth. There are almost infinite variables with barely even any points of reference that I, as one human, know. Earth is our home, for now, and though some may wish we could forecast and predict the state of the world, to either rejoice or dismay, I choose to prepare for possibilities.

We love, we learn, we create, we play, we pray, we thrive, and, most vitally, we live. I typed those seven keywords from the Introversial prerogative in the order they naturally flowed from my awareness into the keys. The difference of sequence is there, yet one essential part is I shifted is the *I* to *we*.

The starting point is love, yet we must continue to learn how to do that far better too. Learning is essential to allow new ideas, thoughts, and feelings to arise, and by doing so, we can encounter new brilliant and beautiful parts of life. We can gain new insights and awareness, and by allowing ourselves also to create, we can manifest congruence in our world with our genuine intentions.

I must allow things to unfold as they shall, yet never quit or give up on improving myself and who I am. That may be self-centred and self-focused, yet I believe the most intrinsic value we may have for ourselves in life is who we are. There are various and opaque parts of our consciousness, yet those parts are also entirely part of who we are and how we are on Earth. I don't want to bend the will of God into my desires. I want to work cohesively and collaboratively, and I want to be sure that I pay homage and respect to those who are real.

Technically, every single human, animal, plant, or even inanimate object is real, yet one of the most fundamentally contested ideas or ideals is God. No matter by what name or religion is calling such, I know it's not me. I didn't create the Universe or anything physically manifested before me.

What each of us can do is learn to play with the words, thoughts, and ideas we have. I need to lighten up and learn how to enjoy life instead of treating it like a series of challenges, concerns, or issues. I need to breathe, centre, and ground myself and allow my heart to edge further into our world. I need to restructure how, what, and why I'm doing this thing called life, and though it's a majestic and marvellous blessing to be alive, I remember to give thanks.

It may not have been Zeus' time to go yet. I hope I don't need to take him to the edge and final crux of his life until, at least, for another decade from now. I wanted to finish writing this book, and I request Zeus can be here at home when I finish the next ones.

Many may not comprehend the significance my pet is to me. Yet, other people also may accuse others of never understanding the significance or importance of other's lives they've known too. Of living beings, those lost up to now receive homage and regard also, even if I don't know.

Well, it may be a bit of a letdown, though, this *is* the last chapter of this book and compilation. In the middle of writing it, I wondered if I'd continue. *Signs of Serenity* took me into the web and out through the soul, and although part of *Mosaic of Miracles* honed the housing model, I hope more ideas continue to creep into future texts.

There is a mailing list for a newsletter about this work. If you want to sign up to follow our work and process, please go to https://mailchi.mp/robertkoyich/introversial. The newsletter is only once a month on the first Friday of the month, and it's a way I share our progress.

For the next couple of months, I learn how to put appropriate actions, ethics, and seeds into allowing us what we need. The Fountains produce the waters of life for much more than I yet know, and as my cat was at home when I wrote this, I hope you also have a loved companion like mine a decade from when this book goes out to the world.

If my kids read this book, they might not like how I talked so much about Zeus and not them, yet it's different when someone is already living with us! I'll tell more, yet another wish, request, and hope are that as we continue on our paths, more come to walk alongside us.

Some people genuinely need a few good friends to be okay, not just one. As much as I love Zeus and my partner and parents, I didn't know who my gal is yet, and I may need to rely on some connection and support with friends I already know. If you're a friend of mine, please give me a call when you finish reading this book! I'd love to hear from you, and I hope you're okay and well where you are.

Although I've had difficulty seeing the near future, the long-range is cast out to the world and shared. I don't want to be cast out, yet being a castaway can be a profoundly deepening experience. Although I can't predict lottery numbers or read other people's minds, you can read mine and remind me that in some ways, I've already won the lottery in life. I have much more than I've yet seen or understood, and gladly, meekly, and with grateful love, I share my books with you.

Take care of your soul; it fuels your spirit. With care, choose what you allow in your mind, though remember, your heart can heal your thoughts. Let your body relax, strengthen, and inform your being with the crucial choices of life learning from your instinct and intuition.

Form your dreams with care and come from the point of honest desire and genuine concern. Delicate boundaries hold firm to our fears, so surpass your beliefs of what's possible into a primal force of greatness, love.

I can't tell you who you are. I merely have an idea we've been orbiting around the same star for a couple of decades. We may not have seen eye to eye up to now, though remember he wants to go out with you, cow! What's the feeling and vow?

I feel like a weird teenager dreaming of their soulmate who told herself to wait beyond the year 1978. *Voyager* is a cool show, yet *Deep Space Nine* could add a link to how I wink into the text to Ruby Sprite. May we both call for what's next? Direction shifts a tribal rift as we sift and move the sands of the dual to help fuel up a cup of a good drink.

Should we link our hearts, it may help to resolve our situations, and though variations of the text may hint a glimmer from a distance, the dream is right. Let us remember such when we wake up and enjoy another peaceful night. What's smack dab in the middle is a riddle I form to allow the warm draft of the sun to speak the keys when I'm done.

Into the meld, we walk, and though I can't take away the pain, like the tears falling in the rain, we can mould, my wife, and return life to Earth. Worth is more than a dollar sign or a line to the divine, yet I incline to include the brood and write for what is right for all of us and not only ourselves.

Though the shelf now holds the book, take a second look into how this came to be. And now, with this to be how I ask you to relight the flame on the candle, I walk with sandals in the snow.

It had been dark for many years. Let us together live the light of life, love, and hope. We learn and allow ourselves to thrive instead of needing only to cope.

ACKNOWLEDGMENTS

I would like to thank people for allowing me to do what I do. My Mom and Dad are two pinnacle supports, and my landscaping boss Brad has been a massive help too. Dear Elspeth, I'm glad for you, I honour you, and I wish you amazing well! Dare we see the Glass House?

My paternal uncles and aunts (Norma, Dave, Lori, Paul and Linda) have given connection through the years, and my cousins, especially Alex and Graham, have been loving throughout my adult life. I may not talk with my family often, yet I wish we gather next year for the yearly party. That includes Troy and his family, plus Damein, Emrys, Lindsay, and Elaine.

Both of my parent's partners deserve mention too because they've both given horrendous support in ways I'm not meant to know. I seem to trust they are on my side looking out and caring for me when I'm meant to be entirely unaware.

I'm glad and thankful for Chilliwack for allowing me to live here after Vancouver spat me out. I landed here in 2002, and hopefully, I can further grow and produce much more for us. I note I neglected Zeus, my best friend, in the first paragraph, though he was sitting on the patio with me as I typed this. I often wonder about saying 'Hey Zeus' as calling out to Spanish Jesus, yet that's not what I mean.

I appreciate my Magic friends, Gideon and Xenegos as two primaries (and Godo), yet I remember soul/life friends Jace, Chandra, and her family. I also best thank the Pede's for being amazing friends and for bringing Zeus into my home. I wonder how and when we'll next connect. I don't know if Ugin would ever read a book I wrote, though I honour him still as a wonderful teacher, master, and guide. Thank you, sir.

For other family friends, Tamiyo, Nissa, and Sorin cue me, and I dare ever forget Kaya, her Mom, and Dovin. Chills, Jerek

285

and Samantha, are kind and cool friends, and dear Diana also gives much. Josie gave me heaps of feedback on *The Sands of Yesterday*, and Ajani and his gal and kids are out there too. The Delcourt brothers have been rare connections, though always great people to talk with, and Mel Kaario, Tim Goertzen, and Colin McCune have been fantastic people with whom to plot and plan. Even if not a reader, dear Ashley has been a marvellous friend too.

Chilliwack friends James and Andrew may not read my book, though they've held influence and seed. Kyle, Robyn, and Colton are good friends, and the landscaping team has put up with me also by letting me talk and process some of my plots and plans for my programs and books.

Adrianne, Bernd, Jeff, and Amanda are four choice people from the preceding months. Although not everyday people, they each have a piece in my work and process. The books are grains of truth that I hope may serve well.

My friend Esper (Sarkhan) was the person who had the $5 idea Providing Point based on, and I wish he may find a way to succeed and thrive. I appreciate other Kyeta friends like Mike, Dan, John and Jon as being social cleats, but I don't forget Dave, Craig, Mark, Cory, Jeff, or Lee either. My cousin Vraska (although not trusted and perhaps dangerous) seeded much of my life in Fountain five, yet words in this work cued me to remember her. PLU8R to her Dad and Lori too. (Hi uncle Doug, Jude, Tristan, and Steffie!)

The Haave's, Wry's and Aandersons (plus Julianna, Paige, and Hope) are brilliant seeds and believers in me and my work, and I hope they see this. Thank you, Chris, for sharing your time, resources, and connection for helping talk and process Providing Point ideas, and thank you, Tyler, for the idea to start the newsletter.

Although I won't mention many Vancouver names, Klang is one I'll never forget, and Leslie Park was also a dear friend when I was in the psych ward. The cast and crew at 23 West Cordova helped me a bunch, and the House of Slack is where a lot of the conspiracies stem. I recall Fair One, Hye-Phive,

Kyle, and NO-BS, and as I think to name other people, I remember hundreds of them work and worked on both sides of the equation. (Where's Waldo?).

Although I'm barely in contact with any friends from high school or before, my friend Mike L has been genuine and honourable support, friend, and connection in the past few months. I love that Mike and his family are well in this world, and even if we've not spoken in person since before the year 2000, it would be rad to have a drink together! Another best friend in the past named Brent is an appreciated friend from Happy-Hippy-Fun-Days, and I'm glad he settled down and found a great life too. Chris Plemel, Chris Seltenrich, and Jason Yamashita were great friends during my SFU days. I wrote to Althea in *Fragments of Intent* and remember her too.

If I mention online guides? Gary Vaynerchuk, Lewis Howes, Jack Canfield, Patty Aubery, Grant Cardone, Gabrielle Bernstein, Marie Forleo, Anthony Robbins, Ramit Sethi, Christy Whitman, and dear amazing and fantastic Rudy of Alpha Investments! Thank you for making sure the Tundra is legit!

I feel a bit shameful for not mentioning Toastmaster friends sooner (because I neglected Arlinn), though some of them should be acknowledged. I'm glad for their support, and I hope we can connect again soon. Dave, Paul, Lucy, Lawrence and Stan are five mentors from the group, though Sue, Ray, Keiran, Yayoi, Joel, Lori, Jerard, Jerry, Keith, and Tanja should also be mentioned. From Snowpeaks, Angelika, Sig, Elva, Carmenza, Sisi, Darren, and Fernanda slip into mind, with Calvin, Stormy, Guhar, Joe, Marja, and Tami as not forgotten either. (Neither have I forgotten you, Mary Ann! I hope we can talk again soon!)

Though I don't want to mention patrons or providers' names, there's a couple in my building who's been tremendous help and supporters of Providing Point for more than a year. There's another who meets up with me in their office for coffee meetings to talk about the Providing Point program. It's not easy running one bus, let alone hundreds that all need

ABC

to intersect at the right time. They know how to do that.

I also wonder, hope, and wish some of those who read this are from my July-October 2020 Canfield/Aubery group who trusted me enough to look into this text. Dear Veronica has been fantastic as an accountability partner in the past month, and we're on a remarkable journey. I hope each of the course attendees gets as much or more out of the course than I do.

And for all the words and worlds that coexist in this Universe, I thank each for allowing this and us to be. For our continued grace, I appreciate all that we're allowed to work with and for the forces of life, truth, and creative understanding that let this book manifest.

As much as I recall, I know it's a cast of thousands, and though I'm not the playwright or director, I appreciate we're all a part of this. Ann Davis, Ruth and Naomi's, Cyrus Centre, Water.org, Pencils of Promise, Ena's Community Cats, and the Chilliwack Animal Safe Haven all gain from sales of my books (the individual books go to different charities), yet I hope much more comes for each of them. Non-profit and for-purpose work assists our world with solutions, and I hope Providing Point and Chilliwack Housing providers are great additions and support networks that can provide people what they need.

And if you think you deserved mention and were neglected (or if I mentioned you and it made you smile), please give me a phone call to connect! It'd be rad to hear from you and talk about what the plans are, both yours and mine.

Learn, Love, Live, Thrive, Create, Play, and Pray

Robert James Koyich

Books, Contact Info, and Links

Fragments of Intent (The Fountains of Yesterday)
Compiled from the first three Fountains
51% of Fragments of Intent's earnings go to Ann Davis Transition
Society

The Sands of Yesterday (The Fountains of Faith)
A compilation of the 4th, 5th, and 6th Fountains
51% of The Sands of Yesterday's earnings go to Providing Point

Shards of My Soul (The Fountains of Fortitude)
This three-part book combining the 7th, 8th, and 9th Fountains
51% of Shards of My Soul's earnings go to the Cyrus Centre to support
youth in need of love, safety, and support

Mosaic of Miracles (The Fountains of Fantasy)
This three-part book combining the 10th, 11th, and 12th Fountains
51% of Mosaic of Miracles' earnings go to Chilliwack Housing Providers

Introversial Mailing List
https://mailchi.mp/robertkoyich/introversial

www.Patreon.com/Introversial
ProvidingPoint@Gmail.com

www.Patreon.com/HousingProviders
ChilliwackHousingProviders@Gmail.com

RobertKoyich.com
Robert@RobertKoyich.com

Peace, Love, Unity, and Respect!

Made in the USA
Monee, IL
26 August 2020